Shelina [...] *Headscarf,* a memo[...]. She is an established commentator on Muslim social and religious trends, particularly around young Muslims and Muslim women, and has written for the *Guardian*, the *National* and the BBC. The vice president of Ogilvy Noor, the world's first bespoke global Islamic branding practice for building brands with Muslim audiences, she was named one of the world's 500 most influential Muslims, and specifically one of the UK's 100 most powerful Muslim women. The Institute of Practitioners in Advertising named her as one of the 'Future Female Leaders of British Advertising'.

idea
Library Learning Information

To renew this item call:

0333 370 4700
(Local rate call)

or visit
www.ideastore.co.uk

TOWER HAMLETS
Created and managed by Tower Hamlets Council

'Shelina Janmoh[...]ed cuts through the misconceptions and fears surrounding yo[...]clear, nuanced analysis of an emerging ge[...]of religion and identity. This book is a [...]g young, modern, and faithful Muslim[...]world a more hopeful place.'

Reza Asl[...], bestselling author of *No God but God* **and** *Zealot*

'A crucial book [...] you far from simplistic stereotypes to m[...]als finding ways to live with their faith in our fast-changing world … full of surprising stories as well as essential insights into what it means to be a young Muslim today. A must-read at a time when understanding the Muslim faith, and why it matters to so many, is more important than ever.'

Lyse Doucet, BBC Chief International Correspondent

'I've read no fresher and truer portrait of Generation M, in all its diverse, sparkling, cosmopolitan ardent faith. Janmohamed takes us across the world to show how young Muslims are balancing their religion with modern citizenship and lifestyles, and trying, despite the odds, to live boldly and courageously, despite the challenges they face from all sides.'

Azadeh Moaveni, journalist and bestselling author

'Shelina Janmohamed is unparalleled in her ability to map markets to Muslims, providing a global snapshot of Muslim commodities that both celebrates the creativity of Muslim entrepreneurship and faces the challenges of community commodification. For those within and concerned with modern Muslim communities this book will inspire and invigorate debate.'

Professor Reina Lewis, London College of Fashion, UAL,
author of *Muslim Fashion: Contemporary Style Cultures*

'A vivid account of what it means to be young and Muslim, and opening readers' eyes to the tone, spirit, and thinking of this critical generation. Her account is timely, well-researched – and highly recommended.'

Farah Pandith, former first-ever Special Representative
to Muslim Communities, US Department of State

'A fresh and insightful perspective on one of the twenty-first century's most important economic forces: young Muslims and how they are shaping their worlds.'

Sir Martin Sorrell, founder and CEO of WPP

'Rapidly representing 25% of the global population, the often misunderstood Muslim consumer deserves all attention and respect. *Generation M* sets out why in a very compelling way.'

Paul Polman, CEO of Unilever

'Shelina Janmohamed here tackles the difficult triumvirate of faith, modernity and identity. In a world shadowed by 9/11 and ISIS, this is a refreshingly honest look at Generation M: modern Muslims whose faith defines their lifestyles. If you want to understand this growing segment of society, this is the book to read. You will see their faith, their priorities, their struggles, and how they navigate their everyday life.'

Muna AbuSulayman, Partner at Haute Elan and Co-Host
of Kalam Nawaem, Middle East Broadcasting Channel

'Shelina Janmohamed has written a hugely positive book on Generation M which breaks down barriers and demands to be read.'

David Yelland, former editor of *The Sun*

GENERATION

YOUNG MUSLIMS
CHANGING THE WORLD

Shelina
Janmohamed

I.B.TAURIS

LONDON · NEW YORK

Tower Hamlets Libraries

91000008008121	
Askews & Holts	
305.235	
THISWH	TH16000651/0006

FSC
www.fsc.org
MIX
Paper from
responsible sources
FSC® C007584

Published in 2016 by
I.B.Tauris & Co. Ltd
London • New York
www.ibtauris.com

Copyright © 2016 The Ogilvy Group Inc., d/b/a Ogilvy & Mather

The right of Shelina Janmohamed to be identified as the author of this work has been asserted by the author in accordance with the Copyright, Designs and Patents Act 1988.

All rights reserved. Except for brief quotations in a review, this book, or any part thereof, may not be reproduced, stored in or introduced into a retrieval system, or transmitted, in any form or by any means, electronic, mechanical, photocopying, recording or otherwise, without the prior written permission of the publisher.

Every attempt has been made to gain permission for the use of the images in this book. Any omissions will be rectified in future editions.

References to websites were correct at the time of writing.

ISBN: 978 1 78076 909 7
eISBN: 978 0 85772 860 9
ePDF: 978 0 85772 841 8

A full CIP record for this book is available from the British Library
A full CIP record is available from the Library of Congress

Library of Congress Catalog Card Number: available

Typeset by JCS Publishing Services Ltd, www.jcs-publishing.co.uk
Printed and bound in Sweden by ScandBook AB

CONTENTS

ILLUSTRATIONS

ACKNOWLEDGEMENTS

Miles Young, CEO of Ogilvy & Mather, and John Goodman, president of Ogilvy Noor, are behind this book becoming a reality. And I'm not just saying that because they are my boss and my boss's boss. Miles saw the rise of this group of young Muslims emerging nearly a decade ago, which eventually led to the establishment of Ogilvy Noor. He's been a consistent advocate of our work.

The emergence of Generation M, and the lifestyle, culture and industries which have developed as a result in this period, are new and for the most part uncharted. John's support for this book has finally given voice to this young generation. He has encouraged me to write the book and given me the time and resources to do so, and these, hand in hand with his reading and input, have been invaluable. This has been alongside devoting his energies and experience towards growing an industry in which we both have a tremendous personal as well as professional stake. Overall, I couldn't have asked for a better support and colleague for this book and for the wider project. Thank you.

My thanks to the indomitable Jeremy Katz, who kept the publication process for this book smooth and was a much-appreciated guide and cheerleader. And an honourable mention for Tanya Dernaika and Nazia Du Bois as the leads on earlier research on the idea of the new Muslim consumer.

My greatest thanks go to all those who contributed the views and opinions which shaped the book, many of which are included in its text. There was no holding back, and their engagement came with such joy and eagerness from all around the world. It was a delight to spend time getting to know these young Muslims, and hearing their stories.

Maria Marsh and Azmina Siddique saw the potential of the book, and their guiding editorial hands helped give shape to its contents. Thank you for making it happen.

Thanks also to those who worked to bring it to fruition, Sara Magness, Jessica Cuthbert-Smith and Rory Gormley.

The inputs of my peers were valuable: Yahya Birt, Fozia Bora, Kazim Zaidi, Tahir Abbas, Peter Gould, Michael Mumisa, Ali Naqvi, Jonathan Wilson and Nahla El Geyoushi.

Naturally, behind the business of the book is the personal story, and the people who supported me in my efforts to create a book-type thing.

Ultimately everything can be traced back to my mum and dad, who from the beginning have always been my support and encouragement. I'm unbelievably blessed to have you as my parents. And how fortunate I am that I have a book in which to publicly express my love and thanks to you. Even in your most difficult times you always gave of yourselves to me.

And, of course, the One. The first book was all for you. But this one too comes wrapped up in your love. I know it was fraught. I know all about working and not working. But you are a double diamond, and what you did for me while I was writing this book I will never forget. You continue to encourage, inspire and create space for me. And for all of those things and so many more priceless qualities you bring to my life, I thank you, respect you and love you.

The final push in writing this book came at a time of immense intensity in my own life. I had just had a little baby, my mini beloved, with whom this book will forever be tied; may she remain always blessed. Even in her supremely cute baby state, she was unbelievably gorgeous and gave me time to write.

My then four-year-old, whilst attempting to sit on my lap while I wrote the book, deserves the most special of mentions for her enthusiasm at my project, even though she couldn't fully understand why I was unable to play with her even at the weekends. But my little beloved did say that she'd like to write a book too, and went off and made one with several different coloured sheets of paper.

Worried about my well-being during the writing process, she asked, 'Mummy, if it's taking you a long time to write a book with so many words, why don't you do a picture book?' It's a good question from a smart girl for whom I have the highest of hopes. She's always had a certain magic about her, and I hope her magical fairy dust and her unbelievably incredible smile, both of which transform the mundane into something extraordinary, will bring sparkles to those around her all of her life. The final word goes to her. 'Is everyone going to read your book?' she asked. I certainly hope so.

To my father
Who has always believed in me,
And gave me the skills and support to do anything that I wanted.
I hope I can pass forward these precious gifts to my daughters,
And to all the young girls around the world.
Most importantly, you gave me your love for Him, for always.
Thank you.

To my girls
Because you can do anything.
Take it from Mummy.

INTRODUCTION

On the morning of 7 January 2015, Said and Cherif Kouachi forced their way into the office of *Charlie Hebdo* in Paris. Armed with rifles and other weaponry, they killed 11 people and injured 11 more in the building. As they fled, they killed police officer Ahmed Merabet, who was a Muslim. According to witnesses, as the gunmen left the scene they shouted: 'We have avenged the Prophet Muhammad. We have killed Charlie Hebdo!'

Four days later, on 11 January, 2 million people joined demonstrations across France at rallies of national unity, with the slogan 'Je Suis Charlie'.

Condemnations of the attack came thick and fast from Muslim individuals, organisations and nations around the world. Muslims were as horrified as everyone else. In France, many joined the national unity rallies and issued statements, tweets and Facebook statuses of support for the victims.

The threat posed by terrorism dominated global news coverage for weeks. In fact, it's never out of the news. The event further entrenched the stereotype that 'all terrorists are Muslim, and all Muslims are terrorists' (both sides of this cliché are wildly inaccurate), turning all eyes to this one act by two Muslims, and away from the diverse, nuanced and mostly quite ordinary human stories of the world's 1.6 billion Muslims.

That summer, when I asked Muslims around the world what they had been doing on the day of the *Charlie Hebdo* attack, I received a deluge of responses: hatred at the disgusting attacks, anger at murder being undertaken in the name of Islam, frustration that all

Muslims were being lumped together as terrorists. They were torn about demands on them to demonstrate publicly that this was 'Not in Our Name', because they couldn't see why they should apologise for people with whom they had no connection. But they also wanted to be clear that this was nothing to do with the Islam that inspires them, and to offer comfort and a sense of reassurance to those troubled by the events. But the outpouring of emotion had something more powerful behind it: these Muslims were finally being asked to share their own stories, relate their own feelings and express what they truly felt without being goaded or scrutinised.

The stories they told me of what they had been doing on 7 January 2015 paint a rich and detailed portrait of Muslims that contrasts with the snapshot that has come to dominate discussions about Muslims globally.

Maleeha was attending the Immigration Court in San Francisco representing a client for a Nepali asylum case, which she eventually won. Nada in Aligarh, India, was writing an article about 'Wars on Children' to tackle the impact of warfare on minors. Henna in Birmingham was giving her grandmother end-of-life care in hospital. Sufian was preparing for an international seminar on interfaith harmony and tolerance, in Kuala Lumpur. Sale was at the main station in Milan, volunteering with a group of citizens which helps and gives comfort to Syrian refugees.

There were more normal daily life activities. Henrietta was in Spain celebrating her daughter's birthday with friends. Sabina had just returned to Sweden from a holiday in the UAE and Oman.

Most poignantly there were stories that bring to the fore how young Muslims are working hard to build bridges and assert their rightful place in modern society but are stuck between the dreadful acts of violent extremists claiming to act in the name of Islam, and a growing anti-Muslim sentiment. Lina says that she was in the midst of talks with the Institut du Monde Arabe in Paris, discussing the possibility of the institute hosting a 'Capture the Spirit of Ramadan International Photography Exhibition' which would highlight the meaning of Ramadan through art and photography. The discussions were shut down with a simple stern warning from an intermediary, not even the organisers: 'The time is not good for this any more.' Lina said she felt that the time was even more right, that people needed to know more rather than less, and what better way to do it than through beautiful, inspiring positive imagery of Muslims around the world celebrating their holy tradition?

When I was growing up in the UK in the 1980s and 1990s, I felt a constant burden to demystify Islam and explain that Muslims are human beings like everyone else. We had alliances with the wider groups fighting for stereotyping and discrimination to be eradicated.

So, for a while, it felt that it was getting easier to be a Muslim citizen of the global village. But for young Muslims today it seems harder than ever. More than one-third of today's Muslims are under 15, and nearly two-thirds are under 30. That means they have spent most or all of their lives under the shadow of 11 September 2001. Then, on a regular basis, along come global events that put Muslims under further scrutiny, like *Charlie Hebdo*, the killing of a British soldier in Woolwich, London, and the beheadings by Daesh. Whether they are young Muslims in America, Afghanistan or Abu Dhabi, these events have had an effect on how they're seen and how they see themselves.

I wanted to find out what it feels like to be Muslim today for these young people around the world, and how the rising barometer of their faith fits into the wider global picture.

Beyond the tabloid headlines and stories of halal meat and jihadi brides, what inspires and motivates these young Muslims? What is shaping their lives and what does that mean for all of the rest of us? How are young people asserting their identity while religion is ostensibly in decline, while political and economic power is shifting eastwards, while Muslim populations are young and growing? All of this against an ongoing geopolitical backdrop of fighting violent extremists claiming Islam for themselves on one hand, and the growing hostility towards Muslims at a social and at times even governmental level on the other. These were some of the questions I set out to answer as I began this book.

If anything, such questions feel to me to be the natural next step in my own very public journey exploring faith, modernity and identity which I began when I published my first book in 2009, *Love in a Headscarf*. It is an irreverent memoir about growing up as a British Muslim woman in Britain. I told the story of the struggles of my identity through the medium of the search for love. I had become tired of seeing piles of stories on bookshop tables about Muslim women who were 'oppressed' and then 'saved'. The book covers invariably carried images of women in face veils (even if the story had nothing to do with a face veil) with sand dunes in the back (even if the story wasn't in the Middle East) and sad mournful-looking camels (yes, even the camels looked sad). I looked at these books and thought, none of these is my story, the story of feeling confident and comfortable in my skin as a British Muslim woman, not conflicted or oppressed. So I set out to author a book, because what was most imperative was to tell my own story.

Persuading the publishing industry that stories of Muslims can be other than misery memoirs was a challenge; they simply couldn't believe that positive stories exist or, more important for them as businesses, that anyone would buy them. The publishing world is, after all, a commercial enterprise. But it also acts as a gatekeeper to the stories available to us about our world, and so its choices impact the shape of our society. That's why I'm so excited that this book, *Generation M*, can bring a whole new worldview and group of human stories into the limelight.

Eventually *Love in a Headscarf* was published, with a feisty pink and purple cover depicting a woman driving her convertible across the London skyline (yes, that's me). It caught the zeitgeist, with my ideas that not only did I have the right to be a Muslim who was rooted in practising Islam, but I also had the right to feel British, to be British and to be part of modern life. In fact, I was living that life. That proud, unapologetic story of finding a faithful modern identity appealed in particular to young Muslims around the world who finally felt that someone had given voice to their beliefs and experiences. The book has been published in ten different editions and languages around the world and reached number two on the bestseller charts in India. More than seven years later, I still receive messages almost daily from young Muslims who say that I've 'written their life' by expressing the combination of being a committed Muslim who is also fully immersed in modern life and sees the two aspects as complementary.

I was very moved by some of the awards that followed. I was noted as one of the 500 most influential Muslims globally, and one of the UK's 100 most powerful Muslim women. They surprised me: what I felt I had done was simply tell an honest authentic story of creating change to make my life and the world around me better. It resonated with Muslims and wider global audiences.

This book is not about me, but rather about Generation M. Imagine this book as a conversation, a series of intimate moments with young Muslims from around the world, drinking lattes on the pavement at midnight in Jakarta, or smoking shisha on London's Edgware Road on a balmy summer's evening. Some are at photo shoots in trendy Istanbul, styling a model in a headscarf posing in front of a fountain. Another is doing a stand-up comedy gig in her Indonesian hometown. Join them as they shop for Ramadan clothes in Dubai at DKNY or indulge in rare halal treats at a night market in California.

Their enthusiasm and gusto for life are infectious. Conversations about love, sex and shopping are as full of passion as those about pilgrimage, prayer and hijabs. There's humour: if your son is called Jihad, don't lose him at the airport – you won't be able to call out for him. But there's also intense seriousness, debate and self-reflection: Not in My Name, Je Suis Muslim, #AsAMuslimWoman.

Ogilvy & Mather, one of the world's leading branding and communications agencies, set out to explore the idea that there is a global Muslim consumer that has common characteristics around the world. We conducted a survey in four majority Muslim countries at different stages of the economic life cycle – Saudi Arabia, Egypt, Pakistan and Malaysia – and then spot-tested the findings across a number of other majority and minority Muslim populations. How important was their faith? What were their attitudes about the modern world? How did they navigate their place within it?

What we discovered was a group of young Muslims bound together by a core underlying worldview: that their faith and modernity go hand in hand. Their faith affects absolutely everything they do, and they believe it can make modernity better. Equally, they are fully immersed in modern life and harness its benefits for both individual and communal good, as well as improving their faith.

So powerful and clear was the definition of this influential group and its growing prominence that the importance of organisations and brands identifying and reaching out to the group was immediately clear. As a result, Ogilvy & Mather founded the agency I work for within its umbrella, calling it Ogilvy Noor. *Noor* means 'light' and in our founding materials we talked of 'shedding light on the new Muslim consumer'.

Ogilvy Noor is the world's first bespoke full-service commu- nications and branding consultancy for engaging with Muslim audiences. Further research on Generation M attitudes to global brands and product categories accompanied our findings. And now this book is designed to build on our pioneering work by offering an in-depth qualitative conversation with Generation M so we can really hear what they have to say. My hope is that it will be fresh, revelatory and exciting in equal measure and will create a marked leap forward in our understanding of today's modern, faithful Muslims.

What most analysis of Muslim attitudes and behaviour focuses on is the role of Islamic beliefs and the political ideologies underpinning their behaviours. Surveys interrogate Muslims about their religious opinions on violence, suicide bombings, the place of women in society or how women should be properly attired. There are precious few mainstream publications about the experience of being a young Muslim beyond politics and theology.

That's why this book is different: it's about the experience and attitudes of being Muslim and their stories are brought to life in their own words. My aim is to bring into sonorous multicolour the voices of this new identity that we have found again and again around the world, that claim faith and modernity are not mutually exclusive and that both make Generation M better human beings.

The quality of our interactions with this part of humanity depends on understanding Generation M's attitudes and their disproportionate influence on the wider (Muslim) population. This is even more acute given current global events. There's also a quantitative perspective of why identifying the emergence of this generation is timely, and why it is imperative to get to know them, whether it's for commercial, social or political reasons.

According to the Pew Research Centre on Religion and Public Life, while the world's population is projected to grow 35 per cent in the next four decades, the number of Muslims is expected to increase by 73 per cent – from 1.6 billion in 2010 to 2.8 billion in 2050; by 2030 Muslims will make up 26.5 per cent of the global population. In 81 countries the Muslim population will exceed 1 million. Six of the fastest growing Next 11 economies are overwhelmingly majority Muslim nations and two more have sizeable Muslim minorities. The BRIC nations (Brazil, Russia, India and China) will be home to just under 300 million Muslims. Minority Muslim populations will add up to a sizeable 500 million people. Countries which are not Muslim majorities but have large Muslim populations are often situated in regions which have a long history of Muslim interaction and understand the dynamics of existing in a Muslim neighbourhood.

At the same time as Western populations are ageing, the Muslim population is young and growing. In 2010, Muslims had the youngest median age, at 23, of any religious group – seven years younger than the median age of non-Muslims which was 30. Muslim fertility rates are also higher, 3.1 versus 2.3, and the higher rates apply across majority and minority Muslim populations.

In 2010, nearly two-thirds of the global Muslim population – 63 per cent – was under 30. That's 1 billion people, representing more than 14 per cent of the global population.

Age is not the only worry of Western populations: front of mind are ailing economies and a gradual shift of economic influence towards the Muslim world and the East. Countries like Indonesia and Turkey regularly feature at the top of global growth predictions.

This growth comes as a result of these nations' huge labour pools and young populations, which can create opportunities for the kind of dynamic change illustrated by the figures above. They also lay the groundwork for social challenges triggered by a youth bulge that is trying to establish its place in society. At a commercial and creative level, the signs of Generation M's influence in their own societies as well as on the globe as a whole are already there. The notion of Islamic branding – building businesses, products and brands to engage with Muslim consumers – is also gaining traction; the halal food and lifestyle industry was estimated at $1.8 trillion in 2014 and predicted to rise to $2.6 trillion by 2020, and Islamic finance at a further $1.3 trillion and $2.6 trillion respectively.

The optimistic excitement of the Arab Spring may have soured with the terrible twists of civil wars and military power, but it still bears repeating that Generation M have grasped an opportunity presented to them to hold their leaders to account and work towards political transformation.

More specifically in terms of numbers, the Muslim middle class, with greater affluence and sophisticated tastes as well as pride in their religion, are likely to triple from an estimated 300 million in 2015 to 900 million by 2030, although these figures remain high-level estimates. The Muslim middle classes are driving a boom in products and services aimed at Muslim tastes, but at the same time they have been identified as acting as a bulwark against Muslim violent extremism.

Against the backdrop of these commercial, social and demographic changes, how should we be engaging with such a vast population? How should we communicate, and what impact are these people going to have on our world? Our research has found that Generation M is the most influential segment of the global Muslim population. Their ideas are pioneering both among Muslims and wider society, and their youthful demographic means that their influence will continue to grow. They will shape and drive the future of the wider Muslim population and by extension will have a significant impact on global events.

Not all Muslims are part of Generation M. We're focusing on a specific section of the world's 1.6 billion Muslims who share this characteristic of believing in faith *and* modernity. Their counterparts might be called the Traditionalists. The latter are more socially conservative, believing in maintaining harmony, more deference to authority and, as their name suggests, trying to hold firmly onto what they see as the good elements of family, community and tradition.

I've let our Generation M protagonists take centre stage in the telling of this story, trying to offer as much of their speech as I can. I've used their first names even where typically their surname might be used – after all, this is a personal conversation – no formalities here, just heartfelt exchange.

Each chapter addresses a different aspect of their attitudes and behaviours, the new culture that they are creating and the trends that they are pioneering. On some subjects I've taken a closer look, particularly when it comes to women and minority Muslim populations, because these are subjects that come up over and over again and which therefore warrant detailed attention. Whilst the sum of the chapters is intended to offer a holistic introduction to Generation M, each chapter is also written to stand alone for those readers who may find a particular subject of interest. For this reason, a point may occasionally be raised in more than one place.

These are real stories, where our storytellers are at the forefront, with my words acting merely as the guide through this colourful, nuanced and vibrant world. To that end, I've quoted only minimally from academics and theories. Equally, I've kept theology and textbook religion to a minimum too. Plenty of religious explanations exist elsewhere, and what we want to do here is focus on what people are actually doing, rather than what is written in reference tomes. I've omitted some of the terminology that Muslims might ordinarily use to ascribe to individuals like the Prophet Muhammad, unless the speaker themselves has mentioned it. Most commonly this would be the Arabic reference (SAW) or the equivalent English abbreviation (PBUH), both of which mean 'Peace be upon him'. This is only for simplicity in the text. I've used religious terms with the everyday colloquial meanings used by Generation M themselves. I've also tapped into the internet and social media to hear our heroes speak to the world, because these platforms play a pivotal role in their identity and self-expression.

This book has been very much the quest of a curious professional excited to get to know a group of people who will be highly influential in our future. But it's also a very personal journey to find out what it means to be a young pioneering modern Muslim today. What are their hopes? What do they feel frustrated about? What would they like the world to know about them? Perhaps the two biggest questions we can keep in mind as we begin our journey together are: what does Generation M want to tell us, and – once we've got to know them – what should we do to engage with them?

So, just as Generation M would begin any journey, let's start. *Bismillah* …

1 THE CURTAIN RISES

The World that's Shaping Generation M

In cold, wintry London, Ahmed and his wife Zahra have recently returned from their honeymoon in the Maldives. In their late twenties, this British Muslim couple had dreamed about an archetypal paradise island escape, but they were looking for something more: a place that would be accommodating, welcoming even, of their Muslim sensibilities.

'We didn't want the headache of worrying about what to eat and looking for halal restaurants,' says Ahmed. He also wanted to ensure that his wife could enjoy swimming while observing her modest dress.

Zahra added, 'This was a place where private pools are available with the rooms.' And, referring to the all-over swimsuit that Muslim women are rapidly adopting around the world: 'Even if I did want to swim in public, I wouldn't have got stared at in my burqini.'

Ahmed and his wife are part of a growing global group of Muslims who feel comfortable with both faith and modern life, and they expect the best of both. This new generation is young, educated, worldly and tech-savvy; they want the finest that life can offer, without compromising any of their Islamic ideals.

There are Ahmeds and Zahras right across the globe, located in majority and minority Muslim nations. They are proud to be Muslim and translate that into the way they interact with the world and the proactive contributions they make. Despite being the trendsetters among a global population of 1.6 billion people, the zeitgeist that Ahmed and Zahra embody remains surprisingly unnoticed. This is a new wave of Muslims who engage in all aspects of modernity through the lens of faith. This shift has been masked behind solid monolithic representations of Muslims which equate faith with opposition to modernity, which frame Muslims as the villains in a civilisational war and which see the global billions as one homogenous group. With the growing global prominence of extremist organisations such as Daesh – the violent group that has set up a so-called Caliphate in Iraq and Syria, calling itself Islamic State – that claim the mantle of Islam for themselves, the efforts, creativity and innovation of our story's heroes remain unexplored. They are frustrated and angered by this discrepancy, and this frustration furthers their ambition to be more creative and innovative. The result is that they want to tell their own stories on their own terms, and to be properly heard.

In London, 35-year-old health professional Amira told me,

> The negative images can be depressing but it empowers me to do more locally, to show through our daily lives that these stereotypes are completely wrong. I hope I can show those who I interact with what our faith really means. The advice I can really give is to be the best ambassador for your faith in your small actions.

Ahmed, Zahra, Amira and their peers are Muslims who see the world in ways that are richer, more complex and far more open than we imagine: ways which we will come to see have great overlap with – even influence over – wider pioneering social trends within civic, corporate, cultural and commercial spaces.

Unlike their Millennial counterparts, there is one significant factor that differentiates Generation M: their faith.

Beneath the dark shadow of 11 September, our young Muslims have grown up under intense global scrutiny. But instead of hiding, the generation that have resulted are passionate about their faith and proudly self-identify as Muslims. They are ardent about defending themselves against what they believe are the misconceptions about Muslims, at the same time as seeing their faith as something that empowers them. They see it as their role to be ambassadors for their faith. They do not see the world in terms of clashes of civilisations. Instead, they see multiple cultures, domains and experiences co-existing inside themselves. For Generation M, faith and modernity together make perfect sense. The proof is that they are living it.

They feel horror at terrorism carried out by Muslims, but also feel scapegoated by the 'with us or against us' rhetoric which underpins the War on Terror; both undoubtedly play a role in shaping their identity. Instead of a story of assimilation and erasure of Muslim identity their hallmarks are pride in their faith, and the assertion of a rich, diverse and inclusive worldview.

When I look back at the publication of my first book, *Love in a Headscarf,* and the reasons that prompted me to write it, I see these attitudes coming through strongly. When the book launched, I wrote,

> I was fed up of seeing the same old stories told all the time, and wanted to share one 'from the inside', and in a way that itself was groundbreaking. I wanted to tell a story that touches each of us as human beings.

This meant stepping away from what I described at that time as 'black and white views' about the stories Muslims are allowed to tell, either about being oppressed by Islam, or about finding liberation only by rejecting Islam. If these are the only stories we hear, I asked, 'how can it ever be possible to create an understanding of our diversity and complexity?'

In the zeal to tell my story I see an echo of Generation M's quest for honesty and improvement, whether that be within their own Muslim communities or across wider global society. I felt we needed to take ownership of our identity: 'If publishers are guilty of monolithic misery memoirs, then Muslims must also take some of the blame for not sharing our universal experiences in a language and context that everyone can relate to.'

Generation M is not the story of all Muslims. Our story zooms in on just one segment who share attitudes and behaviours across the world, a segment who believe in faith and modernity as mutually beneficial and the underpinning guiding principles for their lives. Their energetic and optimistic approach aims to bring togetherness within the ummah as well as outreach across wider society. They are disproportionately influential on the wider Muslim populations.

Generation M are a new story, which makes it exciting to tell. Its characters are vibrant, creative, energetic and optimistic. And the story is a marvellous, inventive and invigorating tale of what happens when unheard voices, under apparent restrictions and with a worldview that encourages creative possibility, are overlaid on a young, fast-growing population that is proud of the new identity it is creating.

In order that they tell us their stories intimately, we must first paint the set of the global stage on which they find themselves, and which has shaped them: religiosity, business, modernity, the spotlight on Muslims which too often veers into stereotyping and Islamophobia, and broader civic trends such as social media and women's rights movements. Before our heroes enter, let us set the scene.

Rumours of the Death of Religion Are Greatly Exaggerated

'American adolescents in the 2010s are significantly less religiously oriented, on average, than their Boomer and Generation X predecessors were at the same age.' This is the finding of a research team led by San Diego State University psychologist Jean Twenge. It confirms waves of earlier studies that indicate that US Millennials are less likely than members of previous generations to attend religious services and more likely to be less supportive of religious organisations. They are also less likely to be spiritual too.

The team suggest several reasons for this, including 'the rise of individualism', the tension between a growing emphasis on independent thinking versus what people believe religions require in terms of 'rule following and submission to authority', and the revival of the debate about science versus religion. They also claim that the sense of belonging that religion once afforded people has now been replaced by social media communities.

The decrease in religiosity in America, and in Europe, which dominate global discussions and culture, makes it easy to assume that religion in general is in decline globally. This assumption is built on the idea that modernity and secularism will eventually win out over religion, and religion will be eradicated. But the reality is that religion is incredibly important for billions of people around the world. As our story unfolds, there are some surprises in store with regard to the factors that the San Diego team posits as triggering the decline in religiosity among young Americans: these very factors underpin the emergence of Generation M. It is this generation's independent-mindedness that pushes them towards a rejuvenation of faith by asking questions; it is their individualism that transforms them into entrepreneurs, social influencers and civic leaders; it is precisely the assertion that science is incompatible with religion that triggers their belief that science has always been a fundamental part of Islamic faith. And digital communities have not replaced the sense of belonging that religion once offered – they have enhanced and cemented religiosity and the sense of a religious family.

According to the Pew Research Forum, over the next four decades, Christians will continue to make up the largest religious group, but Islam will grow faster than any other major religion. By 2050 the number of Muslims around the world (2.8 billion, or 30 per cent of the population) will nearly equal the number of Christians (2.9 billion, or 31 per cent), possibly for the first time in history.

Religion may be waning in numbers, influence and practice in the West, but it is alive in the most populous parts of the world, whether in the form of Christianity, Islam or other religions. With most global media outlets located in Europe and North America, regions that are home to an increasingly areligious – some would even say irreligious, or anti-religious – viewpoint on the world, it is easy to feel as though religion as a whole is in decline globally. But claims of the demise of religion in a post-modern age are greatly exaggerated.

In March 2013, world news was dominated by the election of a new pope. There was a global sense of anticipation and intense engagement from Catholics, who make up 1.2 billion of the world's population. A huge number of people clearly take religion very seriously. What became apparent was that the heartlands of Catholicism have dramatically shifted away from Europe and North America to Africa and South America. In terms of both absolute population as well as growth rates, there was a global realisation that the spread of the Christian Catholic faith had changed, and the way that the Catholic faith was going to engage with modernity was also likely to change drastically.

There are striking echoes of this shift within the global Muslim population. The traditional and historical heartland of Islam is of course in the Middle East. But in terms of numbers, the largest proportion of Muslims (over 60 per cent) reside in Asia. In fact, India will become home to the largest Muslim population, despite Muslims being a religious minority there, followed by Pakistan and Indonesia. This means that, whilst Generation M's values show robust consistency across the globe, there should be no illusion that Muslim is the same as Arab. And neither does Arab mean Muslim. Generation M are not the preserve of any one single culture or region.

Everyday Religiosity is Important

The Pew Forum on Religion and Public Life reports that there are 5.8 billion religiously affiliated adults and children around the globe, which made up 84 per cent of the 2010 world population of 6.9 billion. Faith is growing in regions where the population is growing.

Islam offers a level of prescriptive detail about daily life beyond any other religion. Muslims believe that it covers every aspect of life, and that its overarching reach is one of its selling points. Of course, whether or how much an individual upholds each of these prescriptions is a different matter, and most Muslims will admit that religious practice is a work in progress. What the extension of Islam as a religion into the acts of daily life means is that the kind of products that can be consumed and the daily pattern of life have similarities across the globe. Food should be halal, prayers are to be recited throughout the day, modest clothing should be worn. Again, just because such acts should be done, doesn't mean they always are, but they remain in the fabric of Muslim life, practised to greater or lesser degrees.

The result is a marketplace for the kind of products that deliver this lifestyle. With 1.6 billion Muslims in the world, it makes powerful economic sense for businesses to reach out to them. Critics who say brands and products aimed at Muslims are wrong or 'pander' to Muslims have missed the point: just because Muslims have the commercial world increasingly waking up to their needs does not mean other faiths cannot or should not have the same.

The truth is that engagement with wider faith groups does exist. The kosher industry aimed at Jewish consumers is extremely rigorous in its product development and marketing and is welcomed around the world. In the UK, a Christian dating website ran an advertising campaign with the strapline 'Christians make better lovers'. After a horrific gang rape in Delhi, Save the Children India ran a 'Save Our Sisters' campaign that used the iconography of Hindu deities to show images of violence against women. The posters featured Hindu goddesses with physical injuries on their faces, clearly designed to engage with Hindu audiences.

Modernity Is Not the Opposite of Religion

We look back on the European Enlightenment and see it as a movement that perceived religion as hindering progress, which set us on the journey of leaving religion behind in order to be forward-looking, scientifically minded and embracing of new technologies. Once science, democracy and consumerism are widespread, then religion will disappear, or so the theory goes. So Generation M's attitude comes as a surprise: religion makes modernity better in their eyes. And modernity makes religion better.

The unexpected trend which we will unpick as we get to know Generation M is that, as affluence percolates through the world's vast Muslim population, and as digital technologies open access to information, ideas and solidarity, faith among Muslims is in fact on the increase. Muslims – Generation M in particular – have been looking back into their heritage to see what were once their strengths, and how these can be their inspiration once again in advancing their own place in modernity. The idea that science is deeply rooted in the golden Islamic civilisations is one that allows them to reclaim their position in modern life and offer evidence that not only are religion and modernity compatible, but that religion inspires modernity.

In 2006, the exhibition '1001 Muslim Inventions', and a subsequent book by the same name, set out to bring to public attention the engineers, physicians, inventors and scientists of Muslim heritage that have shaped our modern world. According to the creator of the exhibition, 'The extent to which Muslims have contributed to Western Civilisation is not generally well known.' Professor Salim Al Hassani explains:

> Yet these ancient scholars from the Islamic world gave us many of the everyday things we use today such as coffee, soap and clocks. This exhibition shows that Muslims have always shared the heritage that provides a platform for developments that make the Western World tick.

Although today's young Muslims look back at this heritage with pride, it is the fact that it speaks to their belief that religion, modernity and science are all facets of the same way of life – not in opposition to each other – that is worth noting.

The Religion of Business and the Business of Religion

In January 2011 Mohamed Bouazizi set himself on fire in a small town in Tunisia, and ignited a bigger flame which swept across the Arab world and was dubbed the 'Arab Spring'. He was protesting the restrictions placed on him as he tried to run his business and make money to support himself and his family. It was the urge towards entrepreneurship and autonomy that triggered an intensely human political response.

Today we accept that, within the constraints of the law, people have a right to make money and people have a right to consume. Whilst there is an inherent tension between religion, which advocates ethical money-making, and our current global marketplace, which pushes for constant economic growth, Generation M is inspired by the Islamic imperative to do business.

Commerce is built into Islamic values, but the challenge is to avoid extravagance, overconsumption and waste. After all, Prophet Muhammad was a merchant and so was his first wife Khadijah.

The world's most successful global brands are Western. This puts them in the firing line in cultural and political wars. 'McDonaldisation' is opposed around the world on the grounds that it is a kind of neo-imperialism and has become the lightning rod for questions about whether these brands are suited to other cultures and religions.

For some Muslims, these questions are heightened when they coincide with political events perceived to be in the 'Western interest'. That's why at the height of political happenings such as the Gulf War, or the blockade of Gaza, Western brands are targeted by Muslim boycotts. When cartoons of the Prophet were published in a Danish newspaper in 2005, the ensuing boycott by the Muslim world of Danish brands was predicted by Danske Bank to have put $1.6 billion of trade at risk. Generation M are willing to assert their global democratic right for consumption in order to support their beliefs.

And yet Generation M love brands. They aspire to assert their identity through the brands that they feel best reflect them. They have no problem with Western brands as long as the values they represent resonate with their Muslim lifestyle aspirations. Brands have sadly been slow to understand and respond to Generation M, whether in their products, their communications or their community engagement. As a result, products, brands, ideas and creations that address that gap are being created by Generation M themselves.

Shazia Saleem set up halal ready-meal company ieat foods in the UK (the 'i' representing 'Islamically'). She jokes that she started her food company simply because she was hungry. 'Most of my friends at university were non-Muslims, and when we did a weekly food shop together their trolleys were full of really tasty-looking ready meals, and all I could buy were things like cheese and onion pasties,' she says.

It was really frustrating, and I used to whinge a lot that I was missing out. I thought, why wasn't anyone making halal ready meals, other than the odd curry? That was when I decided I needed to do something about it.

She's beaten most of the global multinationals to create products and a brand to speak to this audience.

The ethics by which modern businesses and economics operate have come under increasing scrutiny in recent years by ordinary people who are pushing harder for business to operate ethically right across the production and consumption life cycle.

In 2013 Pope Francis said: 'There is a need for financial reform along ethical lines that would produce in its turn an economic reform to benefit everyone. Money has to serve, not to rule.' Socio-political movements like Occupy Wall Street also highlighted how ethics and equality need to push reform of the business sphere. Young Muslims see in these movements echoes of Islamic business teachings which have been forgotten, and they are inspired to revive Islamic principles.

The trends we've looked at so far concern the nature of our modern world's relationship with religion: its impact at a macro level in societal attitudes and behaviour; its effect at the micro level of daily life; its relationship with global and local businesses which dominate so much of global development, and whether the trajectory of modernity will be boosted or hindered by religion. The growing affluence of the globe's young Muslim demographic is part of a bigger picture of the growth of the middle class, which will probably shift economics away from the West and will force a rethink among Western brands about how to keep asserting their global dominance. The question is, how will the growing Muslim middle class react?

The Growing Middle Class

According to the Brookings Institution the global middle class will more than double in size, from 2 billion in 2012 to 4.9 billion in 2030. Asia will see the lion's share of this growth, doubling from a current 30 per cent to host 64 per cent of the global middle class and account for over 40 per cent of global middle-class consumption.

By contrast, Europe's middle classes will decline from 50 per cent to just 22 per cent. It's worth remembering that over 60 per cent of the global Muslim population is in Asia, and India's Muslim minority will be the world's largest Muslim population.

The growth of China and India are familiar stories; less well known is that of the Muslim middle class. Figures are scant, although our own estimates suggest that today's Muslim middle class is approximately 300 million people, and is likely to triple by 2030 to around 900 million.

The progression of the global middle class isn't important just as a motor of consumption for domestic and international demand; it also has a social and political role – already seen in India and China. Middle classes are believed to support democracy and progressive but moderate political platforms alongside economic development, in particular those that promote inclusive growth. These are some of the reasons given in the analyses of why the Arab Spring began in Tunisia and Egypt, as this is where the middle classes were growing fastest in the region.

There are also shifts affecting education, sophistication, tastes and concerns. Rising out of poverty means that once the basic needs of food and shelter are met, people are turning their attention to how to invest their values into their production and consumption cycles. As we get to know Generation M, we will see the signs of this growing middle-class taste in products and brands focusing on premium and luxury aspirations.

Vali Nasr comments about the Muslim middle classes in his book *Meccanomics*, 'They constitute people who are better off, who want new opportunities, participate in the global economy, and also want the political freedoms that go with it. Those are the people who use the social media.' What interests this group is not confined to Islamic principles or theocratic identity, but: 'it is friendly to the global values that the United States and the West are partaking in.' Their interests are common to the wider middle-class segment: 'It wants political freedoms, it wants economic prosperity, it wants to engage the world.' Since Vali Nasr postulates that the rising Muslim middle class is the bulwark against extremism, it is economics rather than theology that holds sway. The result is a Muslim generation of entrepreneurs, investors, professionals and fervent consumers.

Changing Attitudes About People, Power and Place

Religion, business, the glare of the world's attention on Muslims and the growing global middle class are some of the overarching global trends from which Generation M is emerging, but there are other shifts that are also having a significant impact: greater interrogation of leaders, the role of the internet and social media, the growing women's rights movements and the shifting nature of identity in a globalised world.

Leaders Held to Account

Leadership and deference to authority have been shaken globally. This might be as cataclysmic as the fall of a dictator, or more apparently superficial such as TV and entertainment celebrities being held to account or religious scholars being challenged about their attitudes. Muslim societies, at both national and local levels, are characterised as more collectivist in attitude, often putting the wider group before their own individual needs. But deference to hierarchy is being slowly eroded everywhere in the world. The internet has played a huge role in this change, opening up access to information, bypassing gatekeepers and removing barriers to people and opportunities.

There has been a fundamental global shift to an open discourse that demands leaders respond to citizens' questions and protests. Whether political, religious or social, leaders no longer occupy the pedestals they once stood on as untouchables.

Social Media and the Internet

With the internet as we know it almost three decades old, the half of the world under 30 has never known life without it, and that is certainly true for young Muslims. The internet is bringing down barriers for everyone and allows access to information and decision-makers. Sharing news across borders, beyond establishment channels, has allowed new stories to be told by new storytellers, such as young Muslims. The limits of family, tribe and geography are dissolved, and values, shared interests and communities of purpose have for young Muslims given rise to the digital ummah, a powerful global space to assert their identity.

Female Revolutionaries

Women in Muslim nations have been part of the shift towards women's rights that started to gain momentum in the twentieth century. However, since majority Muslim nations themselves were fighting for freedom from colonialism, Muslim women faced further layers of struggle as entire societies were attempting to restructure themselves.

In nations that are under-developed, poverty, debt and political clout (or lack of it) have more significant effects on women than on men.

Generation M women believe in the right to equal participation, equal respect and a full role in society, but increasingly demand this on their own terms as Muslims rather than accepting the goals of feminism rooted in the Western tradition. It is undeniable that the global struggle for women's rights influences and is influenced by today's Muslim women. Our female heroes are making an energetic contribution despite – or more likely because of – being on the front line between those who deem them oppressed by religion and those who believe modernity has taken away their femininity. Their inspiration comes from Islam as much as the wider feminist movement, in the way they see it fitting into the modern world.

Identifying Yourself in a Global World, Especially if You're Muslim

In the modern era, the nation state and easy global migration have created a postwar identity politics. Countries were often carved up without regard for the ethnic populations that straddled borders, leading to many of the bloody conflicts we see today. This has caused strengthening of ethnic identities, as well as creating connections of religion across borders and countries. The quest for identity has fed into the search that young Muslims embark on to find their own place in the modern world.

In minority Muslim nations such as the UK, the wider discussions of identity centred around race. The first wave of identity politics focused on black as an identifier and political term. Whilst racial identity has become a strong social construct within which to understand the experiences and desire of different groups, Muslims found that the racial distinctions did not speak to their collective experiences. They found a shared affinity across ethnic groups (including majority groups) by asserting a Muslim identity.

The struggle to assert a religious identity in minority countries has been beset with accusations of 'playing the victim' as Muslims have responded to the growing phenomenon of Islamophobia. Muslims are not given a standing as a race, and given the nature of the ummah as being composed of all races, they reject the idea of being a race anyway. However, in a world where racial identity offers protection, standing and even respect, they feel unjustly treated, being denied the opportunity of asserting their own identity. If anything, all this feeds into a heightened sense of Muslim identity and a demand to be recognised as such.

The Effect of Anti-Muslim Hatred

In September 2015, Buzzfeed published the video 'I'm a Muslim, But I'm Not …' in a bid to tackle stereotypes of Muslims. A number of young Muslim Americans spoke to camera with reassurances that they did not live up to the negative ideas about Muslims. 'I'm a Muslim but I'm not angry,' says one. 'I'm a Muslim but I'm not a terrorist,' says another. There was a whiff of apologism about it, and it was not well received by many Muslims, who feel that far too often they are required to offer up collective penance for actions that are nothing to do with them.

Italian Muslim writer Davide Mastracci put into words what many other Muslims felt, that the video had failed 'largely because it attempts to find exceptions to the stereotype, instead of addressing the problematic nature of the stereotype at its core'. He writes, 'What should instead be challenged is the idea that it's wrong for Muslims to be angry, or that Muslims have no reason to be angry.'

A group of Australian Muslims created their own 'I'm a Muslim, But ...' video to assert how they still have the right to express their social and political beliefs and do not need to apologise. 'I'm Muslim but it's not my job to soothe your anxieties about what I wear,' says one woman wearing a headscarf. Another black woman asserts: 'I'm Muslim but I don't have to justify my right to live here free from racism.' One says: '[...] but I don't need to apologise for random acts of violence that have nothing to do with me.'

They tackle their pride in their religion and their loyalty: '[...] I don't care if you think it's weird that I believe in God', '[...] I don't need to prove my loyalty to you or anyone else.' What really comes through is how they are worn down by the constant onslaught in daily life which they feel makes being a Muslim harder each day. 'It's not my job to educate you on the history of the Middle East or anywhere else [...] I don't think it's acceptable to publish racist "satire" about my faith [...] I'm sick of my community being harassed by security agencies.'

The extent of the hostility that Muslims experience in everyday life, and the frustration it creates, cannot be overestimated. For our young Generation M, this intense negativity has been omnipresent their whole adult lives. Some of the effects are fatal – literally life or death.

After the attacks in Paris on the *Charlie Hebdo* offices, 60 Islamophobic incidences were recorded, with 26 mosques around France being attacked by firebombs, gunfire, pig's heads and grenades. Anti-Muslim attacks in London grew by 70 per cent in the year up to July 2015, with Muslim women suffering the greater share of attacks.

In June 2015, in Dresden, Germany, the anti-Islam PEGIDA (Patriotic Europeans Against the Islamisation of the Occident) party won 10 per cent of the vote in a mayoral election and at its height brought up to 25,000 people onto the streets of Dresden in protest against Muslims. During the 2015 Republican Party presidential candidate selection race in the USA, one of the candidates, Ben Carson, said he would not support a Muslim president. A poll carried out among Republican voters in North Carolina during the race confirmed the level of anti-Muslim hatred. Of those polled, 72 per cent believed that a Muslim should not be allowed to be president of the USA; a huge number – 40 per cent – believed that Islam should be illegal in the USA. The Republican nominee, Donald Trump, advocated that Muslims should be banned from entering the USA.

All of these are of course just a smattering of the growing levels of anti-Muslim sentiment, much of which is institutional discrimination embedded in state policies in various countries around the world. There are also day-to-day impediments caused by deep-seated anti-Muslim hostility that wear away at the ability of Muslims to live ordinary lives. These obstacles go unnoticed by those who are not Muslim.

One of those is 'flying while Muslim'. Soon after Donald Trump's call to ban Muslims from entering the USA, a British Muslim family were prevented from flying from London to Disneyland.

In a similar incident, on New Year's Day 2009, the Irfan family was boarding a flight at Washington DC, heading for Orlando, along with 95 other passengers. As they took their seats, Mr Irfan asked his wife where the safest place to sit on the plane would be – the rear, the front or the wing? The passengers behind them overheard and combined these words with the image of Mr Irfan's beard and his wife's headscarf. The passengers contacted flight attendants, who got in touch with security officials, and the entire Irfan family were forcibly removed from the plane and taken for questioning, detained by the FBI. Eventually they were cleared. But despite the allegations having no substance, the airline AirTran refused to refund the airfare, and also declined to rebook them. After high-profile coverage in the national US press and a huge amount of pressure, the airline apologised to the family and refunded the fare.

Mr Irfan's rationalisation of the experience of 'flying while Muslim' is telling. He said to the *New York Times*:

To be honest, as a Muslim, we do understand how to deal with this, we realize this is an unfortunate aspect in our lives. [...] Whenever we get on a plane, because of the colour of our skin, people tend to look at us with a wary eye anyway. Of course it was very embarrassing.

The Irfans' story is commonplace. In 2015, female Muslim chaplain Tahera Ahmad was refused a can of Diet Coke on a United Airlines flight because she was told she might use it as a 'weapon'.

Dean Obeidallah, a Muslim American comedian of Palestinian-Italian heritage, asked:

> Did AirTran violate any rules or regulations – did they violate the Irfans' civil rights? I'm not sure, but all I can say to the Irfan family – especially Mr. Irfan, who is a lawyer and says he is a proud American – is that nothing says 'I'm a real American' like a big fat lawsuit.

Dean's solution is part of the Generation M way: take advantage of consumerism. Another approach is comedy, as Wajahat Ali demonstrates. Also a Muslim American, of Pakistani heritage, Wajahat is a social commentator and TV presenter:

> Any time I'm depressed or lonely, I decide to go to the airport where instantly I'm lavished with meticulous attention and treated like a Hollywood celebrity. What's not to love about the multiple Transportation Security Administration (TSA) agents who 'randomly' select you for special inspection? Or their curious, unbridled interest in asking you which mosques you frequent? Their desire to express their hospitality and love is so uncontainable that you're treated to several physical pat-downs covering every inch of your body. This includes the thin, inner sewed linings of my pants, which I was told could potentially conceal bombs. Although my adolescent sense of humour prompted an immature comment upon hearing this, I thankfully exercised restraint.

The spotlight is uncomfortably hot for young Muslims and its persistent glare is one of the major trends that we must consider in setting the scene for Generation M's emergence. This is not only because it shapes Generation M's attitudes and ambitions, but also because it shapes the way that those around them have historically responded to Muslims, and continue to do so.

So, even while the Muslim middle classes are being courted because of their growing affluence, business potential and role as buffer to extremism, they are experiencing growing anti-Muslim sentiment and are stuck between Islamophobia and violent extremists conducting horrific acts in the name of Islam.

A New Identity

'I was sick of telling "my story",' says Layla Shaikley. 'Every time I did, I was contending with Islamphobes and terrorists alike, who had equally hijacked the popular narrative about Muslims. So I tried something else: creative action.'

Layla is an MIT graduate who has worked with NASA and the UN and is the co-founder of TEDxBaghdad. With hip hop artist Jay Z's song 'Somewhere in America' as the soundtrack, she created a funky pop culture video about female Mipsterz – Muslim hipsters. She says,

> The video is a celebration of our daily lives. No burqas, bombs, or other symbols ignorantly associated with the hijab on our heads. Instead, skateboards, sunshine, and good times – realities that define us as individuals. We made the video as a self-portrait.

Drenched in sunshine and optimism, the video caught a zeitgeist in depicting a new Muslim culture: how they look, sound, act and what they do, a culture they are defining and portraying on their own terms. It sent out a message that Muslims, particularly Muslim women, embrace modernity, even while the protagonists' aims were nothing grander than to be themselves. But for Generation M, being oneself is totally radical. As Layla explains:

> The video focuses on a couple dozen Muslim women in hijab showcasing their fashion sensibilities and having a good time. Whether biking, laughing, or just hanging out, the people

1. The Mipsterz video was created by Layla Shaikley, who says 'The video is a celebration of our daily lives. No burqas, bombs, or other symbols ignorantly associated with the hijab on our heads. Instead, skateboards, sunshine, and good times.'

in the video were asked to be themselves when they were not shot candidly. The subjects range from an Olympian fencer to a Harvard Dental School student to an attorney to myself. One girl founded a hijab company, and another a jewellery company.

Even though Layla, the participants and the production team set out to do nothing more than offer a glimpse of their lives to a wider American public, the video sparked a discussion within the global Muslim communities. Generation M critics were understanding that being accepted as 'cool' in a climate of hostility is important. But, asked the critics among Generation M, was there a better way to do this, something that was more Islamic, something that pushed the boundaries beyond the current mainstream parameters, something that even pushed mainstream culture to be better? Their worries focused on 'commoditising women', on the soundtrack which through its X-rated lyrics belied the Islamic intent, and on the look of the video, which seemed to imitate existing norms. Generation M's aspiration is always to break boundaries rather than imitate. This determination to push limits both within the Muslim communities and within the wider modern cultures is the epitome of Generation M's drive to enhance modernity through the inspiration of their faith.

This is Generation M in a nutshell: influential, confident in conversation, defining their own self-portrayal, willing to pioneer and lead the community, unafraid of walking difficult lines. Across the spectrum of their own stories and viewpoints there is variation, even in spite of their shared project to live a modern faithful life on their own terms.

As the controversy sparked opinions from Muslims around the world about what it means to be a Muslim and who gets to define it, Layla distilled the attitude into one simple approach: 'Tell your own story, and don't rely on others to do it for you.'

So, prepare to meet Generation M. Here are the stories they want to tell ...

2 GENERATION M

The Young Muslims who Believe in
Faith and Modernity

Outside an upmarket bookstore in trendy Istanbul, the latest editions of glossy magazines are on display. Hip young women are bustling past on their way home from work, in a capital city that sits at the heart of the economic success of one of the world's emerging economies. They are dressed in the latest fashions, accessorised with matching shoes and handbags. As they pick out the fashion magazines that will ensure they stay up to date on the latest trends, they reach over *Vogue*, and ignore *Elle* magazine. Instead, they choose *Âlâ*, a magazine that was outselling the market leaders within months of its launch. Ask them why, and they'll tell you it's because *Âlâ* understands what it is like to be a twenty-first-century Muslim woman. Like them, *Âlâ* is exploring the intersection between modernity and their faith as Muslims. Like them, the models in *Âlâ* wear modest clothes and headscarves.

In a secular country which has only recently slowly started to permit religious symbols such as the headscarf in official spaces – a deeply contentious issue in a nation where expressions of religiosity are growing – the launch and success of this magazine was a shock. An upstart magazine combining Islamic modesty with fashion was outselling leading global publications. *Âlâ*'s advertisers included big brand names such as Gucci, Dolce & Gabbana and H&M.

In Singapore, IT analyst Hasina enjoys reading *Aquila Style*, a vibrant digital lifestyle publication aimed at go-getting Muslim women. Its imagery is bold, unapologetic and striking. Its columnists offer a global snapshot of influential Generation M voices. Each edition addresses big topics for young Muslims: 'The Empower Issue', 'Earth', 'Love'. Other issues offer up stories such as 'Pray, Shop, Cook to Beat the Eid Blues', and 'Love and Intimacy the Islamic Way'.

'I particularly like the fashion shoots with hijab,' says 27-year-old Hasina, 'and the inspirational Muslimah stories.' It makes her feel 'connected with all Muslim societies around the globe'. It definitely appeals to her more than *Vogue*. She reads it online, hooking into the communities which she feels share her values and inhabit cyberspace with her.

Cut 5,000 miles to Chicago, and Muslim YouTube sensation Baba Ali, an American convert who shot to fame with his pithy, humorous yet evangelical video musings on the state of the Muslim ummah, launched *Muslim Quarterly*, a magazine aimed at Muslim men, with front-cover teasers such as 'Foods to Boost Your Sexual Mood' and 'Learn how to Sizzle up Your Love Life'. The difference between it and *GQ*, the inspiration for its title, is that the content – edgy, pioneering, sexy even – is a creative endeavour designed to be entirely halal, Islamically permissible.

What on earth is going on? Technology, sex, creativity, fashion, media …? These Muslims are not rejecting modernity, they are *shaping* it. They are turning their aspirations for freedom, security, employment and engagement into a concrete and formidable reality, and they are doing it at a frenzied pace. Theirs is an entirely new, fresh and self-empowered phenomenon that is going to change the societies they live in, and by extension the wider world. They see their faith as a tool with which to engage with modernity. They are interested in rewriting the rules of leadership, social structures, consumption and communication with one specific factor in mind: faith.

It's a Muslim world we've never seen before: a world where religion affects the way people consume, interact, work and enjoy. It's not a comment on religiosity, or a judgement on the level of piety – it's simply that faith has an effect.

For Generation M, their faith affects *everything*, and they want the world to know it. This is what sets them apart from their non-Muslim peers. It's the single factor that will shape them and a world that they are determined should deliver to their needs. They believe in asking questions, entering into dialogue with authority and crossing geographic and cultural borders to connect with their Muslim peers around the world. They embrace technology and education and believe that, inspired by their faith, they can make themselves, their communities and the world a better place.

Not all Muslims hold these beliefs; not all Muslims are part of Generation M. Whilst most of Generation M are young, it is their attitude not their age that defines them. They are a tech-savvy, self-empowered, youthful group who believe that their identity encompasses both faith *and* modernity. Welcome to Generation M.

Consumption as Core to Identity

'Halal first, everything else later!' is the motto of four young Muslim women in Singapore who founded the Halal Food Hunt website. Their aim is to document all the halal options they can find in order to help people make religious choices more easily, to ensure women get time with their family and, importantly, to ensure there's no compromise on taste. What the website embodies is the significance of being part of the Muslim gang that seeks to live life to the full by buying stuff, and helping others to do so – all the while ensuring it's in line with Islamic principles.

Young, educated and increasingly affluent, the growing Muslim middle class are realising they can assert their right to demand goods and services in line with their Islamic requirements. That can mean anything from the ingredients themselves being halal-compliant, the communications being ethical or even the corporate affiliations of the brand being subjected to scrutiny.

Batul lives in the UK and was looking to take her young family on holiday. She'd previously travelled to Dubai, where the halal food was one of the attractions. Last year, with tight budgets, she looked closer to home at Butlins. 'We requested halal meat and chicken. The catering manager was very helpful indeed, and halal food was made available for us.' The provider also ensured there was no cross-contamination in the way the food was prepared, just as Batul had requested.

The Muslim middle class have become aware of their collective consumer power and have started to flex it. The impact of the boycott of Danish brands after the publication of cartoons of Prophet Muhammad in a Danish newspaper brought about the realisation that this segment can influence global economic rhythms through their actions. In 2003, Mecca Cola was set up in France. Entrepreneur Tawfik Mathlouthi aimed to capitalise on a wave of anti-US feeling by persuading consumers to 'buy Muslim'. The brand promised that 10 per cent of its profits would go to a Palestinian children's charity. 'Don't drink stupid,' read Mecca Cola's label, 'drink committed'. Within two months, it sold more than 2 million 1.5-litre bottles and had orders for 16 million more. Other brands such as Ummah Cola and Zamzam Cola followed. As the names suggest, these were copycat versions of Coca-Cola, even tasting similar. Buying these products was less about the taste and more about the purchase being a marker of identity.

Consumption has always been a way to say something about the self, and this is no different for young Muslims. Buying halal or Muslim-friendly allows them to gain entry into the halal club and wear their Muslim credentials with pride. They wear T-shirts that say 'Don't panic I'm Islamic' and feel comfortable and confident to have the Muslim Pro app on their smartphone blare out the adhaan at prayer time. Engaging in halal consumption as a way of practising religion and being part of the halal club have ensured that the idea of an 'Islamic economy' has gained traction over the last decade.

The halal brand is bigger, more widespread and worth more than any other brand, whether that's Apple, Google, Nestlé or McDonald's. The halal food and beverage sector alone in 2014 was estimated at over $1.1 trillion, and that's before we even consider the wider Muslim lifestyle marketplace. The attempt to define an individual sense of self is a key characteristic of this group. Balancing the tension between the individual and the collective – an important aspect of Muslim cultures – is, however, a source of these young Muslims' power and momentum as the influencers within their wider Muslim, as well as global, communities. Being the individual hero is how they drive the community forwards, even while the community remains crucial to their identity and their motivation.

This strong sense of religious identity is exhibited in every aspect of their lives, and is the foundation of the Muslim lifestyle's sudden bursting onto the scene. The young Muslims' aspiration to imbue every aspect of their lives with their Muslim values means that everything, from clothes to music to travel to food, is an expression of their Muslim identity. Their choices as consumers become a manifestation of their values, which speak both to their flourishing sense of self as Muslims and also to their place in the modern world, where consumerism is a key factor in self-definition.

Creativity from Constraints

Today's products and brands have not, on the whole, been created with Generation M's Islamic needs in mind. Every item that is consumed entails compromise, something that makes Generation M weary and which they are increasingly unwilling to tolerate. With little choice of products available, they have put to use one of their most prolific talents: creativity. They can tailor the modern and the traditional, the cultural with the religious. They can take something ordinary and mainstream and give it a 'Muslim' twist.

Take the case of Muslim fashion. By using what is available on high streets across the world, in different Muslim cultures new looks are being created that share the underlying values of modest dressing with an aspect of localisation. The outcome is a distinctive Muslim fashion look. Born out of an unwillingness to compromise on modest dress, Muslim fashion creators span the range from swimwear to wedding dresses, either showing their Generation M peers how to use existing available clothing, or creating their own fashion lines. These designers include bloggers, YouTube stars, entrepreneurs and models. The 'constraints' of faith have sparked a global multibillion-dollar industry.

This creativity extends to all aspects of the wearers' own lives and that of their communities. They want the best of modern life, and they want it in accordance with their principles. What might seem to be restrictions lead to an explosion of creativity. As British halal ready-meal company ieat foods explains, it is about Generation M making their favourites 'halalified'.

Proud to be Muslim

'I never used to be open with my identity as a Muslim. I wore hijab and always felt that my actions and my character should do the talking for me.' The global spotlight on Muslims was something Somali-born Hodan Ibrahim found difficult to deal with.

'Part of my resistance of ever opening up about my faith to others had to do with being subtly shamed for being a part of a "religion" and even more so, a religion that had a bad international reputation.' Hodan lived in Egypt for a while, and that inspired her to think about economic development. Now based in Ottowa, she describes herself as a 'serial entrepreneur, publisher, author and blogger'. She says, 'I have a passion for living life to the fullest, fulfilling my potential as a human being and supporting the socio-economic empowerment of poor, marginalized and under-resourced people.'

Her faith is the force behind her work:

> Things changed for me when I became an entrepreneur; my identity became a big part of my business. I started realising that when I went into business meetings, when I went into pitches or was looking for investors, my faith became a part of the equation, whether I liked it or not. People judged me, or misjudged me because of the reputation that my community had (and this isn't to say there aren't many people who view Muslims in a favourable light). People were always going to judge and I better be proud of who I am because I would never give it up. I found a strong sense of pride once I had understood the incredible history that I was from.

There's a sadness about the lost greatness, but an aspiration to reclaim it. 'Yes, Muslims might not be in such a good place now, but my faith is strengthened knowing where we came from and what our collective history is.' Her business, Ummah Ventures, aims to build a global Muslim entrepreneurial ecosystem. It's about the ummah: 'I realised that there is too much potential and hope for me to not embrace my community.'

With religion taking on new importance on the global stage, Generation M's response is not to hide, but to assert pride in their religious identity. Of course, not all Muslims will be wearing their religion on their sleeves; they may not feel the need to do so, or may not want to. But the heroes of our story are proud of being Muslim and proud to stand up for their religion.

Unquestioning acceptance of religious practice is not tolerated; instead, debate and discussion of how and why such practice should be undertaken is required. With global scrutiny placed on their choices, this is no surprise to Generation M. When asked why they identify as Muslims and how they justify their beliefs and practices, they have gone in search of answers that can satisfy their interrogators as well as their own questions. They describe themselves as finding their path by reasoning through the discrepancies they see between theory and practice, between culture and religion. They work hard to challenge assumptions that they unthinkingly follow traditions of yore. They bristle at the idea that they are Muslim by conditioning, or as a result of being lazy and ignorant. The result is that they feel that their beliefs and actions are stronger and more robust than those of previous generations.

This characteristic can be seen right across Muslim populations but is most easily spotted in minority Muslim environments. Second- and third-generation immigrant Muslims often exhibit a deeper knowledge of Islam's teachings than their first-generation parents. In fact, one of the core intergenerational dynamics that plays out is younger Muslims accusing their parents of not understanding religion, or of not practising correctly. Rebellious young Muslim women will don the hijab and even the niqab specifically in contravention of their parents' wishes in order to assert their commitment to their Muslim identity. Their pride in being Muslim is sky high.

Zarqa Nawaz, the creator of the hit Canadian television series *Little Mosque on the Prairie*, explains how she started wearing hijab as part of her rebellion against her parents, whom she did not see as proper Muslims in her teen years.

The best thing about hijab was that I had discovered it on my own – my parents had nothing to do with it, which meant that I could beat them at their own game: religion. I wanted so desperately to be different from them. Hijab was the answer.

Clarifying that being Muslim and observing Islam to a greater or lesser degree is a proactive 'choice' – rather than being forced – is something Generation M are constantly battling with in the wider global discourse, attempting to inject nuance via the fact that they have chosen their faith for themselves and should not be categorised with cultures which enforce behaviour in the name of religion. It is a source of frustration that even when voicing their own opinions of their own free choice in embracing and celebrating their Muslim faith, they are dismissed as brainwashed. They feel that this shows a lack of respect for their agency and decision-making. One common mantra that women who wear headscarves often use to challenge the idea that they are brainwashed is 'I am covering my head, not my brain.'

They believe it is Islam that gives them life purpose and direction, that it is by being Muslim that they are empowered. As a result they are proud of the shoes that they stand in, and their religion gives them a defining identity.

They Believe in Struggle and Success

'Maybe there was a hint of mischief when I made the choice,' says Shakeel Ahmed, discussing the title of *My Jihad*, the romantic comedy he wrote for the BBC which aired in the UK in March 2014. He's referring to the fact that a love story is hardly how we imagine jihad to be. There were no wars, guns or anti-Western chants involved in his film. Instead, his story charted the developing relationship of a kind but socially awkward twenty-something man and a chip-on-her-shoulder but charming single mother. They meet at a Muslim speed-dating event and over the course of an evening a tender love story develops as they go home on the night bus.

There are few words that have entered other languages with such fear and misunderstanding as the Arabic word 'jihad'. Jihad literally means 'to struggle', and this directive to struggle includes both thoughts and actions. For Muslims like Shakeel, jihad means something intense, personal and spiritual. He describes it as 'ridding oneself of ugly traits like envy, gluttony, pride, arrogance and conceit'. He adds that engagement in jihad is 'a battle to make oneself a more rounded, productive, merciful and compassionate human being. To make oneself whole.' And here's the rub for Shakeel and his peers, pushing them to try harder: 'In the modern era, I think we could all do with a little bit of that!'

What frustrates these Muslims is how they feel the meaning of jihad has undergone a semantic shift when taken out of its Islamic context and reframed in new languages. They insist on reclaiming the word from its distorted meaning. The 'greater jihad' as dictated by Islamic teachings is the struggle against the inner self. Only in times when physical self-defence is required, whether personal or at a national level, does the physical ('lesser') jihad take place.

The daily struggle means staying true to one's faith whilst pursuing success. Generation M struggle to establish and build businesses, to gain an education, to improve their own lives and their communities. They feel it is their struggle to take advantage of the opportunities that the previous generations did not have, whether it be in education, business or religion. They have no doubt that if they set their minds to it and if they work hard, they can achieve anything.

Asking Questions, Getting Straight Answers and the Pursuit of Knowledge

'I was always an inquisitive child and loved science, although, born and bred for the first decade in Bangladesh, I had little resources,' says Shanam. It was seeking knowledge and educating himself that brought him towards his faith and away from accepting what he was told by his parents.

> The Islam taught to me by my elders was a bunch of mumbo-jumbo; so consciously I chose to be agnostic. At about 13 or 14 years old I had to pretend I was a Muslim to my parents. At about 16 I met some doctoral students and seeing them as Muslims and seeking knowledge, I thought if they believed then I had best get my facts and started reading. [...] It brought back my interest in Islam.

He adds that he is 'not proud, just grateful to find the truth'.

Generation M know that education is the key to asserting their status. Literacy standards in general, but specifically among girls, are rapidly rising. More youth are staying in education for longer. Universities are also being established locally, often as franchises of Western establishments. This is making it easier and often more affordable for young Muslims to advance their education. It is particularly useful for young women in regions where traditionally their higher education would have been frowned upon, particularly if they had been required to move abroad. In countries like Saudi Arabia and Iran, female university students now outnumber their male counterparts.

In fact, so highly prized is education, and so strong the students' commitment to religious values, that sometimes there can be unexpected social consequences. In Turkey, until recently, wearing the headscarf on university campuses was not permitted as it was deemed to be a symbol of religion in what was supposed to be a strictly secular education space. As a result, young Muslim women elected to travel abroad to study, supported by their families. At one time, to leave home and live alone was a taboo for a single woman, but this unexpected confluence of religious values and thirst for education has created a generation of independent, educated and worldly young women.

The commitment to longer periods in formal education has knock-on effects. For women, it can often be the key to entering employment, having their own disposable income if they do start to work, and marrying later. In the UAE, for example, the average age at marriage of an educated woman is 27 years, compared to 18 years for one who does not pursue higher education. Both men and women understand the importance of education for both sexes. In a report on marriage and education in the UAE, one UAE graduate, Hussain Al-Numeiri, aged 22, was keen to finish his higher studies. 'An educated couple is better than an uneducated couple,' he explained.

Education spans the sublime as well as the worldly. Religious education is a key component of self-development, supporting and focusing progress whether it be in careers or society, as well as guaranteeing the spiritual development that is fundamental to these young Muslims' life vision. In fact, it is likely that their increasing religious knowledge is motivating them to assert meritocracy as the social norm, as Islamic values encourage equality and respect based on others' behaviour rather than inherited wealth or position.

They are also very inspired by the new generation of Islamic scholarship that has arisen in recent years. As Ibrahim Kalin at the Foundation for Political, Economic and Social Research, Ankara, puts it: 'This is perhaps the most intellectually active period for the faith since the height of Islamic scholarship in the Middle Ages.' The rise in Islamic universities in minority Muslim nations goes hand in hand with online Islamic universities and courses, supplementing more traditional methods of learning such as study circles.

Whilst educators and scholars remain on an important pedestal, they are no longer beyond the purview of challenge and interrogation. Young Muslims feel liberated to engage proactively in the conversations about knowledge construction.

Online access has forced scholars to open themselves up directly to the faithful. Online courses allow young Muslims to access knowledge that they would not have been able to reach for geographic, time or cost reasons, especially when it comes to women, who may have previously had limited access to religious studies.

Nasima in the UK says that the internet means it is 'so much easier to access information. For example, if I have a question I can e-mail a mufti. I can also search topics on YouTube and watch it being discussed and my questions answered.'

These educated challengers like to make up their own minds. They are unwilling to accept information at face value and need to investigate what they are told for themselves. They are constantly seeking self-improvement through the spirit of self-investigation to further worldly and spiritual development. They will ask difficult questions, and the answers may be uncomfortable. It's vital to avoid 'following blindly' what others do, or what has been done before.

This curiosity plus online connectivity has given them access to more numerous and non-traditional sources of information, and a wider range of viewpoints. This is the most questioning, challenging generation of young Muslims in recent history.

Of course, the internet's democratisation of religious knowledge brings its own pitfalls, as the quality of knowledge can be suspect and the credibility of those disseminating the knowledge is questionable. Generation M continue to debate the opportunities and risks of 'Wiki Islam' and 'Sheikh Google', which can provide answers – but of unclear credibility – to any social or spiritual dilemma.

Like their peers of other faiths, they are constantly checking for discrepancies in what they are told, to the peril of governments, brands, organisations and parents. For these young Muslims there is a driving imperative for verification and even rejection: it determines how they practise their religion.

They are open to ideas and directions from all kinds of experts, and they are also open to the new spaces in which those experts operate. Religious leaders naturally hold great sway, but their sphere of influence is no longer confined to the mosque or other religious domains.

Meet Amr Khaled, an Egyptian Muslim activist and television preacher and probably one of the earliest influencers of our young generation. The *New York Times* magazine described him in 2006 as 'the world's most famous and influential Muslim television preacher'. In 2008, he was voted number six on *Prospect* magazine's Top 100 Public Intellectuals list. He has more than 6 million followers on Twitter, and 19 million likes on Facebook.

He is tall and svelte; his smart suit and tie enhance his charismatic aura. His hair is short and neatly kept, his dark eyes are earnest. He has a gentle, softly spoken approach and his language is everyday and easy to understand, friendly, even humorous at times. He uses traditional as well as digital and social media even while talking about traditional religious values such as honesty, humility and etiquette. 'Faith-based development' is his idea that faith is not for faith's sake but to produce something good for the community.

When Al Jazeera's Riz Khan asked him on his show *One on One* why he attracts 15–35-year-olds, particularly from the middle and upper classes, he says: 'They are the future. They are well educated. And they are ready to change. And they can believe. And think. And put dreams towards producing something. They never say "no".'

Generation M are open to guidance from anyone whose credibility can be investigated and asserted. Even brands and businesses can take the lead in asserting credibility in their products by demonstrating they've listened to Muslim requirements and by explaining how these specifications have been met by the brand in its products.

In 2014, Cadbury in Malaysia came under scrutiny by the Department of Islamic Development (known by its Malay acronym JAKIM), the governmental body responsible for halal certification and monitoring, about possible contamination in its products. Even once the production processes had been cleared, there was still the challenge of restoring consumer confidence. To do so, Cadbury invited three influential Islamic scholars to tour the facility and then to share their findings with their Muslim audience. Both the insight that it was important to get religious scholars involved in the process of verification, and their presence in the rehabilitation of Cadbury's reputation were new strategies and proved an effective starting point in the pursuit of winning back alienated audiences.

These young Muslims do not want to feel that they are purely a source of profit. So if an organisation is seen to have transgressed the parameters of faith, it can be a slow crawl back to forgiveness. Whilst atonement is a tough challenge, it is not impossible if there is demonstrable sincerity, repentance and if discernible and permanent steps are taken to make a change.

Just as making rigorous enquiries in their quest for knowledge acquisition is second nature to Generation M, the same rigour is applied to questioning whether brands are following their rules. They assert their right to interrogate brands to see whether their products and services meet their personal and religious standards. As one Malaysian Muslim I spoke to said: 'The more educated the Muslims are today, the more awareness among themselves to follow the shariah rules.'

The natural consequence of improved education and exposure to wider influences is a more vocal, challenging and confident generation, one that is less afraid to question the intentions of governments, leaders, companies and brands and one that is ready to hold them accountable for their actions.

They Believe in Getting Ahead without Compromise

'I was blessed to be taught to nurture my belief from the inside out so I see where all the scrutiny has actually made me stronger,' says American spoken-word artist Khalil Ismail while discussing the challenges of pursuing dreams. 'There are many different groups of people who have to deal with scrutiny but the tools and guidance of Islam help with perseverance.'

Despite political, social, economic, cultural and even anti-religion pressures, Generation M refuse to compromise their religious beliefs. In fact, some might go so far as to say that they are championing a religious revival in order to revitalise a Muslim world that lies in the long shadow of its golden era. There is a deep distress about the decline of Muslim civilisation over the last few centuries and what Generation M feel is the belittling of Islam and the weakness of the Muslim voice. Those who champion the Muslim voice are rising stars and win widespread support from Generation M, especially if they can use their knowledge of religion, their success and their professional skills to do so. Generation M actively aim to bridge 'East and West'. In fact, this dichotomy itself is contentious for Generation M. Instead they aim to craft a new kind of proud Muslim success.

Rather than wanting to feel protected and cared for by their religion, Generation M believe instead that it is their duty to protect Islam from hostile media influences as they work hard to bridge both worlds. They believe Islam fits comfortably into the modern world and in fact has the potential to change it for the better. Whatever sphere of life they are engaged in, whether it is business, spirituality, civic society, the workplace or the environment, they try hard to uphold and take inspiration from their Islamic values.

They take pride in being ambitious and assertive – they see these as Islamic values. Earlier we met Hodan. Her Facebook profile image as I write this is a picture of a stark white background with nothing but the word 'AMBITION'. They think it is important to be progressive. Their place in the world must be earned, not taken for granted. And, as we discussed earlier, education and career are weapons in earning that place. They believe strongly in the active power of Islam. They are comfortable being loud and voicing their opinions, but this must be done with respect and responsibility. This is not showmanship for the sake of attracting attention to the self. This is proactivity on behalf of the wider community.

In 2013 in the UK, political journalist Mehdi Hasan took part in a debate at the Oxford Union proposing the motion 'Islam is a peaceful religion'. Mehdi was then the political editor of the *Huffington Post* in the UK and a well-recognised and acclaimed journalist in his own right, with credits from Channel 4, Al Jazeera and the *New Statesman* among many others. On this occasion he was seen to be defending Islam in a prestigious public arena. The video of his performance went viral globally and to date has amassed nearly 1.8 million views. Young Muslims felt they had a champion for their beliefs and position in the world. They saw him as forceful, unapologetic and humorous. Their view was that he refused to be on the back foot or to feel a need to apologise or compromise. He represented how they felt about their own faith: proud and assertive. He and his debating partner won the debate by a majority of two-thirds.

One commenter on the videos explained that what he liked was Mehdi's 'masterful preparation, his marshalling of extensive facts, and his powerfully persuasive presentation skills. Being intensely passionate and intensely logical at the same time is not easy, but he seems to do it effortlessly.' Getting ahead is all about talent and skill. And if these can be marshalled to tackle misconceptions of Islam, it is a cause for celebration.

Passivity is not an option. Generation M are energetic and proactive, based on a strong belief that they can and must create change, and that they can get ahead on their own terms. So, while it may appear on the face of it that globalised – Westernised, even – culture is something that they aspire to, it is now invited into their lives only on the condition that it respects their culture and does not compromise their strong religious beliefs and convictions. It is the same question of accommodating modernity and a Western culture that billions of global citizens tackle every day – but for Generation M it is their Islamic values that provide the framework of how to achieve this balance.

Technology, Purpose and the Connected Ummah

We'll come back again and again in our story to the Islamic concept of 'ummah'. It is one of Islam's most distinguishing factors, and hugely powerful in shaping the consistent global attitudes and sense of togetherness of this segment.

Ummah is best translated as the 'global Muslim nation'; it situates every individual within the wider Muslim communities as having an immediate connection to others anywhere in the world. The deep emotion of what it means (in theory, if not always in practice) to be part of the ummah is described by the Prophet Muhammad in the saying 'The ummah is like the body, if one part hurts, the entire body hurts.' The aspiration of the ummah is to act as one holistic entity striving for the same goal.

Throughout history the notion of ummah has held powerful sway, but it was not until the era of the internet that the dreams of Muslims for a connected ummah became reality. Muslims around the world share their experiences almost instantaneously, making the ummah feel real and immediate.

'During the 20th century, the parents of this generation were struggling to define for themselves some conception of a pan-Arab or pan-Muslim unity,' says Reza Aslan, author of *No God but God*, a *New York Times* bestseller on the origins of Islam. 'That was elusive because there are so many things geopolitically that separate the Muslim world. With the internet, those boundaries, those borders, are irrelevant.'

Of course, for Generation M women who have lived in more traditional cultures which might be more restrictive for their gender, the impact has been even more profound, offering opportunities of commerce, identity and confidence. Perhaps more startling is how social media has given Generation M the ability to connect across the gender divide. Not only does the greater connectivity available to Generation M strengthen feelings of solidarity and enhance knowledge acquisition, this greater immersion in religion offers them greater sources of solutions for their everyday problems. It is one of the reasons why religious evangelists who become popular 'on the street', rather than in traditional spaces of religious learning like mosques, can be found addressing day-to-day problems rather than abstract theological concepts.

The family has always been the microcosm of the ummah and continues to be important to Muslim cultures due to the Islamic prescriptions on responsibility to both near and far relatives. But the digital space has expanded the arena for self-expression beyond the home space into a realm where values can be shared by like-minded Muslims.

Islam as a Tool for Positive Change

'In a highly competitive and materialistic world – with which I find it difficult to keep pace – my faith gives me patience and hope,' says Iman, a newspaper journalist in India. 'Allah will take care of everything – this firm belief, alhamdulillah, gives me peace of mind and helps me stay happy in the times I live in.' She feels:

> proud to be Muslim because of the beauty of our faith, our glorious past (the Mughal legacy in my country, India, for example) and the resilience of our community – despite the tough times Muslims are living in, they are carrying on. Certainly, it's faith in Allah that keeps a Muslim going.

One of the most significant features of Generation M is their belief in Islam as a tool to bring about positive change. As we've seen, Generation M are proud Muslims, globally connected, creative 'doers' – this combination is manifested most abundantly in their desire to bring about positive change in the world through their own faith and values. They see themselves as global citizens who have a role to play in improving the societies they live in. They are concerned about the reality of daily life in their own social circles, the well-being of refugees in war zones, economic development and environmental protection. They find their inspiration in Islam. Indeed, for many young Muslims, solutions may in fact become available by applying an Islamic framework to problems. Witness the pride in the Muslim world when Muhammad Yunus won the Nobel Prize for his work in microfinance in Bangladesh. Both Malala Yousafzai and Tawakkol Karman, Muslim women's rights activists who have won the Nobel Peace Prize, describe how their Islamic values propel the work that they do.

Generation M believe their religion empowers them towards change, and that they have a key part to play in the world's future. Islam to them is just as much a force to hold societies together as it is a potent force for political and social change.

In London, 30-year-old Miqdaad is in no doubt about his identity. 'I am proud to be Muslim,' he says. The community aspect is just as important in this feeling as the spiritual element. 'I'm proud not only because of the religious identity it gives me and the spirituality that is strengthened through devotion to God, but in particular when it takes place in congregation such as prayers, fasting and hajj.' Miqdaad explains that it is in the values of his religion that he finds inspiration and energy: 'The ethical principles of Islam remind me of charity, looking out for those less fortunate, the best of character and morality in one's actions.' He adds, 'That makes me feel proud to be a Muslim.'

3 YOU HAD ME AT HALAL

*Why Twenty-First-Century Halal is
Important for Everyone*

Taz, a 32-year-old Muslim, is entertaining her friends with wine, halal wine that is. Alcohol is completely haram, forbidden, for Muslims to consume.

In the local stores around her in Dubai there are signs of Christmas, and her circle of female friends want to have their own bit of seasonal fun. 'I don't go to pubs, bars or clubs. I don't hang out with strange men. I wear hijab. I'm conscious that I represent Islam and I try and behave accordingly,' she says. Whilst Christmas as a religious occasion is something Taz's group don't mark, they do want to get into the festive spirit. Their answer, in order to 'halalify' the celebrations going on around them, is virgin mojitos and bottles of non-alcoholic wine. Some halal beers and wines are specifically produced, branded and marketed for Muslim audiences, others are non-alcoholic variants of drinks produced by mainstream alcohol brewers which carry the 0 per cent label.

'We had a mock-Christmas party once with "secret sunnah" instead of "secret santa" and had some halal wine there as some fun.' Sunnah refers to the traditions of the Prophet Muhammad which, alongside the Qur'an, are the foundations of Islamic teachings. In this context Taz is being playful with her use of the word. 'We also enjoyed mocktails. I always get them when they're available as they are delicious! I also like the way they look, they're really pretty.'

It's not just about how the drinks look, or even that they add 'a sense of festivity to an occasion' for the thirty-something writer.

Part of it is about the flavour. 'I've bought it on occasion to put in cooking as a lot of recipes call for it and my revert friend told me that using the halal version recreates the flavour in cooking.' Since halal wines and beers contain no alcohol she's baffled as to why halal wine 'seems more special somehow'. Halal beers and wines encapsulate the Generation M approach to halal consumption: enjoy life to the maximum and nothing is off limits, as long as you're upholding religious principles. There's no need to compromise – the best of everything is their right.

According to *The Economist*, in 2012, 2.2 billion litres of halal beer was consumed, up 80 per cent on five years earlier. That year Iranians – alcohol is illegal in Iran – drank nearly four times as much non-alcoholic beer as in 2007. The taste for non-alcoholic beer is growing right across the region, including in Saudi Arabia, Egypt and the UAE.

Whilst health is a factor in the growth of the global non-alcoholic wine and beer industries, the desire of Muslim consumers for a growing range of soft drinks is also playing a part. *The Economist* states that the Middle East accounts for almost a third of worldwide sales of non-alcoholic beer, powered by Muslims' 'growing consumer aspiration'.

Generation M don't want to miss out on something that is portrayed as exuberant, celebratory and social by powerful advertising that makes the people who consume it appear modern, fun and edgy – everything Generation M feel about themselves. Take out the alcohol but leave in the social buzz, and you're still left with enough cool for even the most achingly hip Generation M clique. Halal beer and wine are exciting because they offer the consumer something beyond fizzy drinks and fruit juices: something that signifies sophistication and adulthood, the edginess and glamour that Generation M want to express about themselves, while ensuring they don't cross the red line into haram. In Birmingham in the UK, 40-year-old Henna, 'full-time single mother, part-time social political activist', unwinds in the evening with an impromptu cheese and (non-alcoholic) wine party for one. The non-alcoholic wine gives her a feeling of being refined. Plus she says that it's much healthier. 'These are a better alternative to fizzy drinks. A grown-up soft drink but with health benefits of wine minus the alcohol.'

It's not just about being cool, although she smiles wryly and says, 'I must admit I am a snob. These are more sophisticated as far as drink options are concerned.' There's also a more serious reason behind her choice: 'it's like drinking juices but without the heavy sugar content. There's a greater variety of choice and flavours. I don't drink fizzy pop as it's full of sugar and additives.'

In Devon, 42-year-old mature student Adam relaxes after a hard day with a halal beer and a bowl of nuts. He too sees it as an adult step forward from fizzy drinks in terms of taste, but also a way to be more healthy as he thinks soft drinks are 'too sugary'.

The concerns of Henna and Adam for health and well-being are part of a bigger refrain we will hear echoed regularly from this global group. Halal has some technical rules when it comes to animal slaughter and ingredients, but the bigger picture about health, well-being and welfare – what we might describe as the spirit of halal rather than just the letter of the law – looms large in our contemporary, pioneering segment of worldly Muslims. They refer to this concern as 'tayyab', and point out that Qur'anic teachings refer to halal and tayyab side by side. Tayyab has no exact specific meaning, but might be broadly translated as 'wholesome' or, literally from the Arabic, 'good'. For these self-identifying Muslims who choose to observe halal, halal is just the bare minimum they expect. What they aspire to is tayyab. And that is also how they live their lives – observing the rules is the minimum, observing the holistic Muslim lifestyle in spirit is their goal.

So, What Exactly is Halal?

The concept of halal is an anchor in the life of any Muslim who self-identifies as practising. Mentioned in the Qur'an, halal appears to have a straightforward meaning: 'permitted'. Its opposite, 'haram', means 'forbidden' and a neutral area in between is 'mubah'. There are two further nuanced areas: recommended (mustahab) and its counterpart, disliked (makrooh). Mustahab refers to things for which there is no compulsion to do or consume but which will have a positive impact on body, soul and surroundings. Makrooh refers to things that are not forbidden but are disliked and likely to have a negative impact. One makrooh act is to consume copious amounts of garlic and onions before attending Friday prayers – presumably this would make it unpleasant for those standing close within the congregation.

Plenty of foods fall into the 'recommended' category, such as honey and blackseed oil, which are recommended for their many health benefits. They've seen a rise in popularity and consumption in recent years. The halal brand is ubiquitous; halal beers and wines might raise an eyebrow, and there's also halal bacon – but it's beef bacon or turkey bacon – or you can even sip halal champagne at your wedding.

It's understandable that when you think of halal, you'll probably think of food. But Generation M have started to apply these rules to all parts of their activities, creating a Muslim lifestyle. What you wear, where you travel, the financial products you use, the skin products you apply, all of these can fall anywhere on the spectrum between halal and haram. Daily life is a complicated series of decisions about halal acts.

Tongue-in-cheek discussions about love, romance and Valentine's Day prompted a Twitter storm about 'halal' chat-up lines. What could or should you say to someone whom you have a crush on that doesn't cross the boundary of halal? It offered Muslims the chance for some self-parody as they released the tension that is generated as faith and culture tug at each other. They poked fun at themselves, joking that their drive to make everything halal is obsessive and unrelenting. In the #MuslimValentines hashtag, there were mock-confessions that 'you make my heart dance & dancing is haram' and 'you make me have astaghfirullah thoughts'. Astaghfirullah is an Arabic word expressing a deep and sincere repentance for having committed a grave sin, in this case a self-deprecating reference to lust outside permitted boundaries and walking the fine line between halal and haram.

Perhaps most on point was one tweeter (Jerry Maguire, eat your heart out) who proposed the chat-up line 'You had me at halal.'

Food, for Generation M, is of course a very serious matter. And ensuring they get their halal food is more obsessively serious still. A YouTube video released in the UK took up this mantle with a cover version of Lionel Richie's 'Hello'. Faisal Hussein, an activist of socially conscious club nights with the title 'Inqlab' – a take on the Urdu word for 'revolution' – filmed the cover video in North London. It shows him in black and white, walking to a reworked soundtrack for Richie's hit song which now warbles, 'Halal! Is it meat you're looking for?', accompanying the mournful visual journey of a young Muslim man searching for the perfect halal meal.

The Halal Club

As it is for their Millennial peers, consumption is a badge of identity for Generation M. They are in the halal club and wear their badge with honour. Of course, the exact letter and spirit of 'halal' and how it should be delivered to a global audience is contentious, but that's only to be expected from a group that is constantly examining traditional Islamic teachings, applying modern techniques and aiming to inject an Islamic ethos in all that they do.

That's why the story behind the growing popularity of halal beers and wines is so fascinating: it's about how modernity and faith come together, how every aspect of a product's origin, concept, branding and even its packaging are under detailed scrutiny; and what it says about its consumers as Muslims of a new era. The shocked reactions are something Generation M enjoy, combining defiance with conformity. Some might say there's an unconscious hankering for Western culture but with the negative connotations sucked out (literally, in the case of vacuum-distilled drinks, a process which removes the alcoholic content). But Generation M's drive is to adhere to halal principles and to assert that these products are still fully Muslim. It is this kind of nuance in how Generation M see themselves in relation to society that is important to understanding them.

While the characteristics that Generation M exhibit are constant around the world, how these characteristics are manifested depends on the context. In some cases it is the aspect of modernity that is emphasised, in others it is faith credentials, in some it is the very fact that they believe that both go together.

In Saudi Arabia and parts of the Middle East halal beer and wine can set you apart from the traditionalist Muslim majority by highlighting that you are edgy and that you embrace modernity. On the other hand, in Turkey, Generation M are on a mission to demonstrate that, while their religious principles are in harmony with modernity, there is no need for them to embrace – or even look as if they are embracing – the stark secularism that was enforced until recently. Consuming halal beer and wine in Turkey therefore has a different connotation than in the Middle East; in Turkey the emphasis is not necessarily on highlighting one's edginess, but on avoiding the irreligiousness of drinking alcohol, an action connected to the kind of fundamentalist secularism that painted religion as backward and outdated.

In Turkey, the Generation M protagonist is sceptical of halal beer. In an *Al-Monitor* op-ed, Turkish analyst Riada Asimovic Akyol reports:

> When I asked a Turkish friend in Istanbul about it [halal beer], he responded, 'I have never seen non-alcoholic beer in a shop, but I was told it exists.' I asked him, 'If you offered your friends a non-alcoholic beer, what would they say?' He responded, 'My religiously conservative friend would want to double check to make sure it has no alcohol, and only then maybe drink it, but wouldn't be pleased. My secular friend would drink it and ask for a "real" beer when it's finished.'

Even the name and what a halal product looks like when you're carrying it causes controversy. Malaysia's JAKIM won't certify any product with 'beer' in the name, even if it's non-alcoholic. The A&W restaurant chain started calling its root beer 'RB' at all its outlets in 2013. Coca-Cola's Malaysia affiliate renamed its root beer 'A&W Sarsaparilla' in 2009 – one of the requirements to get its halal certificate renewed. By comparison, in the Middle East, the malt drink brand Barbican rebranded its halal beer into green bottles that look like traditional beer bottles. Its subsequent adverts were energetic scenes of groups of young men hanging out, bonding and engaging in typical young male high jinks, all (well, mostly) halal. Here they are on a road trip! Here are the cool young men in the desert! Here they are pimping a ride in the car garage! And here they are (oops!) with some girls in some possibly-halal-but-slightly-dubious shenanigans which less 'cool' Muslim audiences might find controversial – but of course that is the line that Generation M sometimes play with. And it's all thanks to the non-alcoholic beer. With this new 'cool' appeal, Barbican more than doubled its Saudi Arabian sales, from 18 million litres in 2004 to 37 million litres in 2013.

It's not just boisterous post-teen men who want to live life on the (halal) edge with a bottle of non-alcoholic beer. Laziza is a Lebanese non-alcoholic beer. Its brand manager Guilda Saber says that the glamorous image of halal beer means that its consumption is increasing in public places such as bars and restaurants, thereby extending its reach beyond the home and private social spaces. Another brand, Moussy, targets trendy young men and women, portraying them hanging out at a beach resort, which again is an image that sits on the sometimes blurry, controversial edges of the Generation M lifestyle.

A Virtuous Circle of Consumption

'Consuming halal products and doing good deeds have a great influence on me. If I do bad deeds and consume products that are haram, these will have a bad effect on me,' says 27-year-old Sufian, originally from Bangladesh and studying for his master's in English Literary Studies at the International Islamic University of Malaysia.

'Becoming a good person is a continuous process, and consuming halal products and performing good deeds are two of the key factors that define me as a "good" person.' Sufian explains that to observe halal is to be engaged in a virtuous circle of consumption.

Halal products, services and actions have a positive effect on the body which therefore increase the individual's sensibilities for devotion and purity. As devotion and purity grow, the Muslim increases the focus of his or her intention to consume halal products and engage only in halal acts, and so the virtuous circle becomes embedded. The net result is a constant effort to engage only in halal activities, because what Muslims consume affects who they are.

Choosing whether to consume a product or service is a series of trade-offs. What activities and products are available? Am I doubtful about this product? Is it safer to avoid something dubious? Is there an alternative which does not require compromise, even if it's not as good, and would I be willing to downgrade on the quality?

Whilst from the outside life under halal rules might seem constrained or deprived, that's not how it feels to this unwavering, goal-oriented global community. 'I am a Muslim: the issue of choosing a halal product is above everything,' says Sufian, who does not feel this is a burden or a compromise. 'It is saving my spiritual well-being at the expense of the consumption of a few products and services.' He adds:

> No matter how attractive, healthy and cheap a particular product or service may seem, if it is not halal, I prefer not to consume it. It is important to my spiritual well-being to consume products and services according to religious guidelines.

Halal Status: It's Complicated

While the principle that only halal should be consumed is straightforward enough, the rules that determine if a product or service is halal are not always as clear. Like all prescriptive aspects of Islam, there is scholarly dissent on what makes a product halal. The technicalities of what makes something halal or not and how something comes to be certified as halal are modern problems usually arising from the elongated and industrialised supply chain. As just one small example, when it comes to the very specific moment of slaughter of an animal, guidelines vary on whether mechanical or hand slaughter is required, and the associated issue of whether an animal can be stunned before slaughter is also contentious. In non-Muslim countries where stunning is usually a legal requirement, kosher and halal meat that is not stunned is sometimes permitted by a special legal exemption. Even though much of this halal meat is stunned, in these countries there is often opposition to Muslims producing and consuming halal meat. Some believe that it contravenes animal welfare standards – although Muslims who consume halal meat reject this – whilst for others it is a sign of Muslim observance encroaching on their way of life. Both of these attitudes trigger Muslims, and Generation M in particular, to a heightened sense of identity and determination. After all, battling through the difficulties to achieve halal consumption is a social and spiritual badge to show who they really are.

As you'd expect from our protagonists, they've got a lot of questions: What if animals are treated poorly? What exactly is the method of halal slaughter? Are additives halal? And that's just food. What about non-food products like medicines, or personal care products like shampoos and moisturisers, or the financial products they purchase to fund homes and businesses, and even more luxury items such as plane journeys, hotel stays and clothing?

Consumers in general are increasingly concerned about the fact that they know little about the provenance of their food in an era of mass production and synthetic ingredients. No longer can you see with your own eyes how an animal is reared and slaughtered for meat, nor is it clear what a chemical additive described by a number actually contains. For Muslim consumers who observe halal, knowledge of these mysterious processes is even more pressing because it directly affects their spiritual well-being.

On this rocky road to halal in the modern age, there's a huge and growing global fraternity of young faithful Muslims dedicating themselves to answering exactly these questions and attempting to establish agreed standards. These are not just for their own obser-vance, but as a duty to the Muslim ummah as a whole, a duty that weighs heavily on their shoulders, and one that they believe could be a force for good for all businesses and consumers, not only Muslims.

Until they are definitively assured whether something really is halal in its specification, Generation M will exercise scepticism. Some will accept some doubt if the product comes with a halal certification; others, however, are more cynical of the growing number of governmental and civic bodies that have been set up to monitor and certify halal processes. That's why, when it comes to the idea that an inherently haram product like beer might be halal, it's confusing. The Islamic Religious Council of Singapore, for example, went as far as to pronounce specifically that halal beer cannot be consumed as it mimics the culture of alcohol.

Laziza's owner, Almaza, a Lebanese brewery, understands that for Generation M individuals, it is best to avoid such grey areas of uncertainty, and it is taking no chances with Laziza. Although it is marketed as a beer, Laziza is not fermented, since the process of removing the alcohol afterwards can leave traces of it. Its bottles declare it to be '0.00 per cent' alcohol, to distinguish it from the fermented brands, which only promise to be '0.0 per cent'.

Other approaches look at the process of production – and this applies across the board with halal products. In the UK, the start-up confectionery business Ummah Foods created a proposition around quality halal products. To underscore their halal status it ensured that the manufacturing facilities that it sublet were fully shut down from previous products and thoroughly cleansed to avoid even the possibility of contamination by alcohol and other non-halal lubricants sometimes used in the processing of other chocolates.

In the case of halal beers, the focus is on whether even the slightest trace of alcohol exists. Some non-alcoholic beers may have 0.26 per cent alcohol, but usually much less. Saudi and Egyptian religious authorities have all issued permission to consume halal beers, explaining that these products are not produced as alcohol, and the tiny amounts of alcohol present are a natural manufacturing by-product. Vincero halal wine claims to use a new process called vacuum distillation which is 'non-aggressive', retaining the taste but removing 100 per cent of the alcohol. No matter the certifications given, such examples demonstrate why manufacturing facilities are scrutinised, and why many big corporations, including Nestlé and Unilever, have dedicated separate facilities to halal products. There's no need to introduce doubt.

There are other surprises in the world of establishing halal status. For example, halal logistics ensures that halal products are segregated from non-halal products to avoid direct contact with haram and any risk of contamination. This is not just about actual separation but also about the perception by Muslim consumers that contamination has been avoided. This of course affects storage, transport and handling.

The Politics of the Halal Stamp

In majority Muslim countries, the responsibility for identifying a product as halal is usually taken by government bodies, which establish directives with which manufacturers must comply, both domestically and for international imports. Some consumers feel this takes the stress out of checking that every item is halal for consumption. Fatima, who lives in Doha, says: 'I'm happy to leave the decision about halal to the Ministry. They can take responsibility. It is a relief to not look at ingredients and just buy what looks and then tastes good.'

In most minority Muslim nations, such bodies, often several in one country, are independent and governments rarely get involved. Notable exceptions include Singapore and South Africa, where Muslim minorities have strong recognition more broadly in the national consciousness. In minority Muslim countries it has been generally immigrant populations who established these bodies, simply to ensure a halal supply with a recognisable halal stamp. Quality, traceability, welfare and transparency were not front of mind, just as they were not historically front of mind for consumers in general. But Generation M are certainly concerned with all of these matters and believe that certification bodies must be accountable for the standards they set, ensuring they are properly enforced and taking firm action in the case of transgression. They are no longer happy to acquiesce to those who were once deemed to 'know best', finding that many certification bodies are failing to meet the grade. Further, Generation M want assurance that it is not just slaughter, but the more holistic view of halal that is being monitored and certified. In 2014, the politics of halal certification made headlines in majority Muslim Indonesia following accusations that Indonesian officials had extorted money from Australian companies wanting certification, as Indonesia is a huge market for halal goods from Australia. Some claims went as far as to say that bribes are commonplace. Predictably, there was uproar. There is no objection to smart businesses that fill a niche or offer a hitherto unavailable service to Muslim audiences. But the notion that the action of ensuring a basic Islamic principle was being used for profiteering is outrageous to Generation M because they have a strong stance that Islamic principles are something that should be upheld from the heart.

Reputation is important. In France, Nestlé's Maggi brand suffered from accusations that it claimed it was halal but was in fact contaminated. Sales plummeted and the company was forced to withdraw the products. In China, halal certification comes with an added bonus for consumers. The strict inspection process and the halal stamp guaranteed by an authority such as the Malaysian government's JAKIM signal to consumers – Muslim and non-Muslim alike – that the product meets a certain standard of quality. This has made halal products appeal to a wider audience that can trust certified products to uphold hygiene and quality standards. When Chinese companies started stamping their products with Malaysian certification logos, consumers were outraged not only at the compromise of their halal requirements, but also at the compromising of the quality. The companies were prosecuted for fraud.

In an increasingly globalised world, products may arrive from other countries, so their standards of halal also have to be assessed by Muslim consumers. This can be an advantage to export countries: your halal products can be consumed by 1.6 billion Muslims worldwide, and incoming Muslim visitors are attracted by your halal food. In 2012, out of France's total meat and poultry exports, 10 per cent was halal, exporting to its Muslim neighbours in North Africa.

Darhim Dali Hashim is smartly dressed, with a neat trimmed beard and slightly nerdy glasses. You can tell as soon as you meet the Malaysian Muslim that things will be just a little bit different once he's turned his attention to them. In his thirties he became the CEO of the International Halal Integrity Alliance (IHI Alliance), which describes itself on its website as 'an international not-for-profit organisation created to uphold the integrity of the halal market concept in global trade through recognition, collaboration and membership'. The IHI Alliance vision is for 'a stronger global halal industry for the benefit of all', because if halal is the right thing, then it is worth sharing with everyone.

Darhim is also an adviser to a private equity fund that looks at supporting small and medium-sized enterprises (SMEs) in the halal space with the aim of building halal supply chains. His earlier career in global venture capital led him to the livestock industry and the process required to produce halal meat.

It became personal for Darhim: 'I came to learn that we as Muslims really were not in control of the halal supply chain and there was a lack of transparency in the assurance of any integrity.' For the global community – the ummah – he aims to find solutions that reflect the modern world as well as the faith principles he wants to uphold for the benefit of all. He's pragmatic, knowing that establishing agreed guidelines on halal means negotiating diverse and passionate opinions, one of the reasons that so far no globally agreed halal standard exists:

> A single global standard that will be acceptable to all may not be practical as this would mean taking the strictest position, which could be cost prohibitive and maybe even impossible to implement in non-Muslim-majority countries. What is more feasible is a robust system that enables consumers to make an informed choice.

It is an informed choice built on clarity and honesty that Generation M crave, to be clear where others stand. False claims will be harshly punished by them. When it comes to consumption, they want to be sure they are not being left behind and that they are getting the best of today's technology applied to their needs as Muslims.

In order to offer the reassurances Muslim consumers seek, it's likely that we will see the growth of a number of halal global brands in the coming years.

Tayyab: The Spirit of the Law

The Qur'an talks about any food that is consumed being 'halal' (permitted) as well as 'tayyab' (roughly translated as wholesome). Whilst the traditional focus has been on halal, Generation M believe this is not enough: food must also be wholesome. In a modern mechanised world, animal treatment has radically altered, and what was once taken for granted in terms of animal welfare has – pun entirely intended – been sacrificed in the pursuit of mass production. 'Tayyab' would once have been implicitly bundled into the observance of 'halal' but now there is a move to re-introduce it explicitly.

Earlier, we met Henna, who enjoys an impromptu cheese and wine party. She says that focusing on the technicalities of slaughter to define something as halal oversimplifies the issue. There's a bigger picture that she's seeking, which explains the many facets of tayyab.

> I would consider organic wholesome, ethical, non-GMO, fair trade, local economic growth, supporting small businesses and agriculture all as factors affecting my consumerism as a Muslim. Halal is much more than just slaughter. I'm very passionate about this! It's about being a good, decent, fair human being who cares about their world environment.

That is not to say that some segments within Generation M don't exercise the choice to consume non-halal food. Some rulings will permit the consumption of kosher meat, as it is slaughtered in a similar way. Others consume organic and free-range as they feel it adheres more closely to the spirit of halal, rather than ignoring the rearing of animals and focusing on the slaughter only.

As far back as 2010, in an article entitled 'Designing a Game-Changing Islamic Brand' published for the UK delegation attending the Sixth World Islamic Economic Forum in Kuala Lumpur, I explained the importance of values in talking to Generation M and the relationship between something being technically for Muslims and its spirit mirroring their aspirations and values as Muslims: 'Even if you carry out hajj, zakat, salaat or any of the other Islamic activities – even if it is to the letter – but fail to grasp the values that it conveys, then the ritual is empty and feels meaningless even to the protagonist.' I wrote:

> The problem with most 'Islamic' products today is the same. They tick all the boxes that make them 'technically' Islamic. They do this by taking existing products that are not necessarily constructed on Islamic values, tweak them a bit so they 'technically' meet the requirements, and then badge them 'Islamic'. Take the spate of 'Islamic' colas that hit the world – we had Mecca cola, Ummah cola and Zamzam cola to name but a few. What was 'Islamic' about them except the name?

Ethos is crucial, as well as rules.

As we've seen, there's a willingness to invest time and resources in verifying a certification body, the rules of halal, and even each individual ingredient. But beyond this tick list, ensuring the spirit of halal is met is vital, as it fulfils the emotional needs of Generation M as spiritually striving beings. Just as demonstrating their own integrity is important, so is the integrity of halal.

Their scepticism about claims that a product is halal extends to product quality. They tell us that their experience of halal products is that the quality is inferior to non-halal, which leaves them feeling exploited as well as second class. The last thing they want is for their faith to be taken advantage of. Rather, it is important to them that the brand or organisation is on their side, that they are not being cynically targeted as the latest marketing fad, that their demands as twenty-first-century Muslims are really at the heart of the contract. They want the understanding and communication of halal to go beyond superficial stereotypes to what will help them live the kind of lives they aspire to. If people, brands or organisations are engaging with Generation M, they have to be good members of their circle and respect them as a friend would.

Ensuring that products meet an agreed halal standard is hard enough. But enforcing the less quantifiable measure of 'wholesomeness' brings with it bigger philosophical questions, not just about what is in the product, but also about the very nature of the product itself. In the journey to halal and beyond to tayyab, Generation M are on the cusp of wider consumer food trends which focus on dietary specifics as well as provenance. We've seen growing consumer concern and consumption of products such as Fairtrade and gluten-free among a whole range of specialist products increasingly coming into the mainstream.

Big corporations that start to engage with Muslim consumers will be held to ever-greater account, not just to be halal but also to be tayyab. If mainstream consumers are offered organic, ethical, eco-friendly and so on, then Generation M will demand that halal products meet the same standards, and they will not tolerate being treated as second class or substandard. In fact, many young Muslims see themselves as pioneering the ethical consumer movement, specifically inspired by the Islamic teachings on tayyab.

Muhammad Ridha Payne is one of the founders of Abraham Organics, which describes itself as a 'family-run business, established to address the lack of quality halal meat'. The company's aim is 'to provide top-quality, naturally reared, "organic" and ethically sourced halal meat through a business model that supports localisation and contributes to charitable causes through a fixed percentage donation from profits'.

Muhammad describes his own journey from simply looking at halal labels to seeing how meat is actually procured: 'Animals are exploited. If one sees the conditions they are born, bred and die in it would horrify anyone with a good heart.' He doesn't see that this is compatible with the spiritual goals that Muslims are intent on pursuing.

> Muslims need to ask whether this is something they are truly happy eating. Is it good to eat meat that is full of rubbish, that led a miserable life and a stressful end? Is it not possible that all this transfers into the meat? One also needs to ask if this method of farming sits with the ethos and spirit of Islam. Does Islam not teach compassion, kindness and does it not fight exploitation? To me both these elements make most of the meat in the UK inedible. I do not want to subject my body to such produce and I definitely do not want to contribute towards an industry that exploits a community that praises Allah.

It's early days for 'tayyab', as we've seen from the many different facets that go into making a product 'good' or 'wholesome', but it's clearly on the agenda and something that will gain increasing prominence over coming years.

The Islamic Economy: Beyond Food and Beyond Muslims

The Emirate of Dubai announced in 2013 its intention to become the 'global capital of the Islamic economy'. This is a clear recognition of a huge commercial opportunity, but there is a very personal issue for those Muslims involved: that their needs are not being met, and that modernity demands that they should be.

Sami Al Qamzi, the director general of the Dubai Department of Economic Development (DED), believes business can be a driver for improvement and change and that market forces that work towards improved consumer choice can be the impetus for such change. In his view, the Islamic economy does not belong solely to Muslims, but is universal. Production and consumption happen in both Muslim and non-Muslim countries, and halal products can be attractive to non-Muslim consumers too.

Sami highlights in a playful turn of language that is characteristic of Generation M that the 'customer is mufti', a reference to a religious leader or chief, and says that 'the Islamic economy cannot be based on what regulators see fit, but on the needs expressed by consumers.' And those consumers are looking at the holistic application of Islamic values across the supply chain. A colleague of Sami's explains:

> A fish is not necessarily halal. We live in a complex and sophisticated world. What was halal yesterday might not be today. Take the example of a fish: today, it can be raised on a fishing farm and fed a cocktail containing pork meat, wrapped in a pack full of alcohol-based ingredients and transported in a container that carried haram products the day before.

That clearly makes sense. But Generation M feel that sometimes products seem to take the meaning of halal too far, like halal china plates and halal petfood and even water. Whilst these might seem far-fetched, there is a bigger question of how deep halal extends into the supply chain, and Generation M ideally want reassurance that right from the start of the chain, through to what they purchase, the process is halal at every stage.

In 2012 in Brunei, a pilot scheme was proposed to use radio-frequency identification (RFID) technology to improve the traceability of products to ensure end-to-end halal authenticity and to clear up doubt. Doubt is something that bothers Generation M and they are excited by the idea of using technology to enhance their practice of Islam.

The RFID traceability system would authenticate and track the halal status of food products, initially focusing on chicken and raw meat produced in local abattoirs. The authentic halal logo issued by the relevant authority would be validated using an RFID tag embedded into the meat's packaging. An RFID reader would be placed in retail stores for consumers to authenticate the product's status and obtain a range of information, including the slaughtering processes, sources of ingredients, and the manufacturing and expiry dates of the product. With concerns growing about food provenance more generally, such processeses might appeal to wider consumer movements.

Halal Evangelists

Technologies, certification and the greater scrutiny that halal products necessarily entail are slowly persuading Generation M that their own aspirations in following their faith could bring a wider benefit to society, both Muslims and non-Muslims.

Generation M want to place trust in the authenticity and halal status of the products they consume, and their scepticism about whether suppliers are bearing the burden of this trust properly is emblematic of a wider consumer scepticism about modern supply and consumption. The fact that this need for trustworthiness comes from Generation M's faith values is of benefit to the consumer movement as it is non-negotiable and requires companies to find solutions. It is in this space that Generation M's indefatigability shines; it goes hand in hand with their desire to make life better for everyone by applying principles that at first sight seem to apply only to Muslims.

In 2013, Europe faced a scandal about meat products being contaminated with untraceable and unmonitored horsemeat. Halal products did not escape the scrutiny, and some meat certified as halal was found to contain pork DNA, a strict no-no. Muslims were horrified. But the theory of halal inspection and certification offered a framework for improving the authenticity of halal meat, and the monitoring of halal meat looked to have something positive to offer the wider consumer market.

Like kosher meat, halal requires a greater level of inspection of the quality and provenance of products. In theory, both also integrate animal welfare and care at every step of the supply chain, something that Generation M – with their growing focus on tayyab – feel would be beneficial to society more broadly. Generation M feel strongly that their Islamic values can improve modern processes. However, in minority Muslim nations there are those – like the 'Boycott Halal' campaigns – who see themselves defending modernity against the Islam of Generation M. Those people are not willing to listen, believing that Muslim ideas are about imposing shariah law, and fail to embrace Muslim contributions for all consumers.

For Generation M, halal is therefore a personal battleground against the wider world. Halal is also an area for struggle within the Muslim communities in order to establish certification and standards. Halal is a space for self-expression where faith and modernity can be combined. It offers the opportunity to contribute to improved consumption and sustainability for a wider consumer audience. But it is also a front line in the struggle to establish the very identity of a generation that is confident and comfortable in combining modernity and faith.

4   WHAT THE FATWA?

The Four Fs of the Global Muslim Lifestyle

'To me, living a Muslim lifestyle means bringing God-consciousness into every aspect of our lives and trying to model ourselves after our beloved Prophet Muhammad,' says Sabiha Ansari.

> It's how we choose to interact with our friends, family, neighbours and community, it's living a halal and healthy lifestyle, it's about living within our means and choosing to be debt-free and charitable, avoiding ostentatiousness and this culture of 'I want more' and instead living a life of balance.

Sabiha saw her Muslim American peers following a similar trajectory to her own in seeking to live a life in accordance with their religious principles, but they were frustrated by the lack of products and services available on the high street to meet their needs. When it comes to fashion, she says they are 'no longer just satisfied with putting together their outfits by pulling pieces from here and there, perhaps from ethnic shops, they now want brands to cater to them and provide modest lines of clothing'. And when it comes to food, while halal is pivotal, 'it's no longer important to just eat halal from the local butcher's shop, consumers want to know exactly how the animal was slaughtered, whether it was humanely raised, what kind of feed it was given and so on.'

After reading a story in the *New York Times* about how some advertisers were starting to think about Muslims as potential consumers, and that this market had a value of $170 billion, Sabiha, along with her husband Faisal Masood, decided to set up the American Muslim Consumer Conference. It held its first event in 2009, and four more conferences have followed. Their work is more wide-ranging now and they've rebranded as the American Muslim Consumer Consortium. In 2014 they attracted 400 attendees to explore what Muslim consumers are seeking, and held a 'dragon's den-style' event to showcase Muslim entrepreneurs and start-ups, offering the winning company a $10,000 prize. The conference aims to raise awareness of Muslim consumers, their buying power and their presence in mainstream media and advertising, and in turn to influence companies at global, national and start-up levels to develop products and services for Muslims, based on Islamic principles.

'We're hoping it's the start for other retailers to recognise Muslims as a group that is a strong economic force,' Sabiha says. 'Muslim Americans are educated, trendy and economically well-off. They want to integrate the values of their faith with the values of being an American, and this can be a very positive aspect.'

In Ogilvy Noor's research of Muslims around the world, we found that over 90 per cent said that their faith somehow affects their consumption. Where others may see constraints in the rules, Generation M see opportunities to create a whole range of new products and services. The imperative to live a Muslim lifestyle is unleashing a new creative energy. This creativity is extending into four main categories: food, finance, pharmaceuticals and fun.

The growth of these sectors reflects the daily challenges of Generation M and gives us insights into how – from waking up early for morning prayers until late at night – every act is carefully deliberated upon, and choices made. Sometimes these are strict choices ('Should I eat this meat if I'm not sure it's halal?') to more complicated ones, where individual interpretation, flexibility and adherence to letter and spirit of the law can come into play (How feasible is it for me to grow my business if I avoid mainstream financial products?'). Identifying the answers to such questions lays the framework for how products and services should be created in order to meet the Muslim lifestyle.

We asked Muslims who identified as observant in our research about the relative importance of shariah-compliance across a number of product and service categories. We published the results as the Noor Category Index, looking at which categories demanded full compliance, and how the need for compliance varied across categories. Food and drink – things that go into the body – were required to be shariah-compliant at the highest non-negotiable level. If the product is placed inside the body but not consumed (such as toothpaste), compliance is only a little less important. And if it's used on the body but doesn't go inside it (such as body cream) it's important, but less so.

Muslim consumers once thought of themselves as pragmatic in reluctantly accepting that brands such as hotels or airlines, which don't cater exclusively to Muslims, weren't fully shariah-compliant (because they serve alcohol, for example). However, their demand that even categories lower down the Noor Category Index should be compliant with Muslim aspirations has been growing. So travel and fashion are being developed as compliant, plus there is a growing interest in sectors that were not even originally discussed, such as health and homecare.

As we predicted when the results were first published, the importance placed by Generation M on such categories demonstrating compliance has steadily been increasing, and categories where compliance was originally not seen as important are growing in significance. Generation M protagonists in particular believe that assuming improvements cannot be made in products is an attitude of the past, and that, either through their own entrepreneurial efforts or through consumer power, categories that were once agnostic about Muslim demands are now increasingly finding ways to improve their offerings. Even marketing and communications are part of this consumer expression of Generation M, with a huge push to create a new look and feel as well as a new language for these new product and service categories. This expansion of the Muslim lifestyle is something we will see reflected as we explore the four Fs below.

Miles Young, CEO of Ogilvy & Mather Worldwide, noted at the launch of Ogilvy Noor that the appreciation of this growing market was only slowly beginning to dawn on the commercial world:

It was when we sent out a mailer recently, describing Muslim consumers conservatively as the 'third one billion' that the bells started finally to ring in the global HQs of some of our clients. Yes, this is a market bigger than India or China is, and yet it receives a tiny fraction of the attention.

Even though the primary goal of living a Muslim lifestyle is to uphold faith values, this expression of the 'positive aspect' of living a good consumer life, as Sabiha described it earlier, as a challenge to stereotypes through consumption is welcomed. Living a Muslim lifestyle is not that easy – how do you decide which products and services are suitable, where should they be sourced from (especially if they don't already exist or aren't available locally), and how far into your range of purchases do Islamic principles need to be applied? And, on the other hand, how should you deal with the hostility that surrounds the existence of many Muslim-oriented products?

Generation M are conscious of increasing opposition to halal-oriented or Muslim-inspired ways of living, an antagonism which aims to make access to these products more difficult for Muslims. For example, 'Boycott Halal' campaigns are vociferous in many countries, targeting brands that reach out to Muslim audiences and campaigning for the banning of halal products. The 'Boycott Halal in Australia' campaign has been one of the most ardent. The activists threw a tantrum about rumours of alcoholic wine being halal certified, and then were further infuriated when mocked for not knowing wine could not be halal under any circumstances, claiming it was a Muslim trick. As the counter-group to the boycott campaign says, 'The parody writes itself.'

Stories that UK high-street restaurants Pizza Express and Subway, which also happen to be global brands, serve halal meat triggered a response from anti-Muslim consumers that they would withdraw their custom from these chains. Vociferous social hostility, even from a tiny minority, can have a negative impact on businesses already or considering offering Muslim-oriented products and services.

The choice to be halal will depend on commercial considerations. If a Subway franchise is located in an area of high Muslim density, then 'going halal' is likely to be a savvy economic choice. This is often underscored by the fact that a franchise owner may themselves be Muslim and observe halal and therefore will prefer not to handle haram products, nor to sell them.

The Muslim lifestyle sector is being built by young Muslims creating products and services that larger corporations are proving slow to develop. Generation M need solutions, and they're not waiting around for others to solve their problems. Instead, the fusion of their modern consumerist identity with their Muslim orientation is resulting in a flourishing of products and services.

Food

Feeling hungry? Too tired to cook? All you need to do is to pop out to your local takeaway. But if you're Generation M, a lover of the good things in life, and someone for whom halal is important, these seemingly mundane actions become serious challenges.

In 2004 two Muslim American brothers, Zahed and Shahed Amanullah, were fed up of this problem. So they set up a website called Zabihah.com. The idea was simple: to catalogue restaurants serving halal food in the USA and worldwide. This was to be a collective effort, driven from the ground up to help hungry Muslims to tackle the simple but significant problem of finding halal food wherever they were. Today Zabihah.com is one of the oldest restaurant review sites, halal or otherwise, and the oldest site for halal restaurant listings. It has global reach and is also available as a downloadable app.

When it launched, the idea of a halal review site was ground-breaking. It posted a description of the restaurant, including various environmental factors: how did the reviewer assess its halal status? Was alcohol served? What was the ambience like? How good was the food? And so on. Anyone visiting the site could then assess a restaurant and how its Muslim offering fitted with their own preferences. This is Generation M at its finest: an implicit and shared community understanding that maintaining a lifestyle based on Islamic values is hard work, and everyone is in it together. Helping each other through the day-to-day challenges starts with actions as straightforward as finding somewhere to eat.

Halal food finders are now a global phenomenon. In 2015 HalalTrip launched its own global halal food app, Halal Food Spotter, asking: 'Ever searched the internet to find the best halal places to eat on holiday?' Again, the offering is collaborative, relying on the Millennial urge to share experiences and the duty Generation M take so seriously to pass on information that will help others better observe their faith. The new app 'allows Muslim travellers to share halal dishes served in restaurants around the world'. Elsewhere, the Singapore Halal Eating Guide is designed to help Muslims in Singapore find halal eateries. HalalSpot in the UK says it 'makes it easy to find halal restaurants, takeaways and cafes', again emphasising that this is 'more than just an app – HalalSpot is a community'.

Food is clearly a primary driving force, with Muslims estimated to have spent $1.1 trillion on food and beverages in 2014, and estimated to reach $1.6 trillion by 2020. Multinational corporations like Nestlé and Unilever are already getting involved and businesses from within the Muslim world are playing an increasing role. In the Middle East, the managing director of Al Islami Foods, Saleh Abdullah Lootah, says: 'We want to be number one. We want to be the Nestlé of the halal food business.' It's not just about the halal label on the packaging. Quality, variety, taste and a fit with changing family structures and lifestyles are driving the food and beverage sectors.

'I want to celebrate halal dining,' says Zohra Khaku, the founder of digital magazine 'Halal Gems'. Like her target readership, her passion is halal food. 'I want halal food to be the highest quality food in the next 10 to 15 years. It's something to be proud of.' The Halal Gems website includes a restaurant finder, which was the original foundation of the concept, but it's the glossy content that differentiates it, offering interviews and events, and highlighting trends in the halal food scene. 'We're celebrating the whole lifestyle,' says Zohra.

The rise of halal food festivals in both minority and majority Muslim countries, from New York to London to China, is testament to the ingrained desire to seek out good-quality delicious cuisine – as long as it is halal. Trade shows like Thaifex, World of Food Asia have dedicated sessions for the halal marketplace. And Malaysia hosts a halal week for businesses to showcase their wares.

Demand from Muslim consumers means that the export of halal meat and food is an increasingly important part of GDP for many countries. New Zealand, Australia and Brazil have huge halal meat and poultry operations. The US Meat Federation has spoken about exporting halal, noting Muslim consumers show a strong preference for it. In Wales, farmers are seizing the seasonal opportunity by sending animals to Saudi Arabia for the pilgrimage season of hajj when animals are slaughtered as part of the ritual.

The influence of Generation M's demand for halal food extends further: their desire for fusion cuisine that is halal is affecting wider society, and their tastes are influencing the wider Muslim population as well as broader societal tastes. In the UK, fried-chicken chain Chicken Cottage sparked a high-street revolution and there are now halal chicken outlets in towns and villages around the country. Their popularity even led to a mainstream reality TV show called *Fried Chicken Shop*. Similarly, the Middle East chain Just Falafel is expanding into India. In New York City, on almost every street corner, you'll find a streetcart run by The Halal Guys. Set up a decade ago to cater for Muslim cab drivers, the popularity of their shawarma, the Middle Eastern meat sandwich meal, has become widespread beyond New York's Muslim population.

Haroon, a 34-year-old business development director at an internet start-up, says he will never forget travelling to New York and finding himself queuing at midnight at one of the halal food carts.

> People are in good spirits, inhaling the aroma of the meat and enviously watching people who have already been served [...] tucking into their food. After losing track of time I finally got served chicken, lamb, rice, salad, dressed in their special white sauce. I felt taken care of. [...] I love the fact that these guys have great quality street food and that they have inspired a brand loyalty that has transcended the Muslim community and even New York itself. These guys are an institution and I have travelled far and wide on the planet and people have heard of them. What is not to love about that?

In June 2014, The Halal Guys owner signed a deal with Fransmart, the restaurant franchise consulting firm that took Five

Guys Burgers and Fries from four locations in Northern Virginia and helped turn it into a chain with more than 1,200 stores and more than $1 billion in sales. The Halal Guys met their predictions of expanding from coast to coast across America within a year and in the same timeframe had at least four locations outside the USA.

Even while the notion that the food is halal is part of the core branding for the company, what is eye-opening is that the brand's core selling point is considered its 'New York-ness', and that opening franchises will bring a taste of that big city experience wherever it goes. For Muslim consumers, the fact of halal is a tick in the box; it is the Big Apple proposition and taste that are the selling points. For the wider public it is the 'Muslim cuisine' proposition that sells, and that has been created by the mix of faith, modernity and cultures that embodies Generation M. The Halal Guys' food as well as its branding points at the development of a wider notion of Muslim cuisine as a consequence of Generation M's desire for great food and beverages that consistently uphold halal principles.

Other curiosities are also starting to emerge which reflect Generation M's foodie tendencies. In France, for example, halal foie gras is a big seller for supermarket retailer Carrefour. Halal sweets have made confectionery producer Haribo a popular name in Muslim households.

The internationalisation of tastes among Generation M is a marker of their global perspective, their urge to travel and their connectivity to their Muslim peers around the world. Wherever they are, good halal food is important to them.

Finance: Show Me the (Halal) Money

Ismail Jeilani, a twenty-something graduate from the University of London, refused to take out student loans to finance his studies. 'I was personally not comfortable with taking a loan due to the potential implication of dealing with usury.' Commonly referred to as interest, usury is completely forbidden to Muslims. Ismail adds something that a broader range of students would echo: 'I also felt the normalisation of debt is a problem that I wanted to avoid.'

In 2012, the cap on university tuition fees in England and Wales tripled. 'Many Muslim students felt as if they had to make a trade-off between education and religion.' But not so for Ismail, and he set out to solve this new problem in a creative way within the parameters of his Islamic beliefs. 'Islam is instrumental in developing my character, my business etiquette and how I behave around others. I don't feel that Islam hinders my choices or activities, rather it aids the choices that I make.'

He generates revenue by running courses:

Within two years of starting university, I successfully managed to raise enough to sufficiently cover my tuition fees. For the remainder of my time at university, I continued with the work but instead chose to lend the money I earned interest-free to others. In total, I managed to lend almost £40,000. [...]

For each course, we dedicate a percentage towards an interest-free loan pot. The bigger the courses, the bigger the pot. The pot operates under 'takaful' so when the money is repaid, it can simply be re-lent.

Takaful is an Islamic finance instrument that is best described as 'leasing'. There's no interest but rather a relationship between lessor and lessee.

To scale the growth, we hope to increase two further avenues of funding. Firstly, we are speaking to organisations who may want to contribute a fee to the pot. In return, we will provide their students with interest-free loans. Secondly, as the organisation grows and gains a reputation, we hope to gain further funding via sponsorships.

Just as with the evangelism about halal food, Islamic finance is seen by Generation M as a positive contribution towards economics and development in general, not just for Muslims. Indeed, during the global recession of 2009, its advocates pointed to the fact that the Islamic finance industry was untouched and therefore offered worthwhile alternatives to conventional finance.

For Ismail, the idea that there is a different and viable way to do things is powerful, and it only takes someone to show there are options to trigger new thinking. Ismail explains that 'the Prophet was sent as a mercy to mankind, not just a mercy to Muslims. So Islamic teachings have something for everyone. I'd like what we've created to turn this into a source of alternative finance for everyone.'

Islamic banking and finance is one of the oldest sectors of the Muslim lifestyle and in 2014 Islamic banking assets were estimated at $1.3 trillion, predicted to grow to $2.6 trillion by 2020. In Islamic law, alongside usury, investments in prohibited industries like alcohol, gambling and pornography are also forbidden. This means conventional financial products – everything from current accounts and mortgages all the way to hedge funds and sovereign bonds – will be rejected by many Muslim investors. In some regions, either due to these religious reasons or because of a lack of access or low income, many Muslims remain 'un-banked'.

Majority Muslim nations have Islamic finance sectors that are long-standing and even eclipse conventional finance. In Indonesia, for example, finance providers must be shariah-compliant. In minority Muslim nations there is a drive to create Islamic finance products both for domestic consumption and to engage in trade with the growing power that is the Islamic economy. In 2013, UK prime minister David Cameron announced the launch of student loans which would be shariah-compliant for British students wanting to pay for their university fees. He also announced £200m of sukuk, Islamic bonds, which could make the UK the first minority Muslim country with such financial instruments.

The Islamic finance industry does have a marketing problem, as many consumers believe that it is just interest-based finance with an Islamic label pasted on it. For others, the lack of availability and high cost are barriers. And some simply can't get their heads around how a bank can offer both Islamic and conventional products if the back office is run on an interest-based structure. Many believe that an Islamic mortgage is the only permissible way to buy a property, or that conventional current accounts are not acceptable. When they investigate the current Islamic finance offerings, however, whilst they support the spirit of Islamic finance, they express their disappointment in what is available.

Generation M are willing – if pushed by a lack of choice, or persuaded by the benefits of the product – to pay above what a conventional product might cost, but feel extremely upset if there is any whiff of being exploited for their faith.

Like halal food and Muslim cuisine, Islamic finance is an area where 'values' are highlighted rather than Islamic technicalities. In Turkey, Islamic finance is called 'participation banking', with reference to the community aspect of the finance. In Malaysia, campaigns about finance focus on the modern and progressive nature of such financial instruments. Middle-class Malaysians epitomising Generation M are concerned, for example, about shariah-compliant savings investments for their children.

Technology is offering new ways for Generation M to access shariah-compliant financial products where their options would otherwise have been limited. In the USA Noriba ('no' and 'riba', the Arabic word for interest) was set up in 2012. CEO Ahmad Bassam displays the Generation M traits of fully partaking in modern life while maintaining Islamic values:

> Noriba Investing was created because American Muslims and those who have faith in the Islamic way of investing, while welcome to contribute to America's prosperity, have up until now been unable to 'get their share' when it came to investing in the markets. American Muslims, taxpayers, consumers and members of society, should be able to freely participate in the market without having to compromise their core principles.

The consumer push for ethics in industry extends into the financial services sector. Crowdfunding investment vehicles which harness the community to finance businesses are reminiscent of Islamic ideas of 'qard-e-hassana', the 'goodly loan', where money is given out of goodness rather than necessarily only to make a profit, and is also founded on the idea of profit-sharing.

Halalfunder was launched in October 2012 and describes itself as 'the crowdfunding platform for halal projects and ideas'. It makes it clear that it's not exclusively for ideas and projects that are aimed only at Muslims, as long as they're Muslim-friendly. Again, this underlines Generation M's desire to bring good to society as a whole, while being conscious of Muslim needs and values. Halalfunder has larger brothers and sisters in crowdfunding such as Shekra and Yomken, which are based in the Middle East.

Pharmaceuticals: Halal and Healthy

In Malaysia, 30-year-old Sara is playing with her toddler, reminiscing about her pregnancy. 'I used to take Vitamin C, Vitamin B complex, folic acid and iron when I was expecting, on the recommendation of my doctor.' Sara explains that there is a range of options for vitamins and supplements available over the counter, but the only ones she considered were 'certified halal by JAKIM'. The others didn't meet her requirements.

> As a Muslim, I will try my very best to make sure that what goes into my family's stomach is halal and tayyab as it is an order placed upon a Muslim to seek and eat halal food. It's an obligation to first and foremost find the best and that is being halal.

> Does it really matter? To Sara, it's crucial: 'With regular intake of non-halal food or vitamins you'll find it hard to be in touch with religious obligations as it will leave a dark spot in your heart that will grow bigger each time you consume non-halal food.' She's keen to emphasise that the choices made about health are dependent on what is available and what is required to preserve life. It's an important Islamic principle that preserving life trumps all other considerations, even if that means consuming haram products like alcohol or pork.

> Vitamins are unlike vaccinations or other medical drugs where we may have no other choice in terms of the ingredients used. Until we have other options that use halal formulae and ingredients then we will settle with what's permissible by religious scholars. So within the choices that are available, it is very important to buy only halal vitamins as it is part of being a Muslim.

It is this determination to observe halal, the awareness that the medical and pharmaceutical industries should be more responsive to Muslim needs, along with a belief that voicing their requirements for halal products and services can make tangible changes, that are driving new developments in the healthcare segments.

Generation M believe that state-of-the-art healthcare provision should be delivered in ways that are more suited to their Muslim sensibilities. Despite healthcare and pharmaceuticals not appearing on the original Noor Category Index, the conclusions of the index – that what goes into the body must absolutely be halal – would apply in this case. Even while the exemption on halal observance applies in the case of healthcare, why should they choose second best?

Every year anything up to 3 million Muslim pilgrims from over 180 countries make their way to Makkah in Saudi Arabia for hajj. The conditions of intense overcrowding, heat and cross-fertilisation of viruses make this time rife for the spread of infections, particularly meningitis. Saudi Arabia has made it mandatory for all visiting pilgrims to have been vaccinated against the illness. But what should the host country do if the vaccine contains porcine elements? In 2012 an alternative halal variant was approved, and in 2014 production began in Malaysia in conjunction with three Saudi companies to bring to market a halal vaccine.

This is merely the beginning of the pharmaceutical industry's engagement with the requirements of Muslims. While global pharmaceutical brands are yet to fully embrace Muslim healthcare requirements, smaller businesses are taking matters into their own hands. Muslim American company Noor Vitamins focuses on halal vitamins for children. Ensuring children are healthy and halal is a prime concern for Generation M and they are more likely to focus on the halal requirements of their children than even their own. In Malaysia, Safwa Health is inspired by a similar vision of offering halal choices in health management. It explains: 'Enabling families to lead happy and healthy lives is our goal, and we hope to improve the quality of life of the Muslim community in Malaysia and beyond.'

The value of the entire end-to-end halal healthcare industry, which could cover over-the-counter to hospital care to medical tourism and in-home care, has not been estimated, mainly because of the relative infancy of these ideas and the difficulty of estimating how quickly Muslims would take up the services if offered. However, with regard to the pharmaceutical sector specifically, the Muslim consumer spend in 2014 was estimated at $75 billion. This expenditure is expected to grow to $106 billion by 2020.

The significance of this sector is underscored by global-level efforts to establish a 'halal pharmacopeia' which details the halal variations and availability of the core building blocks in pharmaceuticals. Malaysia, for example, released its 'Halal Pharmaceuticals General Guidelines', which aim to address halal integrity in the pharmaceutical supply chain from manufacturing through to distribution and even the storage and display of medicines and health supplements. Only a handful of other countries including Saudi Arabia, Indonesia, Thailand, the Philippines and the UK already have one.

There are increasing consumer movements for medical care, or medical tourism, from regions such as the Middle East to Muslim-friendly healthcare providers – for example, in the Indian subcontinent and Asia. Thailand is one of several hubs for medical tourism, and one hospital alone receives upwards of 125,000 Arab visitors. This has spurred the development of halal cuisine and Muslim-friendly services as well as creating jobs for local Muslims who interpret into Arabic. In India, where medical tourism is also growing, the importance of catering to Muslims prompted Chennai to open the first halal-certified hospital.

For Generation M, healthcare is a holistic activity that takes in the spiritual as well as wider family involvement. In Malaysia, Dr Norshinah Kamarudin is the chair and managing director of Al Falah Care, which launched an Islamic home-based nursing care service. 'There are many patient-care agencies, but most of them only focus on physical health and needs alone,' she explains. Muslim patients receiving Al Falah's services will also have access to a spiritual approach from the attending doctors and nurses to help assure their speedy recovery. Al Falah provides Muslim patients with a book on prayers. The nurses attending to Muslim patients will support them in prayers. Additionally, patients will be advised on how they can perform their religious obligations when they are ill.

In coming years, Generation M are likely to drive the development of 'holistic healthcare' in order that both their physical and spiritual needs can be met. In addition, gender sensitivity in treatment, family-friendly environments, conscientiousness in the medicines provided and the facilities being Muslim-friendly are likely to be at the forefront of developments in treating Muslim patients.

Generation M are not requesting religious segregation – far from it. In our own research as well as anecdotal feedback we find they seek quite the opposite: to be included in the mainstream, but for sensitivity to be shown to their spiritual requirements. During childbirth these may be as simple as giving space to birth rituals such as playing Qur'anic recitations during labour, or giving space to the father after the baby is born to whisper the call to prayer in the child's ears. Family and visitors are an important part of a patient's treatment, but most hospitals have little room for visitors and their needs. As young Muslims assert their healthcare requirements we may see new hospital concepts emerging which create spaces for family support, living areas for visitors and accessible prayer spaces for patients and visitors alike. Spiritual welfare is a core component of physical recovery. Even in healthcare, Generation M are keen to uphold the virtuous circle of consumption.

Fun: The Final Frontier

Marwa is eating at an Indian restaurant in Cairo with three of her friends. Her bright pink headscarf and floral blouse are easy to spot from the other side of the room. The friends' animated conversation ebbs and flows while they savour the curries in front of them and discuss relationships, politics and current events as well as nutrition and fashion.

'I'm very interested in exploring other cuisines,' Marwa explains as she tears a roti into pieces with her fingers and dunks it in the curry. 'Just like I love to understand different people and how they view life.' Marwa says her social circle includes Muslims both practising and non-practising, Hindus, Christians and those of no faith at all. But she quickly gets back to the seemingly more important subject of food. 'I don't like to eat at fast food restaurants as I'm health conscious, so no junk!'

She loves to travel, both within and outside Egypt. She relishes reading and learning foreign languages, and she's a fan of the opera, movies, theatre and 'any multicultural event'. Her energy seems to be endless as she also enjoys working out at the gym and yoga. But, says the 33-year-old English-language instructor who works at a private university, her 'major fun activity' is dancing. 'I attend belly dancing classes as well as Zumba at a ladies-only gym. My dancing instructors are so professional. They are all religious and the majority of them wear hijab too.'

It's important to her that this energy she has for life is reflected in her style, and she believes the attention she must pay to fashion is rooted in her Islamic beliefs. 'I love to look cheerful. I don't believe in having to wear dark colours to look religious. Islam didn't impose any colours on us because what we wear reflects our individual cultures around the world.'

She laughs when it's put to her that this fun-loving energy she demonstrates does not fit with ideas that Muslim life is about following strict rules.

> Lots of people think Muslims don't have fun because we don't drink alcohol, smoke or take drugs or have sex outside marriage. But I believe that Islam allows me to enjoy life to the utmost as long as I'm not breaking any religious rules. And I believe that all the rules are consistent with our physical, spiritual, mental and emotional needs. So breaking any of them will hurt no one but ourselves.

She pauses and beams brightly. 'God created us to live a happy, joyful life.'

Generation M believe that having fun is a God-given right. All activities are up for grabs as long as they adhere to the parameters set forth by their faith. Before our very eyes, the world is developing a new cultural cool.

Sex, music, drink, art, travel, fashion, personal care, home care, Muslim media such as magazines, TV and online life, culture creation, video games, comics, even branding and charitable giving are all facets of a Muslim lifestyle that goes beyond the technical requirements of halal food or shariah-compliant finance. Every aspect of attitude, behaviour and consumption can be demonstrated in the growth of these categories that affect every angle of daily life. When aggregated together in financial terms, they are worth billions of dollars.

Muslim fashion was estimated in 2014 at $230 billion. Muslim travel was worth $142 billion. Muslim personal cosmetics and care over $54 billion. While these numbers are huge, they reflect a wider truth: fun and self-expression are at the centre of Generation M's life ethos. Yet the propensity for enjoyment that is a defining factor of this segment has been woefully overlooked. In fact, what troubles many young Muslims is that they are criticised for being humourless and sour. It's an image that particularly bothers them, because they believe it's far from the truth, and therefore is a myth that they have to work hard to dispel.

Saleem in England explains how these new sectors of halal fun and culture are being embraced as core to their identity: 'If Muslims can't have any fun, then why did Allah create it?'

But it's Fatim in Singapore who cheesily sums up that fun is central to the fusing of their Muslim faith and comfort with modernity: 'Muslims put the fun back into fundamentalism.'

5   #MUSLIM

Building the Digital Ummah in
Dar-al-Internet

A typical day for Usman begins when his smartphone wakes him up to perform fajr, the morning prayer. 'I have the prayer timings app on my phone. If I'm travelling it connects with the Google location service and updates any changes in prayer time.' Later, if he wants to recite some verses of the Qur'an, he has installed the Qur'an app. 'It has over twenty reciters to choose from.'

'The internet has made me a better Muslim,' says the 30-year-old civil servant, who lives in Nigeria. 'It has given me a sense of belonging to the global ummah that has helped shape my life. [...] I get my news from the internet,' he says, preferring its immediacy over traditional print. 'I also learn more about news globally. It is very important to keep up with news from the Muslim ummah around the world because it may be your responsibility to defend them in your community.' It's a subject that is close to home, particularly in the shadow of horrific actions carried out by extremist group Boko Haram.

'We could see the unity of the ummah and even non-Muslims globally in condemning the act of the Boko Haram sect when they kidnapped over 200 girls in Chibok with the #BringBackOurGirls campaign; this is all thanks to the internet.' Even the first lady of the USA, Michelle Obama, tweeted a picture of herself holding the hashtag on a placard. Usman continues:

When the media labels Muslims as terrorists, non-Muslims back that up by referring to warring Muslim countries around the globe.

For example, in the southern part of Nigeria where Muslims are few, they can't defend the religion of Islam. This is something that motivates me to learn more about the ummah globally.

The connectivity to the ummah has been one of the most powerful effects of the internet on today's global Muslim community, and explains why Usman mentions it again and again. It has offered up a shared identity despite distance, language and culture. He's not shy of modern tools that help him improve his faith. 'It's good to take advantage of what the twenty-first century has to offer and learn as much as we can. We can now reach beyond learning from just friends, families and local communities. We can learn globally.'

There are more practical impacts of the internet. 'It helps us advertise what is halal and what is prohibited, promote upcoming events, share Islamic experiences like eid celebrations with the kids, prison visits, hospital visits and so on with other communities, which might inspire them to do [the same] in their own community.'

It's his own personal development as a Muslim that is at the heart of Usman's internet interactions. 'I use the internet to gain Islamic knowledge. I search fiqh rulings that seem complicated to me so I can get other views which are maybe explained in a different way that would help me understand it better.'

There's Islamic-inspired entertainment to be had too:

I enjoy different Islamic songs from different artists around the world – Kamal Uddin, Junaid Jamshed, Zain Bhikha, Sami Yusuf, and so on. These CDs are hardly seen at CD stores around us here in Nigeria but the internet has made it easy to get them.

The internet has also opened up channels for younger Muslims to explore topics which may not have been culturally acceptable, where suitable scholars were not available, or which could only be discussed in places from which younger people are excluded. 'There are also questions that I feel shy or awkward to ask at the Islamic school, study group or at home. The internet gives me the freedom to ask these questions.'

Usman shares a worry that has plagued the ummah because the internet allows anyone to take the mantle of knowledge and spread (mis)information: 'The only problem I face with the internet is I might fall prey of fake sheikhs or websites with false information. I try and know more about a website and sheikh or read some of their articles and people's comments to be sure they are genuine.'

Affordable, accessible and democratic, the internet, mobile and social media are tools for Generation M to achieve their aspirations and become part of a worldwide network of peers who share their values. This global reach is part of their new identity, and for Generation M women in particular it opens up previously unavailable domains.

Generation M are tech-savvy. The internet has undoubtedly been the glue which binds them together and creates the critical mass that turns them into a globally influential force. Technology is a tool for self-empowerment. They use it to educate themselves, to connect themselves, to build networks and cut across geographies and cultures. They use technology for research. They use it to hold people and companies to account. It breaks down barriers and, more than anything, it creates the community on which Generation M is built.

Dar-al-Internet, Home of the Generation M Ummah

The Muslim nation, the ummah, described in the Qur'an as a fundamental part of the Islamic faith, aims to be a global, borderless community that feels the sufferings and joys of its members no matter where they are. The internet has dissolved the barriers of time, distance, culture and ethnicity and has finally made instantly available the spiritual love and social consciousness that underpin the notion of ummah.

Generation M do not feel – as their parents and forebears may have done – that Muslims are located in unreachable territories and lands. Rather the e-ummah puts their sisters and brothers at the tips of their fingers. They can immediately access news coverage from across the minority and majority Muslim world, picking up stories not carried in mainstream publications. During the invasion of Iraq, it was the voices of online citizen journalists that let us hear the authentic words of those under siege. During the waves of bombings of Gaza, Al Jazeera experimented with combining the stories that its reporters in the Gaza Strip were filing along with their GPS co-ordinates in order to create an online map of the war zone. Young Palestinians spread news via Twitter and Facebook of what would have remained undocumented aspects, creating what was noted globally as a change in global media coverage. The wider Muslim activist movement co-ordinated boycotts through online means.

This community of purpose, brought together by its interests and principles, is eschewing the constraints of geographic boundaries in favour of a shared worldview called Islam. Traditional scholars in early Islamic history divided the world into Dar-al-Islam and Dar-al-Harb, the land of Islam and the land of war. It was an easy split to make in a world where Muslims were connected by where they lived, even though they exhibited great variation in culture, and in a time where civilisational powers were generally characterised by one religion. Even then it was a contentious distinction – after all, Muslims and non-Muslims lived, participated and travelled easily in each other's territories.

Today, scholars, academics and experts debate whether these divisions are relevant and how these notions affect mindsets, politics and even wars. The concept of Dar-al-Aman, the land of peace and safety, holds greater sway. Those early distinctions are irrelevant as far as Generation M are concerned, particularly when it comes to navigating the vast oceans of cyberspace. In fact it is Dar-al-Internet, the land of the internet, that is at the vanguard of creating social, spiritual, religious and political change in the Muslim world.

The Democratisation of Religious Access and Knowledge – and its Effect on Religious Authority

Umm Hamza is a 26-year-old Egyptian from Alexandria, a blogger who goes by the name 'PinkPerla'. She says: 'The internet makes for a true understanding of the ummah from every nation and hue, and a better sense of one body as the hadith implies.' She enjoys the immediacy of the internet for building her faith: 'On the level of worship, the internet has made available information on fatwa and hadith authenticity much needed in an ever-changing world.' She strikes a note of caution that Muslims need to be careful 'not to rely too much on Sheikh Google or subjective "fatwa shopping"' – a term that denotes taking your question to multiple religious scholars until you get the answer you want. But she points out, 'it's just more convenient to check preliminary rulings at your fingertips.'

Like her Millennial peers, Umm Hamza sees the internet as offering an alternative to broadcast TV. 'I thrive on the thought of finding quality da'wah shows on YouTube without the need to put up with tons of ads on the TV channel, available on demand,' she says.

The access to information, as well as the ability to publish or broadcast news and opinion, has brought positive benefits to those who have been traditionally excluded from the spheres of religion and politics. In both the corridors of power and in mosques, it is women and youth who historically have been denied access, alongside groups that might stand outside powerful orthodoxies. But in the broad, welcoming e-ummah these groups have found a place for expression and belonging. Some of these involve the creation of entirely new spaces for self-expression, which began with early bloggers and group portals and has now morphed into Facebook and WhatsApp groups.

There is also the opportunity to ask questions, challenge social mores and explore ideas without the fear of being judged.

Alia says, 'I live in a small Swedish town and do not have access to Islamic lectures in the languages I am more comfortable with but even being in a small secluded Muslim community, I can use the internet, make my own halaqa (study group) online or use any other virtual forum.' It's a kind of religious freedom that these futuristic Muslims cherish, to be able to escape from a single limited brand of proselytising to a broad range of viewpoints and materials.

The prayer congregation, study group and social community that once characterised the proliferation of mosques around the Muslim world have slowly been complemented by virtual spaces. Websites have sprung up offering a wide range of religious education, something that was once restricted to a limited locality, often only for men. Now online courses are available anywhere in the world and to anyone, and women in particular have benefited. These groups span the theological spectrum and offer courses on anything from reading Arabic to learning how to become a Muslim entrepreneur.

Umm Hamza, whom we met earlier, explains how she combines the internet with her real-world life: 'My approach to online Islamic knowledge is complementary to my weekly visits to the mosque study group, we sometimes even use Skype to recite the Qur'an to my teacher a bit more often.'

Websites also act as resources for Islamic rulings, again reflecting different theological viewpoints. Zainab bint Younus calls herself the 'Salafi Feminist' and describes herself as a 'Goth, (Steam) Punk, wannabe-biker niqaabi feminist'; her blog image is of a woman in a black cloak and niqab sitting on a motorbike. She looks fierce (in the sense of Beyoncé rather than of a jihadist, although she might be rightly unhappy at both of these comparisons). She's one of a growing number of prominent internet voices who use the platform to share opinions they feel go unheard. In her case it is the voice of a woman who is a feminist but whom some would describe as hailing from the most hardline of modern Islamic viewpoints, Salafism. She relishes the variety of religious opinions and people online.

> Facebook has connected me to so many different types of Muslims, whom I would never have met in real life. And though I may disagree with them on many matters, I have learned a great deal about different types of Muslims and what the concerning issues of the day are, and how to respond to them and deal with those concerns.

It is increasingly common for scholars to have their own websites, Facebook and Twitter accounts, often with massive followings. Well-known names carry heavyweight authority. The controversial but highly influential Yusuf Al Qaradawi has 1.1 million Twitter followers. The even more controversial Saudi cleric Mohamad Al Arefe has 14 million Twitter followers, which is currently more than the Pope (8.6 million). Indonesia's Abdullah Gymnastiar has 1.7 million followers; Iranian cleric Khamenei draws a much more modest 190,000; while Iraqi ayatollah Sayed Hadi Modarresi who opposed Saddam Hussein has around 160,000 followers.

The flat structure of the internet and the lack of gatekeepers to the discussion of faith can be a breath of fresh air in religious discourses that younger adherents complain are stuffy or out of date. But there is a growing recognition of a new problem, mentioned by Umm Hamza above – how do cybercitizens recognise true expertise and credibility if they are looking for direction and truth? Those who are ordinarily vulnerable can become even more so. The e-ummah – much as it is distasteful to admit – is also full of charlatans and hatemongers. The anonymity which is the hallmark of the internet offers many the room to explore ideas and learn about themselves, but it is sadly exploited by others to hurl abuse and spread nefarious ideas.

In the book *Islam and Popular Culture in Indonesia and Malaysia* (edited by Andrew Weintraub), Muhamad Ali writes that Islamic religious authority has not been lost but transformed. It allows for a more active struggle between supporters and challengers. Muslims may follow the views of their peers as 'fatwas', even if they're not intended as such, if they think of those peers as being more learned than themselves. He says that there is a plurality of subjects that are discussed, and the egalitarian way in which views are put forward has been part of shaping a wider decentralisation of religious authority.

In short, as Alia in Sweden explained, it is no longer the local imam who holds sway; adherents can pick and choose from the scholars they wish, wherever they are. The scholars have websites, videos, blogs, Facebook pages and so on, and are open to direct contact in many cases. In fact the internet has seen the rise of many celebrity preachers whose messages are circulated by video and their phrases are turned into memes by fans to use on status updates.

Generation M worry that it's easy to forget that the e-ummah doesn't really exist; it is critical that those who take their religion seriously engage in the physical rituals and human interactions that are the foundations of Islamic activities. They see the internet as an enhancement to the highly physical presence required in congregational prayers, at hajj and in other social activities.

Seeking Like-minded Muslims

Looking for love and marriage on the internet is no longer the occupation of the sad, lonely or awkward. In many Muslim cultures, seeking partners through family and friends has been commonplace, so the expansion into online matchmaking and matrimonial services has been a natural extension of these methods. It is extraordinarily popular, with thousands of profiles posted by love-hungry Muslims, or their worry-laden parents, in the pursuit of a happy marriage. Young people are no longer willing to meet their spouse-to-be on the wedding night, but instead want to find someone who shares their views without having to engage in 'Western-style' dating. The internet seems perfect, giving access to countless prospects, within the framework of a formalised marriage search.

There's a little blush in Umm Hamza's words when she talks about how the internet played an important role in her getting married.

> I kind of actually did use the Internet to get to know my husband! It was a family recommendation matchmaker who thought we would work as a couple; yet at the time he was halfway around the world doing his studies. So it was suggested that we start to get to know each other long-distance through Skype. It turned out to be a blessing, alhamdulillah. Of course there were the frustrations of technical difficulties and missing out on body language but once we saw each other face to face we had already known each other quite well, so that I agreed to our engagement. Two years later we were married.

Because Generation M are defined by their Islamic faith rather than ethnicity or tribe, matchmaking websites allow them to look further afield rather than relying on traditional matchmaker networks. SingleMuslim.com, for example, is just one of a huge number of matrimonial sites which allow young Muslims who no longer want to be bound by strict and traditional arranged marriage norms to find a partner in an Islamic fashion.

As for those who want to know more about the world around them, no longer do they have to wait for the epic travelogues of the likes of Ibn Battuta. Nor is the limit of their information their circle of friends.

MuslimTravelGirl.com is run by Elena Nikolova to help 'Muslims explore the world in style'. She says: 'There is a famous verse in the Qur'an: "and We made you into nations and tribes, that you may know one another". With travelling I feel this is what we achieve,

getting to know people, nations beyond our towns and countries.'
Her blog is a mix of travel tips and sneak previews into new and
exotic places through the eyes of a young hip Muslim traveller. Her
website offers Muslim-friendly traveller tips: 'There is no excuse
for not praying especially when travelling', and then gives her top
hints on how to fulfil this obligation. Although for most travellers,
credit cards are seen as a travelling essential, Elena suggests 'the
best card for Muslims to travel without interest'. The internet gives
her the technology to offer up her expertise in one neat, appealing
and accessible place, and for would-be travellers to have a guide
that resonates with their needs.

Of course none of this is necessarily unique to Generation M;
these are the benefits of the internet for everyone. But it has been
crucial in the formation of Generation M's identity and continues
to be essential in the way they communicate, engage and propel
themselves forward. This is the ummah writ large, and this is how
they connect with those of similar values and aspirations. With sites
like MuslimTravelGirl, the internet offers them a chance to see other
young Muslims like themselves, to hear their alternative viewpoints
and trust them, and to be buoyed up in their own faith practice.

To Internet or Not to Internet?

The digital space has been an important step forward for Muslims,
along with other minorities who feel excluded from the mainstream
press in Western countries. Breaking into the media is tough anyway,
and promoting an alternative view harder still. Joining the e-ummah
is at last a way for Generation M to be heard on their own terms.

Governments in general have been slow to talk to their populations in cyberspace, but this is more so in Muslim countries, where
historically the imbalance between authority and follower has been
highly asymmetric. However, there is a recognition that communication infrastructure is an economic and commercial need, even while
it is less clear how exactly its social implications should be managed.
In a 2009 Economist Intelligence Unit survey of e-readiness among
70 countries, the UAE was ranked the highest majority Muslim country, coming in 34th, with Malaysia at 38 and Turkey at 43.

What Generation M tell leaders is that they must realise that the mobilising cross-boundary power of the internet is unstoppable and they should use it instead as a force for dialogue and reform. In 2011, social media was hailed as one of the catalysts of unprecedented change in the Middle East, bringing down entrenched political systems and uniting populations in a way that no one could have foreseen. But by 2012 it seemed that social media was already being denounced in the Muslim world.

Saudi poet and journalist Hamza Kashgari sent out three tweets about the Prophet Muhammad on the occasion of the Prophet's birthday. His apparently controversial words provoked fury and even calls for him to stand trial for blasphemy, the outcome of which could have been a death sentence. Kashgari fled to Malaysia, and has since been extradited to Saudi Arabia. After two years in prison he was released. The grand mufti of Saudi Arabia issued a fatwa against Twitter, demanding that 'real Muslims' avoid it, calling it a 'platform for trading accusations and for promoting lies'. It seems somewhat ironic that a Facebook group was immediately formed to call for Kashgari's prosecution after the tweets, with tens of thousands of people joining up.

The mufti wasn't the only one calling for 'real Muslims' to abandon social media. In Pakistan, the CEO of a website called Millat Facebook called on Muslims to delete their accounts on the 'blasphemous' Facebook. Speaking at a conference on the subject of 'Blasphemy by Facebook and the Role of Muslim Youth in Social Media', he said Facebook had caused offence to millions of Muslims in 2010 by hosting a competition to draw the Holy Prophet.

Yet the greatest irony of all is that social media has opened up the opportunity for young Muslims to engage with their faith and their co-religionists in a manner that their parents could never have imagined. Nigerian-born Hadiza says, 'I recite Suratul Kahf alongside the Imam of Makkah, Sudais, thanks to YouTube.'

Despite this being a fraught relationship, there is recognition at a state and civic level that the internet is important and must be correctly harnessed. According to the World Economic Forum's Global Information Technology Report in 2015, the UAE, Qatar, Bahrain, Malaysia and Saudi Arabia now all make it into the world's top 40 network-ready nations.

Social Experiences Lead to Greater Piety

Whatever reluctance traditional social and state institutions may have about the internet, whether religious or social, the fact is that young Muslims have already rushed ahead and embraced it. During Ramadan, people 'tweet the Qur'an'. During hajj there are passionate Twitter feeds offering emotional and intimate accounts of what it is like to be present. Both give people around the world the opportunity to engage with important rituals and to share their experience with fellow Muslims.

Jenn in the UK uses an app which 'gives you a prayer time notification and some Qur'an to read every day'. Umm Hamza says she uses 'an app called Prayer Times to keep updated with prayer calls and qibla directions at home and all my travels. I also tune in to my local mosque website for updated prayer times.'

Nigerian Yusuf Hassan created the Tutlub app as a social forum where 'Muslims meet with friends and families who share the same belief with them. With this set of people, it is religion that forms the basis of their social interactions.' One of its key features is the ability to post a dua, a prayer, and for Muslims around the world to respond by clicking the 'amin' ('amen') button.

Generation M's Millennial peers, as we noted earlier, are much less religious than previous generations. Millennials are less likely to attend services, less likely to say religion is important in their lives and less approving of religious organisations. According to the author of the University of San Diego report we mentioned earlier: 'Individualism can be an uncomfortable fit with religion.' This may well be because religion usually emphasises social norms, but religion also offers a sense of community and belonging. This need to belong hasn't changed, but rather than going to the church or mosque, Millennials are turning to the internet and social media for community.

While some parts of this analysis hold true for Generation M – they are more individualistic than their parents and grandparents, and traditional institutions do not always meet their needs – the internet and social media have enhanced rather than diminished their religiosity. Their sense of ummah is heightened by the internet; social media offer them opportunities to revel in the group experience of religion that is in-built in Islam.

This group experience is powerful. Fatimah in Nigeria says, 'Knowing that I am not always alone in my thinking has emboldened me to voice my opinions more, learning and impacting in the process.' Umm Hamza adds that she is buoyed up by the kind of social support networks that can be built via social media: 'I found Facebook pages like "Surviving Hijab" and "Making up Missed Fasts Club" completely inspiring.'

Ramadan creates a dramatic shift in interactions online. Usage moves to the early morning hours in the Middle East, around 3 a.m. to 6 a.m., just before suhoor in Saudi Arabia. In Indonesia, the hours in the run-up to lunch and lunchtime focus on online shopping. Online engagement is also far more positive, with negative subjects talked about less, and activity about positive community aspects rises. This positivity spills over after the end of Ramadan too.

Brands have started aligning themselves with the social media experience of religion. In 2015, Coca-Cola Egypt ran a Ramadan campaign encouraging consumers to tweet a photo of themselves holding up one finger with the phrase 'One second makes a difference' (*thaniya tafarruq*). The campaign aimed to highlight how prejudices and stereotypes build walls between people, with the habit of judging and labelling people being far too common. The 'One Second Makes a Difference' campaign aimed to encourage the audience to spend more time learning about one another before they passed judgement. The digital ummah is constantly linked to the real world too, and so Coca-Cola tied in its social media campaign with a change to its cans, removing all branding apart from the red background and white stripe, adding simply the phrase 'Labels are for cans, not for people.' In addition, instead of advertising its product on TV, Coca-Cola announced that it would only post its video ads on social media. The savings made by not buying TV advertising slots would be put towards developing underprivileged villages in Egypt.

New Content, New Culture and Getting Your New Identity Heard

One of Generation M's potent frustrations in light of their perception that the Western media stereotypes Muslims is their sense of exclusion from public discussion. Muslims of course are not the only ones to complain of this; however, it is very front of mind for Generation M.

Generation M feel that gatekeepers in the global media speak for Muslims rather than allowing them to speak for themselves. Equally, gatekeepers within Muslim communities chide 'modern' and experimental ideas for not being 'properly Islamic'. The internet has brought down these barriers on both sides. Personal and group blogs have created spaces to be heard, and, over recent years, this has expanded into all forms of online content, notably video content.

In 2014, global pop star and producer Pharrell Williams released the hit song 'Happy'. It prompted cover versions from around the world, with ordinary people dancing along to the catchy beat. As part of the global trend, the Honesty Policy, an anonymous Muslim blog based in the UK, created a #HappyBritishMuslims video. The creators of the video said their aim was to show that 'British Muslims are just as happy' as anyone else. Feeling comfortable in their own skin as faithful and modern, they believe that, if only people could know them as individual human beings who are interested in the same things that interest the mainstream, they would be able to eradicate the growing tide of anti-Muslim hatred. The video sparked a wave of similar covers from around the Muslim world.

The video also triggered a social media storm about whether Muslims really could – or should – be happy, and whether critics of the video were by definition unhappy because they were asserting legitimate political, religious and social concerns. Some Muslims felt there was no need to dance along to the insistent beat, that Muslims should not constantly have to demonstrate how 'normal' they are. There is undoubtedly pressure put on minority Muslim populations in particular to constantly prove their patriotism and normality.

Others felt that the very essence of the video was contrary to their principles as Muslims and that 'proving' they could be happy didn't require those principles to be compromised. They pointed to the problematic sexualised culture of popular music. These critics were quickly labelled as 'unhappy' about fun and accused of not accepting difference of opinion and variation.

Again, the debate demonstrates that, even within Generation M, Muslim identity, place in the world and religiosity are still under fierce discussion, and fluid. More notable for our examination of the e-ummah is that the digital space allowed these voices to be published and discussed. Generation M was heard on its own terms.

This new space has given rise to a whole range of Muslim lifestyle activities ranging from Muslim fashion blogging, to YouTube diaries to new Muslim music, to charitable campaigns. The new content brings to life a new look, sound, language and culture for our futuristic faithfuls. The internet gives them a shared home for this culture and reinforces their shared identity right around the world.

The New Celebrities

In the virgin territory of the internet, new celebrities have been born. They aim to satisfy the hunger for everything to do with building a Muslim lifestyle, whether it be hijab tutorials, poking fun at their own lives or creating rap music and religious sermons.

In the UK, Humza Arshad created the Diary of a Bad Man video series, taking a wry look at the daily antics of a young Asian Muslim man living at home with his parents. It's now been commissioned as a TV series. The videos were so popular amongst teen Muslims that the UK government worked with Humza to create a special episode addressing the issue of radicalisation. He now speaks in schools about the dangers of terrorism. Humza's YouTube channel has chalked up over 68 million views.

Palestinian-American Yousef Saleh Erakat is better known as FouseyTube, with more than 8 million subscribers. His videos mix humour with social commentary, such as his most popular 'Yoga Pants' video, which was created when he noticed that girls at the gym in yoga pants got stared at. So he put on a pair himself, concealed his face and upset a lot of men whom he caught off-guard staring at his bottom. He has more serious videos too, such as one where he pretends to harass a woman in a hijab, and others exploring his Palestinian identity.

Alongside the rise of celebrity scholars and sheikhs online we're seeing a growing number of female celebrities, like Yasmin

Mogahed and Yuna, who would previously have been unknown. There are online bloggers and influential tweeters too, including a huge raft of Muslim fashion icons and Instagrammers.

Not Always a Force for Good

Umm Hamza is aware that the positives of the internet come with dangers too: 'the internet is a "land" of opportunities but we should use it wisely.' This darker side is something that is increasingly worrying for Muslims as they see the positive benefits of the internet being perverted by extremist organisations like Daesh for violent and blood-thirsty ends. Daesh (also known as Islamic State, ISIS or IS) has used the internet as a key tool in its propaganda and recruitment wars.

Robert Fisk, veteran journalist of the Middle East, says, 'ISIS has turned the internet into the most effective propaganda tool ever.' When it comes to repackaging violent extremism, the group's mastery of branding, YouTube videos, Facebook and Twitter is extraordinary. Instead of young Muslims going to mosques, they had simply to visit the darker corners of the internet to imbibe their propaganda. This point was made by a French lawyer for returning jihadists who are now imprisoned. The lawyer described how his clients were sucked into the Daesh extremist narrative by spending hours on the internet looking on YouTube and other social networks at messages and images from the violent extremist group. It was not the mosques that radicalised them.

The slick online operation used by Daesh to spread its message and to recruit people is a challenge to counter-terrorism experts. Its high digital production values and use of social media means that its messages are swiftly spread. High-definition films are finessed with 3D graphics and musical scores featuring jihadi music. The look, the music and the language are highly attuned to the audience and these are deployed through social media with tweets and hashtags into spaces where people are seeking identity, knowledge and belonging. This appeals far more to the tech-savvy YouTube generation than the grainy videos posted by Al-Qaeda to TV stations. Thousands of Twitter accounts are opened and shut down in order to keep perpetuating the message.

Generation M finds itself forging a path between Islamophobia and stereotyping on the one hand, and on the other the hijacking by violent extremists of the tolerant, modern inclusive Islam that they believe in. The #NotInMyName hashtag kicked off in Britain, but spread around the world as Muslims tweeted, Facebooked and Vined their own personal denunciations of Daesh. Even President Obama referenced the campaign.

In Singapore, A'qilah Saiere said: 'Because of ISIS, many Muslims globally have become victims of Islamophobia and other forms of hate,' adding, 'ISIS is doing an injustice to the Muslims and non-Muslims. So, we are standing up in our own way to show that these are not the teachings of Islam.'

The Muslim Youth League UK launched a 'Jihad against ISIS'. It called the group a 'cancer' and stated in a seven-point rejection plan posted on its Facebook page that 'We declare their killing of human beings, whether Muslim or non-Muslim, to be un-Islamic.' They also noted: 'We reject all generalised Islamophobic labelling of Muslims as extremists or terrorists by the media, politicians and the general public.'

Digital humour also got an outing as a means of exercising jihad against both kinds of extremism and hatred. In the #MuslimApologies campaign Muslims mocked the incessant demands to condemn terrorists who have nothing to do with ordinary Muslims. As one said: 'As a Muslim, I apologize for World War I and World War II, even if it has nothing to do with Muslims, but just in case.' Another said: 'Sorry for trigonometry and astronomy.'

Our tech-savvy Muslims also recognise a less menacing, but none-theless difficult problem: that the internet has no quality control or regulation. Anyone can post anything, and when that comes to dic-tats about religion, this can pose danger for those who may be duped into following websites or online figures who can easily mislead.

In the UK, Muslim convert Gemma says that the internet:

Can be bad and good! The internet displays the fitna which before we wouldn't see so much of unless it was on the media so it can distract one from worshipping Allah. And there is also a lot of misinformation online especially for reverts and youngsters, if used correctly then yes it has immense benefit!

'Religious Commerce': Creating a Viable Marketplace

'I use the internet to buy Islamic clothing, kids' nasheed CDs and Islamic books,' says 35-year-old Sveta in Melbourne, Australia. These might seem like niche products, but technology opens up a global Muslim futurist segment, and suddenly such items become economically viable.

Start-up costs for online businesses are comparatively low, and with the growing ease of international delivery and online payment protocols, products can be made available to and purchased from almost anywhere in the world. Muslim fashion is a fantastic example of the shared digital space making a new market possible. High-street retailers have yet to understand the size and spending power of the Muslim fashion consumer. Even when they do, they will have to ensure that Muslim consumer footfall in a particular area can justify an in-store range. Online Muslim fashion boutiques, of course, have a far wider target audience, which encompasses both Muslim and non-Muslim consumers who want modest wear.

In the UK, the internationally renowned London College of Fashion conducted research into the project 'Modest Dressing: Faith-Based Fashion and Internet Retail' as part of the Religion and Society research programme, to look at the growing market for modest clothing among faith groups within Islam, Christianity and Judaism.

'The research shows that the market is growing, with new companies starting up, diversifying and segmenting even during the course of the project,' said Professor Reina Lewis. The study found that the reduced overheads of online retail and marketing made it possible for specialist clothing businesses to reach a national or international market. The increasing range of items has made it possible to shop online as an alternative to the high street.

Because of the more fluid nature of the internet, 'The market for modest clothing is not limited only to religiously motivated shoppers or companies,' Reina Lewis pointed out. 'We found that there is a significant group of modest dressers who do not identify as religious, or who, if they are religious, do not see this as the main reason why they choose to dress modestly.'

The same commercial principles apply more broadly to the business ideas that Generation M are developing – inspired by the e-ummah and the exchange of ideas, as well as a response to a growing commercial marketplace. It's no surprise that the flourishing of the digital ummah and Generation M's interest in consumer goods are creating a thriving online economy across all the lifestyle categories. Every imaginable product that has a Muslim lifestyle twist is available online because the economics and the audience reach stack up. These outlets range from Facebook sellers, across Etsy and even to niche brands covering everything from Ramadan decorations to personal care to Muslim nannies.

A notable stake in the ground – at least symbolically, if not in commercial receipts – came when the Malaysian prime minister, Najib Abdul Razak, announced the launch of Zilzar.com in 2014. Its aim is to offer a platform for businesses and consumers to sell to each other, bringing together entrepreneurs, youth and SMEs. Razak explained: 'The environment and conditions are perfect for this partnership for economic growth. The halal industry is made up of small and medium enterprises who are globally dispersed and crying out for connectivity.' As our blogger Umm Hamza explains about her online consumption:

> Searching for hijab-friendly clothes takes me through Debenhams (where there is no local store near me) for a maxi dress and cardigan as well as Islamic Design House with the nearest stockist an hour away. Now it's Ramadan; I watch some da'wah programmes on YouTube. I listen to Maher Zain and I got the chance to download his Amazon album for my wedding before it was even available in stores. I check profiles for US Muslim activists like Linda Sarsour, follow thinkers like Zainab bint Younus, and a few Muslim mummy bloggers from India, Indonesia, Canada, France and Palestine.

What is most important to her when it comes to being part of the digital ummah is that:

> it makes me feel a better, more-informed Muslim. The Prophet (PBUH) praised the strong [knowledgeable] Muslim over the weak. I think in an age where knowledge is power, the opportunities the internet brings could mean I become a stronger Muslim.

6   GOD GAVE (HALAL) ROCK AND ROLL TO YOU

The Soundtrack of Generation M

It's just after the celebration of Eid, and Wembley Arena is packed with 10,000 Muslims. Teenage girls are waving glo-sticks and swaying their raised hands side to side, mobile phones held high to record the performance. But this is no ordinary teen concert.

As Maher Zain walks onto the stage – one of today's best-known global Muslim music celebrities – the crowd goes wild. Everyone in the audience, from toddlers to grandmothers, is a fan of his songs. His music explains his attempts to be a better Muslim, how to live life as a faithfully inspired twenty-first-century citizen. It's clean-cut living at its finest. Some might even call it corny. But in a music marketplace that is still in its infancy, the audience is mesmerised. No raunchy music videos or lyrics to be found here – instead these concert-goers are seeking ethical inspirational music, which in turn is creating the soundtrack to a new Muslim culture.

Maher Zain is a Muslim Swedish R&B singer, songwriter and music producer of Lebanese origin. His videos and music are a mix of soft-focus love and sentiment sung with a clear melodious voice. He wouldn't have looked out of place on an *X-Factor* stage. A quick visit to YouTube finds that his songs gather tens of millions of views. His tracks include one thanking his mother, another about how this life leads on to the eternal afterlife, yet another to accompany an Islamic wedding. So far, so ballad-like. But he also talks about freedom, the challenges of terrorism and how to live as a Muslim in the modern world. His music is his method of expressing how to combine faith and modernity: 'We [Muslims] are not a boring people, you know. We don't just sit and pray,' he said. 'I want to make music because I want to send a message.'

Maher is aware that such culture creation is important both for the growth of Generation M and as a vehicle for Muslim interaction with wider society. 'People would rather listen to songs than screams,' he says, reflecting his listeners' strong consciousness of their rightful place in the world and how his music can wield its appeal for the wider good. Usually wearing casual clothes, Maher does not have the overtly religious appearance often associated with traditional Muslim musicians, and he says his choice of attire is deliberate: 'The way I dress, inshallah, is a way of showing that people can be good Muslims no matter how they look.'

Before he was a singer, he worked as a music producer in New York. Despite landing a job with a prominent producer, he says he was uncomfortable in New York's music scene. He decided to quit and pursue a career as a singer, a job that would allow him to express his true identity. He went to new music label Awakening Worldwide, whose slogan is 'faith-inspired and value-driven'. Maher's popularity skyrocketed after he made a Facebook page and put his music videos on YouTube. Within a year and a half of going online, he had become the first Muslim musician to reach 2 million fans on Facebook and his videos had notched up more than 8 million views on YouTube. The internet also helped popularise him in South East Asian countries such as Brunei, Malaysia and Indonesia, despite the fact that at that time he had no promotional campaigns in the region. Today he has over 10 million Facebook followers and over 100 million YouTube views.

The clean-cut Islamic boyband genre is hugely popular. While handsome young men attract screaming teenagers, talk is of marriage rather than boyfriends and girlfriends. Seven8Six is a Muslim American boyband that is best described as the Muslim answer to the Backstreet Boys. Mo Sabri is another Muslim American teen heart-throb. His best-known songs include the cheesily sentimental but extremely popular 'Heaven Is Where Her Heart Is' and the cross-faith rap song 'I Believe in Jesus'. Some of his videos depict him in soft focus or in black and white performing on stage to an audience of screaming female hijabi Muslim fans.

The band Outlandish hails from Denmark and is made up of three young men of Moroccan, Pakistani and Honduran origin. They say their style is 'life music' and offers a mix of hip hop, folk, soul and pop, and they talk about topics from love to racism. 'You can say we are social realistic and we always talk about the society which shapes us all for the better or worse.'

Humood Al Khudher is from Kuwait and sings in Arabic. His song 'Kun Anta' talks directly to this generation that won't accept the mutually exclusive choice of being either modern or religious. Instead, he says, 'be yourself':

> I accept people but I don't imitate them
> Except for what I agree with, to satisfy myself
> I will just be myself, just the way I am, this is me
> My conviction suffices, this is my certainty.

No list of Muslim boybands would be complete without mentioning Zayn Malik of the global chart-topping group One Direction. Even though he openly acknowledges he is Muslim, Zayn does not profess any kind of deep religiosity for himself. He's caught between being a mainstream Muslim pop icon (often seen being chased down by Muslim girls in headscarves) and being accused of 'boyband jihad' or 'pimping Islam to your daughters'. Young Muslims see the fact that they are stigmatised with jihad no matter what they do as both frustrating and hiliarious: Sheila Musaji, who writes the website 'The American Muslim', quips: 'I thought that the Islamophobes had run out of crazy jihad plots but I was wrong.'

The MTV-esque sound, image and lyrical content is a huge feature of this new genre of Islamic pop music, highlighting how modern trends are embraced as long as they adhere to Islamic principles. Of course, there are times where this combination becomes controversial. The Muslim teenage groupies at Wembley Arena concerts have come under fire for their 'un-Islamic behaviour' in screaming at their heart-throbs. Some, apparently, threw their hijabs on stage (although how they achieved this baffles me).

The growing Muslim celebrity culture echoes wider trends, but some ask how it fits with Islamic principles. There's an irony in stars singing about humility and modesty at the same time as being

2. *Generation M popstars are global celebrities. Artists like Outlandish (Denmark), Maher Zain (Sweden) and Yuna (Malaysia) sell millions of records.*

mobbed by fans. YouTube sensation Adam Saleh runs TrueStoryASA with his best friend Sheikh Akbar. Their channel, which now has over 1,275,000 followers of their real-life pranks, was set up to challenge misconceptions about Islam. Their most popular video has had over 15 million views. When they travelled from New York to London in August 2014 for a social-media-publicised meet-and-greet with their fans, the famous Marble Arch had to be closed because of the hordes of teenage Muslim girls who flocked to see them. In the ensuing ruckus, the two stars had to be escorted away in police vans. When they returned to London in March 2015 they had to be surrounded by a heavy police presence. Londoner Ameera Al Hakawati describes what she saw when she accompanied her 16-year-old sister to meet Adam and Sheikh in 2014: 'One fan pulled his baseball cap off and another grabbed his hair, and that was it. The mob had completely surrounded him. He had nowhere to go, his words inaudible over the shrieks of hysterical hijabis. Scarves were being torn off heads as girls desperately tried to grab a piece of him.' Using a strong religious image, she notes that 'The last time I'd witnessed something similar was at Masjid al-Haram [in Makkah] with hordes of Muslims trying to reach the black stone.' This contentious celebrity culture affects Muslim musicians, internet stars, fashion icons, even Islamic scholars who get mobbed by fans.

Maher Zain's music label Awakening Worldwide had shot to global prominence when it created the look and sound for Sami Yusuf. The company began by publishing books from its UK head office in Swansea but, after spotting a void in the music industry, it hasn't looked back. 'Our ideas and music were fresh, our standard was the Western standard,' says Wali-ur Rahman, one of the founders of the company. 'We wanted to raise the bar and compete with our western contemporaries, as most other nasheeds were cheaply produced.' The result was British Armenian Sami Yusuf, with his suave good looks, silky smooth voice and intense stage presence. He was arguably the first global Generation M pop star singing in English. He's sold over 20 million records and is now signed to Sony. *Time* magazine pronounced him 'Islam's biggest rock star'.

Like his artistic counterparts, Sami Yusuf's music is built on expressing religious ideals for living a good life. He is engaged in numerous charitable activities, acting as an ambassador for Islamic Relief, one of the world's largest Muslim-inspired charities. As his career grew, the breadth of his themes expanded into universal human experiences, although always Muslim inspired. It's a journey that is echoed in many prominent Muslim musicians' and artists' work, and is perhaps a metaphor for Generation M's constant refinement of the boundaries and method of its engagement with the wider world.

Layla in Yogyakarta, Indonesia is a huge fan. 'I love his music, not only the content and style, but because he composes with mainstream music sounds. And also his songs are universal at the same time as having a religious touch.' The 37-year-old loves the music so much that her internet pen name is 'Layla Hijab Sami Yusuf'.

It's Sami Yusuf's dedication to the ummah that makes him so meaningful to her, and his recognition as an equal on the global stage as a Muslim: 'He was the first Muslim artist appointed by the UN to be one of the World Food Programme ambassadors. As

Muslims we are proud of him.' Her devotion is also rooted in the fact that she believes his music has helped her to be a better person.

His song 'Free' was inspired by our sisters in Europe who were discriminated against for wearing hijab. I had been thinking for a while about wearing hijab and when I heard the song I thought, 'Why not now?' My sisters are fighting for hijab and here I am in the biggest Muslim country. When I heard his music it made me want to be a better Muslim on that day, and I'm still trying.

It's Not All Pop, Pop, Pop

Critics of the Islamic pop genre say it is sanitised and doesn't express the broad range of Muslim musical subcultures. There's no doubt that the saccharine lyrics and upbeat tunes ignore the grittier genres that are developing. There's a clear hunger for music that inspires and motivates but also asserts young Muslims' identity in a world that cannot comprehend the notion of being faithful and modern. Some of these genres are familiar to us, like hip hop, which has been wholeheartedly embraced by young Muslims seeking music that is rooted in the spoken word, has limited musical accompaniment (some Islamic rulings deem instrumental music other than drums to be haram) and reflects the growing number of converts coming to Islam who find resonance in hip hop's words and rhythms.

Some developments are altogether more surprising – Muslim punk, for example. A novel by Muslim American convert Michael Muhammad Knight called *The Taqwacores* (taqwa meaning piety, plus hardcore) spawned a whole genre and also a documentary following the development of this scene. Michael writes of Islam and punk: 'They aren't so far removed as you'd think. Both began in tremendous bursts of truth and vitality.' This is probably best expressed in his song 'Muhammad Was a Punk Rocker'.

When he delivers sermons
the kids think he's a bore

> but when he smashes idols
> everyone cheers for more
> Muhammad was a punk rocker
> he tore everything down
> Muhammad was a punk rocker
> and he rocked that town.

American musician and professor of history Mark LeVine comments in *Heavy Metal Islam: Rock, Resistance, and the Struggle for the Soul of Islam* that these multiple genres reflect the variety of ways younger Muslims are expressing their presence in the modern world and attempting to assert their place in it.

> One can see a teenager with green spiky hair and baggy hip-hop style clothing standing next to one in goth makeup, and a few feet away yet another in a black metal T-shirt who's watching the show with his mother or aunt who may be dressed in a black, full-length abaya.

Safa Samiezade'-Yazd is the culture and music editor for Aslan Media, which says that its aim is to inform, educate and engage the public on political, social, religious and cultural issues related to the greater Middle East and its diaspora communities. She pushes hard for the definition of Muslim music to reflect the fact that today's Generation M artists don't just address faith but explore global issues like identity, political oppression, Islamophobia, navigating tradition and modernity, wrapped up in calls to action.

'The reach of global Muslim music is much broader than that represented by Awakening's album,' she argues, in reference to the single sound this label's music tends to have.

> Missing from this compilation is the emerging niche that represents Islam as not just part of a tradition, but as critically engaged in the social issues that drive today's social events [...] They address their Islamic identities from a more universal stance – that is, as a culture and faith that guides them to create their socially-conscious and activist tracks. Islam, as these artists depict it, is not so much dogma or

even religion, but rather a moral compass, something they connect with on a more personal, philosophical level. For emerging generations navigating both parents and peers, the lyrics offer a safe space to question identity, grapple with religion and ultimately renegotiate the role of Muslims in post-9/11 society.

New Culture, Counter-Culture and Self-Expression

So in times of defining moments take this moment to define
    yourself
Tell your own stories
Sing your own psalms
Re-write the headline …
Saying NO … THIS be Islam.

Dasham K. Brookins is an author, poet and writer whose work focuses mainly on adult fiction and spoken poetry. Born and raised in Brooklyn, New York, in a family he describes as 'spiritual', he was gradually attracted to Islam and became Muslim. His poetry covers topics from the everyday activities of life to more philosophical topics like race and discrimination as well as the meaning of life. He explores the challenges of attempting to live a spiritual Muslim life and the engagement Generation M Muslims want to have with a world that feels harsh, discriminatory or stereotyping about them. He urges a move towards empowerment and redefining the perception of Muslims. The lyrics quoted are from his poem 'Headline Islam'.

Poetry has long roots in traditional Islamic communities, and it is undergoing a potent revival. The Qur'an when presented to the pre-Islamic Arab tribes who were contemporaries of Prophet Muhammad was posed as a challenge to their advanced poetic talents. 'Bring another ten chapters like it,' says the Qur'an to the tribes, in reference to its poetic stature. It is within this tradition that today's Generation M sees their spoken-word efforts.

Million's Poet is a reality TV series based in the UAE that looks for the most talented Arabic poets and has been described as

'American Idol for the GCC' and as one of the most successful Arab television shows ever. It aims to revive the tradition of poetry. Lina Khatib, an Arab media expert at Stanford University, explains the social and political appeal: 'Because it's poetry, one of the most respected forms of expression in the Arab world, you can push the boundaries much further than you might with popular music.'

Those boundaries were pushed even further than expected when in 2010 Saudi mother of four, Hissa Hilal, dressed in black abaya and niqab, became the runner-up for the series. She stirred up huge controversy with her critique of conservative clerics in Saudi Arabia. 'I have seen evil in the eyes of fatwas, at a time when the permitted is being twisted into the forbidden,' she said. The clerics and, in her mind, by extension, suicide bombers who wrap explosives around their waists 'are vicious in voice, barbaric, angry and blind, wearing death as a robe cinched with a belt'.

She earned the acclaim of both judges and public, collecting death threats along the way, but stood by her words: 'My poetry has always been provocative. It's a way to express myself and give voice to Arab women, silenced by those who knock our culture and our religion.' Her bold reclamation of religion, and her unwavering confidence in bringing a female perspective, are echoes we see more and more in this new Muslim cultural cool that is emerging.

Part of the appeal of genres like spoken-word poetry, rap and hip hop, apart from conforming to even the strictest rules of music production which prohibits instruments, is their 'outsider' culture status. These works appeal to young Muslims who feel excluded from mainstream culture by its apparent demonisation of Muslims and by Muslims' own rejection of some of the aspects of those cultures which they feel are incompatible with their faith – such as explicit lyrics and sexualisation. Despite their sometimes violent and sexual language, these genres are being reclaimed as vehicles to convey a more Islamic lifestyle without losing their appeal.

Deen Squad is an Islamic hip hop duo that takes mainstream songs, removes the explicit lyrics and imagery and turns them into something they feel is in line with Islamic values. Jae Deen, one of the Canadian pair, says that that the songs they rework are 'not clean spiritually' but 'the beat is amazing, the melody is amazing'.

3. *Canadian hip hop duo Deen Squad take songs where 'the beat is amazing, the melody is amazing' and rework the lyrics to discuss the Muslim experience. 'Imma pray salaat with my lady,' they sing in a remake of the song 'Trap Queen'.*

Their song 'Friday' is a rework of the Drake song 'Tuesday'. Instead of hitting the clubs, Deen Squad sings about going to the mosque, engaging in Friday prayers, and bonding with the brothers. In another remake, this time of a Fetty Wap rap song 'Trap Queen' they sing about wanting to get married to a 'Muslim Queen', praying to God to unite them with their perfect wives (halal diva), because 'Imma pray salaat with my lady'. He says that young Muslims tell him that his videos have helped them to 'start praying again, inspired them to be better Muslims'.

In London, 16-year-old Yusra, wearing a deep-purple headscarf and dressed in the latest fashion, says listening to Deen Squad songs that describe young modern Muslim life is 'comforting' because 'you're doing these things, and you know that other people are doing these things,' adding, 'it's very cool.' She feels it's a good alternative to mainstream rap and disagrees with more traditional voices that look at music as haram.

> Jay-Z [type] songs, they usually talk about love and sex and drugs and whatever, and if you're starting to agree with that you need to step back and think 'Yo! This is wrong.' But if Jae Deen songs are telling you to go to Friday prayers, there's nothing wrong with that. It's all about your intentions.

Eighteen-year-old Mehdi says, 'Putting Islamic teachings into it is genius. And it's very catchy.' Like many of the new Generation M influencers, Deen Squad have come to prominence via the internet and social media. They are shared across channels like Snapchat and YouTube and have the hashtag #DeenSquad. 'They've used a medium which is really appealing to young people. Most of the time Islamic teachings are in chunky books and not very easy to read through and digest,' says Mehdi.

Both Yusra and Mehdi see Muslim-inspired music as offering a positive recognisable sound and image. 'To see two Muslims spreading a good message about Islam, I really do like that,' says Mehdi. There's a deep worry for Yusra about being seen as an outsider by society because of her visible Muslim identity, and music is a way of reaching out. 'Jae Deen's intention is to show that we are just normal human beings. I'm not an extremist, or a jihadist. Him doing re-mixes connects us to everybody else.'

Yassin Al Salman is known by his artist name 'The Narcicyst'. His parents were from Basra, Iraq, and moved to the UAE, where he was born. When he was a child, they relocated to Canada, and he spent his early years between the two countries. An artist himself, he noted there was a growing global phenomenon for 'using hip hop as a vocation and a social mediation, to translate experience into music'. He reflects on the turbulence in his ancestral region of the Middle East: 'in the last five years with everything that has gone on, from the several war theatres that were projected upon the Middle East to the revolutions that are happening right now, hip-hop has been a prominent voice in all these things.'

One of his best-known songs is 'Hamdulillah', meaning thanks to God. The video is a bold, brightly coloured montage of Muslim faces; the lyrics intertwine religious and political commentary. The song is a mix of English and Arabic. He says that one Ramadan he thought: 'I want to put out a video to show the diverse faces that are within our culture […] that share one common thing, which is an identity struggle.'

Music as a means of asserting identity, claiming power and smashing stereotypes through real human connections once again comes through:

You know, a lot of the time our faces are painted on television the way, you know, the media want to represent us. In this case, we wanted to show our faces ourselves and have that power within our hands. So we put a call out on Twitter and Facebook to videographers all around the world, saying, 'If you want to partake in this video, here are the guidelines that you have to follow.'

The strong sense of duty, of wanting to share their humanity and their identity in the face of what is felt to be stereotyping, came through in the way that contributors responded. 'Next thing you know, we had people's faces from Australia, London, New York, Los Angeles, Montreal, Dubai, Jeddah. People from all over the world started sending us footage.' The end result: 'They showed us how powerful they can be.'

This emerging culture unites its adherents across languages, geographies and cultures. Of course, the artists and insights given here offer just a taste, and there are many more in many languages and nations. They are all driven by the same urge to create music rooted in Islamic teachings, spiritually oriented and connected with wider social activism, which gives shape to their new modern faithful identity and the experiences and attitudes this lifestyle brings with it. At the same time it offers something that connects to wider society.

There is a more worrying musical development that is being driven by organisations such as Daesh. Their binary 'Muslims like us versus everyone else' view of the world, and their bloodthirsty and merciless kind of jihad – which Generation M believe is warped, evil and entirely in contradiction with Islamic teachings – has its own soundtrack. The nasheeds draw on traditional Islamic beats but are mixed with the rhetoric of counter-culture warfare and victory set to hip hop, and are best described as 'jihadi rap'. The most well known of these is the infamous 'Dirty Kuffar' (non-believers) released in 2004 as a jihad-style extremist rap video produced by British Muslim rappers Sheikh Terra and the Soul Salah Crew.

Professor Peter Neumann from the International Centre for the Study of Radicalisation and Political Violence, at King's College London, explains:

[People] often start engaging in hip-hop as a form of protest
and rebellion against a situation where they feel they are
marginalised in society, and that, of course, is exactly the same
sort of feeling that the jihadists are also exploiting. They are
trying to recruit people who are feeling lost. Who are feeling
marginalized. Who feel that society doesn't accept them.

The production values of this music are also high, to appeal
to a vulnerable global audience that is seeking media quality as a
benchmark of Daesh's utopian claims, using the internet to reach
out to a global audience. In a further complicated twist, the US
and British governments are exploring if and how to co-opt Muslim
artists to use their musical talents to counter jihadi music.

Neumann points out that the outward rejection of all things
Western while embracing the music of hip hop and rap is a part of
Daesh's ideology which is 'completely contradictory'.

As much as these guys who go into IS saying that they want to
return the world to a seventh-century state, they are actually
creatures of their own society and their own cultures. They
cannot stop using the Internet and they cannot bring themselves
to stop expressing themselves in 21st-century western forms of
expression, which, of course, hip-hop and rap are.

Neumann continues: 'It's a kind of form of gangsta rap, only for
jihadists.'

Fusing the Modern and the Traditional

To suggest that this short exploration of Generation M's developing
music encapsulates the entirety of Generation M's musical choice
or playlist would of course be absurd. Their musical tastes are just
as inclusive of mainstream and niche genres as their non-Muslim
peers, and many will listen with just as varied tastes – some with
more and some with less comfort regarding whether it is deemed
in line with Islamic values or not. There are also some distinct
sounds specifically being developed by and for our young Muslim

audience looking to find and express a modern faithful identity, demolish stereotypes and project themselves. They believe music is important but can be socially and ethically conscious, inspirational and motivating. It can draw on wider contemporary trends, and equally they feel it can contribute to those trends.

The new soundtrack draws on traditional Islamic music genres, which is no surprise, given that this is a segment that takes pride in its Muslim credentials and reviving its history. One of these forms is the nasheed. These are religiously themed songs, similar to hymns, usually sung without any musical instruments. Background harmonies are often derived from other people humming in melodies. Perhaps the most famous of early modern nasheed artists is the Malaysian group Raihan, whose debut album is still Malaysia's most successful in terms of album sales, having sold more than 3.5 million copies since its release in 1996. Their motto squarely represents the Generation M philosophy: 'Pray hard, work smart'. Raihan is signed to Warner Music.

In his book, *Countering MTV Influence in Indonesia and Malaysia*, Kalinga Seneviratne quotes a Warner executive regarding Raihan's success:

> Before Raihan there were many nasyid [*sic.*] groups, but they did not promote themselves by going to radio for radio play, so this time we tried. We treated it like a normal pop album. We used normal marketing tools like TV, radio then magazines.

The executive added that, before this, nasheed songs were marketed on cassettes which were sold at underground music stalls at mosques on Fridays, which meant that the wider public was not aware of the genre. Once Warner Music started promoting it, radio stations were playing it 'ten to twenty times a day', not as nasheed songs but as pop songs: 'It was like a phenomenon, everybody, everywhere was playing.' Other multinational recording labels in Malaysia, including EMI and BMG, started signing up similar acts like Hijjaz and Rabbani. Seneviratne explains that the station manager of IKIM Radio, Malaysia's first Islamic radio station set up in 2001, said that while nasheed was once considered an alternative music genre, it is now part of the mainstream.

The nasheed genre is now huge globally, with the range of artists too numerous to list. The genre uses Arabic devotional words, which connect it to listeners across languages. Whilst Raihan came to prominence singing mainly in Malay, other global artists sing in languages such as Arabic and English, which have a wider global reach. Ahmed Bukhatir is an Emirati artist who sings in both languages. He topped the Virgin music chart in the Middle East for seven weeks and his music is popular around the world. Like his peers' works, his music covers spiritual and religious themes, including death, the importance of respect for mothers and forgiveness. He sees his creativity and public platform as intertwined with community and charitable issues.

Whilst nasheeds are the most traditional form of musical expression for Generation M, even artists like Ahmed, who abide by the strict non-use of musical instruments, sound and look quite different from their traditionalist counterparts. The videos accompanying their songs situate them in today's visual environment where the artist and the illustration of his words are important. The videos are slick, well produced and of international standard, and they appeal to Muslims across cultures. They are clear, unapologetic statements that the aural and visual identity of Generation M is quite different from those of past generations.

Nasheeds and devotional music, forms of music founded in the heritage of today's Muslim generation, are being fused with other forms to create new sounds and meanings.

Rafli is an Indonesian singer from the province of Aceh. He started his successful music career as a rock star. 'I wore tight jeans and jumped around on stage,' he says. In the summer of 2000 he spent hours praying in a mosque; he felt he needed to leave rock music and serve God and the people of Aceh. Then in 2004 came the tsunami, after which he decided to travel from camp to camp visiting surivors, aiming to get people's attention just by the strength of his drum. In this Rafli follows the tradition of sixteenth-century Sufi masters who roamed from village to village with rapa'i in hand, spreading the teachings of Islam.

Pakistan-born Salman Ahmad has sold more than 30 million records of his self-labelled 'Muslim rock and roll' through his band

Junoon ('Passion'). He topped the music charts, bringing rock to Pakistani teenagers, and his band has been described as the 'U2 of Asia'. Ahmad says his music brings together his love of modern Led Zeppelin with the traditional sound of qawwali devotional music. He too uses his music for charitable ends and was a UN ambassador on the subject of AIDS, a thorny topic in the Muslim world, and one which he has sung about.

In the USA, Kareem Salama fuses his mystical Islam-inspired worldview with a country and western sound. In one of his earliest songs, 'Generous Peace', he quotes an early Islamic scholar's famous analogy that undergoing difficulties makes you into a better person: 'I'm like incense, the more you burn the more I'm fragrant.'

Across the many genres, what unites Generation M musicians and their audiences is their expression of an inner yearning for a bigger meaning. Generation M feel that today's popular music is spiritually void, concerned with the vulgar and profane, illustrated with X-rated images that do not speak to their inner drive to be better people. Time and again, Generation M musicians attempt to bridge their faith experiences to the modern world through their music. Notably, they see their expression not just as a way to connect themselves and the Muslim communities they are part of, but also as a way to reach across divides and speak to the wider world. They do this to give voice to the feelings of those who are not Muslim but whom they believe also seek spiritual expression beyond what they see as today's empty pop lyrics and semi-pornographic videos. And they do it as a way of dispelling stereotypes about Muslims through the power of the spoken and sung word.

Kamal Saleh is an Australian Muslim who has become a YouTube sensation with his spoken-word explorations of how we relate the questions of Islam, meaning and popular culture. His video 'The Meaning of Life' has had over 3 million views. He asks:

What are we doing here? What is the meaning of life?
Besides we just woke up one morning, and then it's welcome to
   the show [...]
These are just simple life questions and I'm just searching for
   some answers

Like what are we doing here? What is our purpose?
How did we get here and who made us so perfect?

In one video he opens his music by reflecting on the top Google Australia searches for 2013. The top search, he explains, was 'What is twerking?' and after that the second most popular query was 'Who is God?' His multimillion-view videos intertwine popular culture references to explain questions which Kamal and Generation M feel popular culture itself does not tackle but instead distracts from via the kind of values Generation M attempt to escape – money, sexualisation and commercialisation. He talks not about Islam per se, but about values, exactly what Generation M see as their approach to modern Muslim life. He talks of the struggles to avoid the highly sexualised surroundings we are faced with, of managing relationships, even difficult subjects like domestic violence and of building bridges with those of other faiths and none.

There are voices from within Generation M that are critical of what they see as relative religious conservatism – something that those who love these artists would disagree with as they see themselves as thoroughly modern. Generation M are in a state of flux, constantly challenging themselves from within to ensure that they are pushing the boundaries while remaining truthful to core Islamic values. This seeming paradox is what drives them.

The Female Voice

One of the most controversial areas of musical development is that of female artists. In conservative Muslim cultures, the female voice is considered 'awrah', an attraction that should not be shared in public, which is a big reason why female public voices – both musical and in the civic space – have been so rare. There is a growing trend to change this, particularly as Muslim women themselves want to take advantage of their increasing access to the public space to express themselves. Spoken word and hip hop are popular because the lack of music or singing helps overcome these issues.

UK duo Poetic Pilgrimage is made up of Muneera Williams and Sukina Owen-Douglas, both born and brought up in Bristol,

4. Female hip hop duo Poetic Pilgrimage say of their audience, 'it takes about three songs before they get over the shock of hijabis running across the stage, telling them to throw their peace signs up.'

England, to Jamaican migrant parents. Their hip hop music explores gender, faith, citizenship and heritage. They say they became Muslim in 2005 after reading the autobiography of Malcolm X. They are conscious that seeing Muslim women perform on stage can cause astonishment. '[We] often joke about performing to new audiences and how it takes about three songs before they get over the shock of hijabis running across the stage, telling them to throw their peace signs up.' They feel with hip hop that the 'initial purpose of this art form fits us like a glove', explaining,

> hip hop began as the voice of the underdog, the voice of the ones whose story is never told, of those who are spoken about but not spoken to […] these pioneers became narrators of life on the poverty line, storytellers of those who are victims of an oppressive system.

Spring 2015 saw the release of the film *Hip Hop Hijabis*, which followed the duo on tour. The filmmaker, Mette Reitzel, wrote: 'Their story is an example of how geo-political forces impact the daily lives of individuals in a very personal way.' Whilst the themes of identity, belonging and faith fit into the wider musical trends we are exploring, the two women are conscious of being up against a culture where women's artistic and musical expression is deemed by some to be culturally inappropriate. At the same time, they constantly face negative stereotyping for being Muslim women, especially as they wear the hijab. They've even been criticised for converting to Islam in order to further their musical success.

Reitzel writes that when the women converted,

> Some of their own doubts were appeased when they learnt that hip hop and Islam share a genesis as being the voice of the oppressed, which included historically progressive rights for women. They concluded that many of the problems faced by Muslim women across the world are the result of cultural misinterpretation rather than an inherent misogynist bias; and they set out to 'release [their] faith from the hands of thieves', as Sukina puts it in her poem 'Aborted Daughters'.

'Some people think the … West and Islam can't meet,' says Sukina. 'But we can't ever have that stance because that's who we are.'

South East Asia currently has a stronger track record of creating female Muslim artists. Malaysian Shila Amzah sings in Malay, English and Mandarin. Photogenic in her stylish headscarf, she had success in a string of reality TV competitions, and then decided to move to China and more recently to South Korea in order to expand her potential audience. She says: 'there aren't any singers there who wear the hijab, so that can be my selling point.'

Indonesian singer Fatin Shidqia won the first season of Indonesia's equivalent of *X-Factor* and is now signed with Sony Music. She said she planned to use some of her prize money to pay for her parents' trip to hajj. Cute and colourful in her girlie clothes style and decorated headscarves, through her music and voice Fatin reflects an upbeat youthful image. In Ramadan 2014 she released the track 'Proud of you Moslem'.

Layla Hijab Sami Yusuf, whom we spoke to earlier, says she is inspired by Fatin Shidqia's success.

> I like her spirit to keep on doing what she's doing. I think she broke all the stigma here that a woman in hijab couldn't

and shouldn't sing Western music, that they should only sing religious [songs]. When she succeeded it was a breakthrough. Now many women in hijab have the guts to show their talents and want to be famous like her and still be religious.

In Malaysia, Yuna is a household name; with a soft jazz voice, she chirps as she plays her guitar, a serene look on her face, her body covered with a headscarf and modest clothing. She's proud of her music, but just as proud of her Muslim identity, and she wears it front and centre. Her colourful headscarf, stylish demeanour and easy music have made her globally popular, with 2 million Facebook followers and 1.4 million on Twitter. She is certainly pushing boundaries. Her 2012 hit 'Live Your Life' was produced by controversial but globally hot-property artist Pharrell Williams. 'Live your life,' says Yuna. 'Don't hide from who you are.'

Think of the Children

The development of the Generation M soundtrack has two further notable trends, the first being the growing number of converts to Islam who come from musical backgrounds. Most famous of these is Yusuf Islam, formerly the global pop star Cat Stevens. On conversion, his music – which was always ethically inspired, even before he came to Islam – took a sharp turn towards the most conservative expression of musicality, with the voice only. Even then, its melodies, lyrical allegories and rhythms were still very much anchored in a Western music tradition which was new to many Muslims used to traditional nasheeds. Slowly he has intertwined his earlier musical style and instruments to return to more ethically oriented music designed to appeal to a wider audience, singing in terms of human values rather than religion.

Similar artists include Dawud Wharnsby, a Canadian folk singer who followed a musical journey like that of Yusuf Islam upon his conversion. He brought his experience and folk rhythms to his Muslim musical expression, beginning with musical approaches that were fresh even while they maintained a more conservative line. His more recent musical releases have seen him return to his folk roots, again speaking in the language of universal human experiences that can cross boundaries.

The second notable trend is that the origins – and ongoing development of Generation M's music – can often be traced back to a generation of parents looking for music for their children which could tie their children's presence in the modern world to Islamic values. Yusuf Islam's 'Alif is for Allah' is a childhood memory for a whole generation who grew up listening to this rare gem in a then unheard-of genre of English-language Islamic nursery rhymes. Other artists in the growing area of Muslim children's music include South African Zain Bhikha and Subhi Al Shaikh, who created the Zaky animations for his music.

These children have grown up with the idea of such broad and 'Western' experiences of Muslim music and, as they have matured into today's Generation M adults, it has spurred them into expecting and creating boundary-breaking music. Generation M would describe these works as expressing their values as Muslims leading modern lives, blessed with a global ummah outlook. To be able to express themselves on their own terms, to eschew what they see as the empty pop cultures of twenty-first-century life and instead imbue it with value-laden exploration that appeals to Muslims and non-Muslims, building bridges between the two, is at the heart of the new culture that Generation M are building.

As Dawud Wharnsby has said about his work, 'It is always a prayer of mine that the work I produce will help, in some small way, to better the world or provide others with hope in themselves or trust in The Creator's mercy to us all.'

7 HALOODIES AND HIJABILICIOUSNESS

The Language of Generation M

'I'm making a film about a pilgrimage called the hajj,' Anisa told the nurse administering her vaccinations in advance of her visit to Saudi Arabia. A Muslim American filmmaker who focuses on religion and the arts, Anisa describes herself as someone whose life and work are 'enriched by great educations plus a loving family'. She was on her way to film the documentary in Makkah.

'What language do you speak there?' asked the nurse, sincerely baffled. 'Do you speak Muslim?'

Anisa muses: 'The answer was embarrassingly obvious to me. Makkah is located on the Arabian Peninsula. People speak Arabic there. And since Muslims are from the world over they speak myriad languages. In fact, Arabic is not the primary language for most Muslims. More Muslims speak Indonesian and Chinese dialects and Urdu than Arabic.'

Yet Arabic remains one of the uniting factors of the ummah. Whilst the number of native Arabic speakers is small, many more will learn it to be able to understand the language in which the Qur'an is written. Substantially more will learn simply to read it, even if they have no comprehension of its meaning. In 2013, The British Council named Arabic as the second most important foreign language going forward. It's a unifying factor across Muslim populations.

So is there such a thing as 'speaking Muslim'? Moving past literally speaking the same language, there does exist a common language currency, both verbal and non-verbal, literal as well as conceptual. Some of this occurs across all Muslims, not just Generation M. The greeting 'Salaam alaikum' (Peace on you) and phrases such as 'alhamdulillah' (thanks to God), 'Allahu akbar' (God is greater), 'La illaha illallah' (there is no god but God) and the ubiquitous 'inshallah' (God willing) trip off the tongues of Muslims around the world, Arabic speakers or not. Shared belief in a divine purpose, an orientation towards God and community and repeated rituals central to Muslim life mean words have subtle meanings and cues.

Anisa describes the non-verbal communication that exists too:

> It may be a language of practices that most of us understand, like some men placing their hands on their hearts rather than shaking hands with women and vice versa. The language of eyes filled with knowing pride and compassion during the month of Ramadan when we go hungry and thirsty during daylight hours for an entire month.

'Speaking Muslim' has an added level of playfulness, fusing religious terms with ordinary language. Earlier I used the phrase 'What the fatwa!' to replace the less polite English expression of shock and horror. Taking something and making it suitable for their own consumption, our lively linguists have coined the terms 'halalify' 'hijabify' and 'sunnahfy'. There's a sense of poking fun at themselves too. Many Muslim cultures are notorious for running behind schedule; GMT is often jokingly translated as 'Generous Muslim Time'. An inability to organise is sometimes described as 'couldn't organise a prayer in a mosque' (a quote first coming to mainstream attention in the British hit sitcom *Only Fools and Horses*). Fashionable young Muslim women are referred to as 'hijabistas' or 'muhajababes'.

There's a more serious existential reason why language is important to Generation M. The stereotyping of Muslims in the way language and imagery are deployed is one of the greatest challenges that they feel they need to step up to. Anisa describes this as 'a language called Muslim that speaks in defence of Islam in the face of fanatics and cults that seek to use faith to generate social unrest and political gain'.

Stereotypes, Loaded Meanings and Reclaiming Words

In 2007, the book *The Islamist* was published in the UK. It is a memoir of British Muslim Ed Husain, explaining his flirtation with 'radical' Islam in the 1990s whilst he was a college student. The book's title reintroduced the term 'Islamist' into colloquial parlance to refer to 'extremist' Muslims, and in particular to Muslims who express themselves and their values politically.

The term Islamist has risen to prominence, in particular after the Arab Spring, to rebrand political parties in a way that had not existed before, parties which politically and contextually may have little in common. For example, the Tunisian En Nahda Party works in quite a different way to the AK Party in Turkey and the Muslim Brotherhood in Egypt, but all have been grouped together as 'Islamists'. To describe these movements as Islamist – a term with shifting meanings – tints them with certain negative but unspecific ideas: hardline views, anti-democratic, violent, opposed to the West.

The term has come to carry an emotional weight that entrenches the 'West versus Islamism' dichotomy, one that is created by far-right as well as violent extremists claiming the Islamic mantle. Other variations of this either–or are Islam versus the West, Islam versus democracy and Islam versus modernity. These dichotomies are seen as facets of the same exclusion of Muslims (or segregation, when forwarded by violent extremists like Daesh) and are therefore vehemently challenged – after all, it contradicts the very core of Generation M's being, which is grounded in modernity *and* Islam.

It's one example of a word that has shifted semantically to carry a loaded meaning. Similarly, many words that have entered the Western (and English) lexicon in relation to Muslims and Islam have been given a meaning that is alien to our modern faithful Muslims. They believe language is being used to negatively tar Muslims and also to frame the relationship between Muslims and the wider world in a distorted way. They want their beliefs to be understood as they understand them, not defined by others. It is this distortion and what they see as the deliberate misunderstanding of the Muslim mindset that affronts them. They are acutely aware of the power of language and misframing.

The term 'Islamism' is another example of the paradox they face. Whilst today's technical academic meaning is Islam as a political ideology, Generation M feels incensed that it is used with a vague equivalence to Islam itself. As civically engaged, proactive individuals, they are frustrated that their engagement in the political domain therefore risks being labelled Islamist, and that their activities in the public space thus carry with them a suspicion of extremism and danger to society. It is this negativity which fuels Generation M's passion to put the world to rights, but specifically to address how language is used to shape others' and their own ideas about Muslims.

Lazy use of Islamic terminology – defined by others rather than what Generation M see as the 'true' meaning of the religious terms that guide their behaviour – alongside stereotypes is a source of frustration for them. They are also the motivation for young Muslims to portray themselves as 'normal' and to burst the bubble of hostility. They recognise the power of language and how it can be used to build ideas and relationships and hence they are very sensitive to its nuance, fierce in its use and opposed to its abuse. They work hard to reclaim the meaning of key Islamic terms like ummah, jihad and shariah both from negative stereotyping and from extremists.

It's interesting to note that the term 'Islamism' was coined by Voltaire in the eighteenth century as a synonym for Islam, and a preferable alternative to the then popular descriptor 'Mohammedanism' which Muslims were unhappy with because it echoed Christianity's elevation of an individual rather than Islam's focus on the centrality of God.

If we are to be able to truly understand Generation M then it is imperative to understand what they mean by key terms, and how they respond to language that is used by others to describe their experiences, and then how they use language to describe themselves. Several terms have entered Western discourse and languages such as English, either undergoing a radical semantic shift as they move from Arabic to other languages, or simply being coined with a palpable negativity built into their usage.

In 1989, during the Salman Rushdie crisis, the term 'fatwa' entered the English language as a result of Iran's Ayatollah Khomeini's statement about the author of *The Satanic Verses*. It's a good example of how Islamic terms used in the wider world take on a completely new meaning which does not correlate to Generation M's inner compass. In the case of 'fatwa', the term is now part of mainstream culture, but continues to have a sense of absolutism, death even. So when any cleric, even of minor (or non-existent) stature, claims to issue a fatwa, it is given disproportionate weight. In fact, 'fatwa' means nothing more than 'opinion'. From those who have no religious standing, a fatwa has no validity and power. Even if it did, fatwas are not binding on anyone unless they choose actively to follow them.

There are words and phrases that Generation M will immediately identify as leading to frustrating stereotyping: words like jihad, jihadist, Islamic terrorism, Islamic fundamentalism and shariah. Almost as a stream of consciousness, ideas are then associated with these words, which are used to indicate negativity against Muslims even while they may apply to many wider groups: FGM, honour killings, forced marriages, oppressed women, opposed to democracy, clash of civilisations and so on.

Generation M are extremely conscious of the power of these ideas and are constantly battling to reconnect original Islamic concepts to their core meanings of goodness and humanity. The use of negative and hostile language and stereotyping is not just a linguistic issue; it can trigger real-life and fatal consequences through the ideas it seeds, unleashing anti-Muslim attacks, creating restrictions on access to resources or products and communications which speak to their needs and thus excluding them from the enjoyment and advantages of modern life.

'I am Muslim and from Bangladesh. That does not mean I am a terrorist,' wrote Sumaiyah Mahee in her high-school essay. To be misunderstood and misportrayed is exclusionary, and Generation M will not tolerate it. Sumaiyah's frustration is palpable:

According to society and everything else going on in the world, I am not who I say I am. I am not an innocent girl who walks around not hurting the world. Because of violence, from the Boston Marathon bombings to the almost bomb that went off in New York by a Bangladeshi boy, I am apparently the 'child' of the terrorists who did these acts. I am getting judged and misread by all the stereotypes in the world going on about my religion. I am

Muslim and I am not going to hide that because of everybody else's perspective about what it means to be a Muslim.

Fighting stereotypes is a constant battle. Numerous 'I am Muslim' campaigns have been run around the world in connection with words that Generation M believe give them nuance in the public discussion. 'I am Muslim and I am against homophobia', 'and I give blood', 'I'm Malaysian', 'I stand against ISIS' and 'I'm #blacklivesmatter' are just some examples that aim to bring forward their multifaceted identities as modern faithful Muslims.

In Thailand, 35-year-old Furqan Isamael is part of the Halal Life group that launched the campaign 'No space for violence'. The group members wear T-shirts with the slogan 'I am Muslim, not a terrorist'. 'It's not an easy task, but we know that there are problems concerning the perception of Islam.' Furqan explains that the campaign will send out two messages: first, to communicate that they don't agree with any kind of violence, and second, to promote Muslims who interpret and apply the religion's messages in the right way.

We are the defendants. It's hard to refuse that some acts of terrorism have been committed by Muslims. However, the rest of us, most of us, are not terrorists. We want to be safe. We want peace, like you all. We want people to know us in other ways.

We will focus on a futher handful of terms that Generation M feel have had their meanings shifted in a negative direction, to understand how they understand them: shariah, jihad, ummah and zakat.

Shariah

In 2013, The Pew Research Center released the results of a survey conducted between 2008 and 2012 which focused on 38,000 people in 39 countries from the global Muslim population. A solid majority, notably in Asia, Africa and the Middle East, were in favour of shariah – traditional Islamic law – being adopted as 'the law of the land' in their countries.

The headlines fed into a global narrative that is deeply worried about 'medieval' and 'backward' shariah law that apparently chops off hands and encourages stoning. But beyond this headline there was more variation in the study itself. First, the support for shariah as 'law' varied by country. For example, 12 per cent of people polled in Turkey supported shariah as the official national law, as opposed to 56 per cent in Tunisia, 71 per cent in Nigeria, 72 per cent in Indonesia, 74 per cent in Egypt and 99 per cent in Afghanistan.

Second, commenting on the research, Princeton University professor Amaney Jamal, a special adviser to the Washington-based Pew Research Center, emphasised that there is no one common understanding of shariah among all the world's Muslims: 'Shariah has different meanings, definitions and understandings, based on the actual experiences of countries with or without shariah.' I've found that Muslims see a marked distinction between what is described as shariah, the inner moral compass, and its implementation, which is shariah law. On top of this, shariah law itself has many different interpretations depending on the theology of the legal experts deriving the law from religious source material.

What the headlines rarely reflect is what this utopian life guided by shariah actually means in the eyes of Muslims. For them, shariah is the personal moral code that guides them in their daily lives. It is the 'path to God' that Muslims should follow, a holistic set of practices that influences every aspect of one's life, from politics and business to family and social issues. This is quite different from the tabloid concept of 'shariah courts' and beheadings.

Shariah is not something scary or 'backwards' to this group, but rather something that is seen to be core to their modern, faithful identity.

Jihad

In 2013 Chicago activist Ahmed Rehab launched the 'My Jihad' public education campaign to 'share the proper meaning of jihad as believed and practiced by the majority of Muslims'. When Muslims talk of jihad they are referring to the struggle to better themselves, the inner fight. Generation M feel that this meaning has been completely lost in Western discourse – or worse, distorted. Jihad al akbar, the greater jihad, is the struggle against the inner self. Jihad al asghar, the lesser jihad, is the physical fight in self-defence. Generation M are fighting the modern usage of the term jihad as a catch-all term for war, a usage which is reinforced by the modern derivative terms jihadi and jihadism.

Ahmed's 'My Jihad' campaign was carried out through ads on buses and trains, through educational videos on YouTube, speaking initiatives and a Facebook page as well as a Twitter campaign that aimed to capture imaginations with the hashtag #MyJihad. The ads featured real Muslims expressing their own personal struggles. 'My jihad is to never settle short of my best effort,' said one. 'My jihad is to stay fit despite my busy schedule,' says another featuring a hijab-wearing woman lifting weights. 'My jihad is to break stereotypes with humour,' says another with a black-and-white picture of a woman wearing a headscarf and holding up comedy glasses and moustache over her face.

At the other extreme, Generation M are also fighting the rise of a disturbing trend of 'jihadi cool'. This is the way language, imagery and videos are being used by violent extremists to rebrand the idea of jihad as only war, the idea that violent struggle is obligatory and that war is fashionable and cool. US National Public Radio described jihadi rap videos as 'more MTV than mosque'.

Ummah

Ummah is another foundational concept which Muslims feel distinguishes them from other faiths and ideologies. It is the notion of a 'global Muslim nation' that unites Muslims across geography, culture and language. The shared journey towards the Creator, following the path of Islam, is a powerful unifying factor. It is why, when Muslims travel around the world, they can meet other Muslims and step into a mosque to be greeted as friends rather than strangers. It is why Muslims feel pain about far-off conflicts as sharply as if their own family is being attacked. The Prophet Muhammad explains that the ummah is 'like a body', and if one part feels pain the whole body is in pain.

Belonging to the ummah is a privilege but it also brings duties – duties to care for the ummah, duties to share resources and money, duties to defend, duties to educate. Of course, whilst at an individual level Muslims will express this deep-rooted love for the ummah, practicalities and politics mean that intra-ummah relations are more complex. The idea of the diverse, strong, self-supporting ummah generates huge emotion. Any number of products and services will be named for the ummah: Ummah Welfare Trust, Ummah Chocolates, Ummah Babies, Creative Ummah, Ummah.com, Ummah FM … the list goes on.

The ummah is of course most visibly on display at hajj when the diverse global Muslim population gathers, its focus on the same spiritual goal, its clothing all the same, its physical togetherness something that those around the world who cannot attend long for. We cannot underestimate the magnetic draw of the ummah for today's Generation M. In fact, it's so crucial that I've dedicated a good deal of Chapter 10 to the subject.

Particularly when it comes to communication, Generation M feel a strong duty to share information with the wider ummah. If a business or brand, for example, has made an effort to understand Muslim consumers, Generation M will be quick to spread the word. By the same token, if the brand has made an error – whether it be including haram ingredients, improper advertising or supporting causes which Muslims feel oppose their principles – Generation M will be quick to pass on the news and shut down the consumer relationship. International organisations must be especially careful in their engagement, as what is communicated in one region to Generation M will quickly spread to other regions via their communications channels.

Zakat

'I want zakat to be one of the first Arabic words the entire community in the UK associates with Islam. We want to put zakat into action,' says Iqbal Nasim, a thirty-something former investment banker who took an 87 per cent pay cut when he was appointed director of the National Zakat Foundation in the UK. The Foundation was established in 2011 to help collect and distribute the annual 2.5 per cent charitable contribution mandated by the Qur'an. It is unusual in that it is one of the first of a growing number of charities that, rather than sending money abroad, collect and distribute to local beneficiaries in the UK, prioritising local community improvement and investment as core to the Islamic spirit.

Alongside collecting donations and creating community projects, the National Zakat Foundation aims to raise awareness about the ethos and importance of zakat. Iqbal explains, 'No other organisation was focusing on zakat and we felt it was a misunderstood concept.' Now they not only want to reclaim the word zakat, they want to engage in social change in a way that is core to Generation M's belief that their Islamic lifestyles should be of benefit to everyone, particularly to the local communities of which they feel they are an intrinsic part.

Zakat is the obligatory giving of charity from one's own wealth and earnings to those in need, but is also intended to meet community needs such as schools and hospitals. In recent years the term zakat has been hijacked by the far right to suggest that zakat payments are in reality funding terrorism. The radical 'Boycott Halal' campaign managed to confuse several Islamic concepts at once by asserting that 'If you buy halal, you are indirectly financing terrorism via zakat.' Understandably, this type of fear-mongering has caused upset among Muslims, as it attacks the core concept of charitable giving.

The Language of Values Rather than Religiosity

Like their aspiration to introduce the concept of zakat into the English language, Generation M also want Islamic concepts to become part of the language of values, believing that in this way they can connect to wider civic movements and inspire society to become a more value-based system. One of these values is purity, which is rooted in Islam's emphasis that everything must be maintained in a state of constant cleanliness. There are very strict rules around the person and objects being clean. When Muslims pray, for example, a ritual washing is required for each prayer. If clothes become contaminated with impurities they must be washed to become pure, otherwise they can no longer be worn. These include contaminants such as urine, faeces and blood. Obviously, everyone cleans these, but for Muslims there is an added imperative as it is mandatory to clean them thoroughly in order to pray.

Other values that are constantly cited as important are honesty, humility, discipline and togetherness. These are crucial in both substance and in communication, for both the individual and corporate entities. Organisations do not have exemptions from the behaviourial values that govern individuals and as a result they are held to the same account as individuals for their actions and language.

These 'shariah' values are simply good sense for all organisations and businesses. To be honest, transparent and accountable in business is crucial to Muslims but is just as important to the wider consumer movement. By using the language of values, Generation M are actively and deliberately engaging their Islamic values to join forces with wider society. The urge to improve society as a whole and make their own motivations accessible is important to Generation M, and the language of values is one mechanism they have used to do this. This has proven particularly powerful in minority Muslim countries where Generation M have been working hard to find common cause with wider social movements to overturn stereotyping of Muslims and also to gather broader coalitions for change. The ways that Generation M have been using language are absolutely crucial to this project, as I describe in this chapter.

One example of translating religious language into the lexicon of values is that of tayyab, which is referenced side by side with halal in the Qur'an. Muslims who are working on promoting the concept of tayyab often use familiar terms like 'ethical' and 'organic' to build understanding with other activists.

Another obvious value-oriented approach taken by Generation M concerns the hijab and Islamic wear. A term that is increasingly used to counter the accusations of 'oppression' and which is less overtly Islamic in flavour and more consciously part of the discourse on body image and sexualisation is 'modest wear'. Generation M are keen to use language in this way to pare back an action to its core value and make their ideas accessible and contemporary.

Self-Definition and Deprecation

Against the backdrop of the stereotyping there is a new playful language that Generation M are using to describe themselves. For example, following a TV interview with a member of the far-right British supremacist group the English Defence League (EDL) who talked about 'Muslamics' and muttered something unintelligible which sounded like 'ray guns', Generation M have started jokingly referring to themselves as those 'Muslamics' who carry 'Muslamic ray guns.'

Muslim women are fed up of being portrayed as oppressed or brainwashed and are tired of spending time explaining modest clothing in worthy and pious terms. Instead, new phrases are being coined to convey their passion and empowerment. 'Hijabilicious' is one expression of how Muslim women take pleasure in their modest wear. It comes from an early Muslim fashion blog set up by two British Muslim sisters who wanted to share their style tips with the growing community of Muslim women who were trying to intersect faith and fashion.

The growing number of Muslim women in business has created the word 'hijabpreneurs'. Other derivations include 'hijabistas' and 'hijabers' but also the pejorative 'ho'jabis'. Women who wear hijabs with a little hair showing might be called 'frinjabis'. The swimwear designed for full modesty and head cover is known as the burqini ('burqa' and 'bikini').

The ubiquity of the discussion about hijab and niqabs and engagement with Muslims doesn't only affect women. In fact, one North American man of Asian descent took on the moniker 'Hijabman' precisely to tackle that issue. His playful use of language extends beyond simply his name, which is designed to rattle assumptions made by both non-Muslims and more traditionalist Muslims. The unexpected word play is a way of shaking up perceptions.

Hijabman markets T-shirts with curve-ball attitudes: 'Make biryani not bombs'. He expresses what Muslims experience: 'Go ahead, profile me' and 'My name causes national security alerts.' And again, tying the subject of values and linguistic expression together, he prints straplines such as 'Halal for me means sweatshop free.' He even sells women's hip-hugger underwear with the word 'halal' printed on it. Perfect for bridal showers, says the description.

The title of the tumblr Superhanallah, which showcases cartoon work, is a play on the Islamic term 'subhanallah' (praise to God) and the obvious superhero connotation.

The subject of halal can be contentious, for reasons we discussed earlier, even while being core to Generation M's identity. Again, instead of being defensive about their adoption of halal, Generation M are increasingly proud of upholding this core Islamic concept. Phrases like 'fabulously halal' are used.

In the UK, a food brand has been launched under the name Haloodies, combining 'foodies' and 'halal'. The descriptor was launched at the UK's first Halal Food Festival, held in London in 2013. It encapsulates a rising trend of Muslims who take their food very seriously but are struggling to have their passion catered for by the mainstream food industry. The launch campaign aimed to introduce playfulness by referencing 'Sheikh Speare' and his 'well-known' oeuvre 'Much Ado About Naan'.

Comedy

There is a lightness of touch in these linguistic twists, reflecting a sense of pride in Muslim identity and fun. In fact, comedy, self-deprecation and satire are on the rise as a way of releasing the angst in the Generation M communities, but also as a way of reaching out to the wider world. In the USA a troupe of Muslim comedians named themselves Allah Made Me Funny. The title of Australian author Randa Abdel-Fattah's first book, aimed at teenagers and tackling the subject of the headscarf, teen romance and adolescent angst, was *Does My Head Look Big in This?*

Sometimes, despite Generation M's desire to answer hostility, stereotyping or even simple curiosity about Muslim opinions and practices, they feel that being worthy can only achieve so much, and that they can only deal with queries for so long. Their best approach is to use humour to respond to what they feel is obvious or even silly. We have already heard some of their voices in dealing with the challenges of flying while Muslim.

A rather baffling question that is often put to Muslims – who generally belong to quite sociable communities – is: 'If you don't drink, how do you meet people?' And what is one to make of the question: 'Is it true that light green is the official colour of Al-Qaeda?' Perhaps my favourite of all time is: 'Now that you're engaged, will you have a forced marriage?' These questions project such a one-dimensional, stereotypical understanding of Muslims that it is hard not to laugh. And Generation M are turning it into comedy.

There's a growing number of comedy festivals, films, internet videos and blogs being created by Muslims around the world. Abu Dhabi hosted an international comedy festival featuring the Lebanese stand-up Nemr Abou Nassar. In the UK, acts like Imran Yusuf, an East African Asian, and Sadia Azmat, first seen as part of the BBC's HaLOL Ramadan festival, vie for attention on the national stage. There are also stand-ups such as Riaad Moosa in South Africa. In Australia the mainstream comedy show *Legally Brown* featured the Muslim comedian Nazeem Hussain.

Slowly but surely we are seeing Muslims depicted on Western screens in comedy, rather than just as scary terrorists. Mainstream productions include such films as *The Muslims Are Coming!*, which follows a Muslim comedy troupe around the American Deep South. *The Infidel* tells the story of a Muslim who finds out he has Jewish roots while his daughter is being courted by the son of a deeply conservative Muslim family, and *Looking for Comedy in the Muslim World* follows the actor and comedian Albert Brooks to South Asia. But perhaps the most widely known film is *Four Lions*, an acclaimed British satire about four young Muslim men who plot to carry out a suicide bombing.

In 2010, the American journalist Katie Couric suggested that what her country needed if it were going to normalise its understanding of Muslims was a 'Muslim Cosby Show'. Her wish may be about to come true, as Preacher Moss of Allah Made Me Funny is crowdfunding such a show, currently titled *Here Come the Muhammads*. He says that 'by making it funny, you make it accessible. People can say: "You mean I can actually laugh at that?"' In a similar vein, Aasif Mandvi, one of the actors from the US hit news comedy series *The Daily Show*, created his own web TV comedy show called *Halal in the Family*. In the UK, the BBC commissioned a series of British Muslim comedy film shorts to showcase new talent.

Satire is increasingly popular. At the beginning of this chapter we looked at the book *The Islamist* and how this language was creating stereotypes. In response to the book and its own narrative, which many Generation M protagonists found stereotypical in its content, a popular blog was launched to satirise the book – not through political or journalistic methods, but through comedy. The blog was called The Islamicist.

The Power of the Arabic Language

The globalised ummah means that Generation M are constantly looking for ways for their language to point to their shared religious values and common purpose. It's natural that this common language derives from Arabic. In their conversations there is a resurgence of using Islamic and Arabic terminology. This is in part due to the strengthened identity that Generation M feel from their Islam, but it also draws on commonalities with their Generation M peers across the world, where other languages and cultures might otherwise create differences. As the language of their uniting religion, Arabic connects them on a deep, almost subliminal, level.

There are words that have migrated from Arabic into multiple languages. For those brands, businesses and campaigns that want to tap into this target audience, using Arabic cues and visuals can be a shortcut to making that connection. That's why so many brands that specifically want to connect to the Muslim identity of their target audiences have Arabic or Arabic-inspired names. Visual cues also build on this Arabicisation, often using Arabic or Arabic-style scripts. In Indonesia, one of the first halal cosmetics companies was called Wardah Cosmetics, *wardah* being the Arabic word for 'rose'. Another example is my own agency's name (Ogilvy Noor), which uses the word *noor*, meaning light.

The power of the Arabic language to Muslims beyond Generation M can have some suprising consequences. In Bangladesh in 2015, a public service campaign to end the unhygienic but rampant problem of urination on public property deployed the reverence of the Arabic language for the public good. It involved writing in Arabic nothing more sacred than 'Do not urinate here'. Since Arabic is used mainly in sacred contexts, and because the majority of the population recognise but do not understand the language, Arabic writing is given reverence. The campaign appeared to be a success as young men saw the writing and moved on. The video accompanying the campaign put its insight succinctly: 'Same message, holier language'.

Violent extremist groups are attempting to own Islamic terminology, and so are traditionalist voices. Our worldly, modern, faithful Muslims have been working hard to reclaim these meanings from both extremes, believing they should be shared by all. In 2013 Malaysia's Court of Appeal ruled that only Muslims could use the word 'Allah' and other groups were legally prohibited from doing so. The ruling brought fury and ridicule from Muslims who were more interested in the meaning than in ritual and difference.

'This is not Islamic. There is no compulsion in Islam,' said one Muslim Malay commentator, Dr Faisal Hazis. He asked other 'moderate and level-headed Muslims' to speak up against 'this fear-mongering and chest-thumping Islamic supremacy'.

Malaysian blogger Ariff, who says about himself that 'when he grows up he wants to be Zorro', thinks the ruling is both hilarious and baffling. 'Why this fear of Muslims converting? Is the faith of Muslims in Malaysia so paper-thin that just seeing the word Allah in a Bible would make them run to the nearest church to be baptised?' Here writ large in Ariff's words is Generation M's confidence in faith as something that is not blindly followed but is thought out, evaluated and hence robust. The confident use of language reflects how innate such beliefs are to Generaton M. 'Surely as a moderate Muslim country we have intelligent, discerning Muslims who can tell these things apart, and the meaning of the word Allah within the context?'

Obviously, Arabic is a uniting factor across the ummah. But a more recent reason for the spread of Arabic is the export of Gulf culture in the latter part of the twentieth century. Signs include the proliferation among Muslim women around the world of the Gulf style of dressing, such as abayas and black clothing. There is debate about whether the popularity of such styles is because they are more 'authentically' Islamic, or because Gulf preachers have spread across the Muslim world and their local culture has been adopted by the global Muslim population to represent Islam, while all it really represents is Gulf culture.

The financial clout of the Arabic-speaking world has certainly had a role to play, rewarding Muslims for their spiritual investment in the language of the ummah with worldly economic benefits. But in the end, cultural and financial exports aside, it is the fact that Arabic is the language of the Qur'an and the ummah and an element of faithful aspiration that gives it ubiquity and deep roots in Muslim life. And since we are talking about Generation M, their most likely response will be: and if it brings financial benefits too, why not?

'When I was very young, I started to learn more about Arabic and more about Islam. It's a lifetime obligation for me, that's why I wanted to study at the Arabic school,' says Yang Jianyang. He works in a trading company in Yiwu, about two hours from Shanghai, China. The 25-year-old from China's Hui Muslim minority spent four years studying Arabic and now makes a living as a translator. He's one of thousands of Arabic-speaking Chinese people serving the growing number of Arab traders from the Middle East. When the merchants arrive, translators like Yang help them navigate the markets to get good deals. Yang's wife is also an Arabic translator and broker. Why shouldn't their faith be of economic benefit, think Generation M. 'I think Allah has brought me to Yiwu. It's a wonderful place for business and for living.'

This balance of Arabicisation to reflect subliminal Muslim cues for Generation M versus Arabic culture trumping local culture as being the 'right' way to be Muslim is one which is increasingly contested. In minority Muslim populations – particularly where the Muslim communities come from diverse language backgrounds – Arabic cues are seen to bring together cultures which have different languages, as well as being a unifying element establishing a common Muslim identity. In these areas the debate about importing Arabic linguistic references is less fraught because there is a positive benefit in creating a unified identity. The tension in non-Arabic but still majority Muslim populations is much fiercer. There is an urge to retain local identity even while being part of the ummah.

In India, the Muslim journalist Irena Akbar explores the language shift that is changing 'Ramzan' to 'Ramadan'. The latter is the Arabic pronunciation whereas the former is how Indians have traditionally referred to the month of fasting. She notes that one of her online friends is increasingly incensed by this shift away from how Indians typically refer to the holy month: 'Wish you all not Ramadan, but only simple, true Indian Ramzan Mubarak.' The friend later even suggested that those who prefer 'd' over 'z' are followers of 'Saudi Islam', and that choosing 'Ramadan' over 'Ramzan' is not just a spelling preference but a 'political decision' favouring Arabs over Persians.

Mina Malik-Hussain in Pakistan complained of a similar affliction, noting that abandoning the local language traditions of Urdu and adopting alien Arabic in common parlance was leading to 'the sheepification of Bakistan'. Not Pakistan, of course, since native Arabic speakers do not have a P in their language.

Using Arabic as a cue for a campaign, concept or brand that is aimed at appealing to a Muslim identity is widely accepted and uncontentious. What Generation M see as problematic is their own local culture not being reflected in their expression of Islam.

Our filmmaker Anisa, whom we met at the very beginning of this chapter, asks the subjects of her hajj documentary:

> How can the power of all the love and intention to 'speak good Muslim' be channelled into making the world a better place for everyone?

These appear to be questions she also poses to herself and her Generation M peers, in appreciation of the fact that the language they are creating in opposition to stereotypes and extremists must go beyond firefighting. The foundations of the language are in the common rituals and phrases: 'The greeting of peace among strangers; the give and take for position in the crowd; the resentment of folks who push too hard to complete their rituals.' But, as in everything that Generation M pursue, it is the ethos that is important. 'Speaking Muslim should mean being careful not to endanger anyone. To aid someone in need. To be hospitable, generous, charitable.'

8 WAGING BEAUTY

Visual Identity in an Age of Stereotypes

That's Not What I Look Like

During the production of my book *Love in a Headscarf*, the time came to commission the cover. It's an upbeat humorous tale that I wrote to bring nuance, warmth and humanity to the multitude of stories about Muslim women that too often only relate stereotypes of being oppressed and wearing long dark cloaks, absent of facial expression. Imagine my surprise when the first mock-ups came back in washed-out colours, a ghost of a woman looking blank in the front, her dark mantle filling up the page. 'I wrote the book and even I feel terrified of the woman in the picture,' I told my editor. The next round of covers were brighter, but again reinforced stereotypes. This time it was two hands painted with henna. 'But that's not the story,' I explained. 'This is the tale of a woman who goes out to embrace the world on her terms of faith. Where is that in this image?'

My editor and I worked through the existing images of Muslim women on book covers to see how to convey these ideas. There were plenty with faces demurely veiled, eyes peeking through. Sand and camels were popular backdrops. I found it hard to reconcile how someone who had actually read my story could erase the humanity of a face from the cover. It wasn't just about me; it was obscuring the identity of Muslim women through a visual stereotype of anonymity and oppression.

Several months later, I was working on the cover for the Indian edition of the book, which eventually went on to become number two on the bestseller list. This time the mock-ups were an artist's depiction of the headscarf, beautifully rendered with texture and detail – but there was no face, just a scarf. It encapsulated the problem: more focus on the scarf than the woman herself; Muslim women erased from our visual space.

I explained on both occasions that Muslim (women) want a face, an identity that is bold, feisty and full of personality, with a gusto for life and a fierce sense of confidence. By looking beyond stereotypes of drab colours and mournful figures, the cover of the UK edition underwent a metamorphosis into a brightly patterned pink and purple cover, a young headscarfed woman driving a sports car against the London skyline. The background was a subtle layer of reworked Islamic geometric prints to weave in an Islamic visual identity, but this time interspersed with hearts to reflect the love story. In the Indian edition, the Muslim woman drawn on the cover was bold and brightly coloured too, in bright pinks and electric blues, looking cool and stylish in her Jackie Onassis-inspired sunglasses.

I'm not alone in my exasperation at the uncreative tropes trotted out about Muslims. Egyptian Muslim Marwa says: 'I do feel frustrated with the visual stereotype of hijabi Muslim women. I can't understand how some people still view us as oppressed creatures especially after many of them have visited and met Muslims and have seen and dealt with aspiring liberated open-minded women.'

At the risk of veering into adult matters, Muslim women in veils are often depicted as exotic, and even become the object of fetishes. The alluring veiled headscarf- or niqab-wearing woman has been depicted with a sexual frisson since colonial times. And, yes, hijab porn is a thing. Whether portrayed as over- or under-sexualized, subversive or submissive, these depictions grate on Generation M. The author of the blog Badass Muslimahs says: 'I've had enough of the sensationalist, exoticised, demeaning portrayals of Muslim women seen all throughout the media, and this is my way of countering all the nonsense.' Then she explains: 'This is not an attempt at "breaking stereotypes" or trying to enlighten people, if you're ignorant enough to believe that Muslim women are oppressed and subjugated by Islam then that's your own problem.'

It is a problem that is more far-reaching than just the depiction of Muslim women. Libyan-born Hend set up tumblr LibyaLiberty to highlight racial misprofiling. Whilst she says that her blog is about 'Arab' stock photos and how they go 'terribly wrong', much of the imagery is used interchangeably to refer to Muslims. One shows a woman in a dark grey shirt and a scarf wrapped around her head and across her face. 'The shirt is from Marks & Spencer. The turban is from the year 1185 AD,' she mocks. Another has a woman draped in a red headscarf swathed across her face and is described by the photo library as 'traditional Middle East fashion'. Hend points out, 'This photo is none of these things.' Another depicts a woman looking directly at the camera while pretending to hold up her hands in supplication. Hend mocks: 'Unless you're addressing the photographer, you might be doing this wrong.'

One front cover of *Newsweek* magazine pictured bearded South Asian men, their hair covered with turbans and Arab-style scarves, their mouths open wide and shouting, with the strapline 'Muslim Rage'. Muslims responded on the hashtag #MuslimRage to counter the stereotypes being perpetrated of the 'angry Muslim man'. Responses included a picture of four Muslim women building a snowman, another of a Jordanian girl swinging from a tree. Muslim rage from Iran showed a young couple cuddled up on a hillside overlooking a cityscape. Hend chimed in: 'I'm having such a good hair day. No one even knows. #MuslimRage.'

Australian Muslim Silda set up Sanat Craft, which produces tote bags with clean crisp images and the slogan 'Extreme Muslim'. She says she wanted to reclaim the phrase because she was frustrated at the way the term was used. One design features a woman in a headscarf, holding a helmet about to climb onto a motorbike. Another bears the image of a man in a turban, sticking out his tongue and holding out his fingers, in punk-style. Silda says: 'I created this collection to question and re-define an Extreme Muslim through a funny and sarcastic statement.'

Muslim American artist Saba Taj produces bright bold canvases of Muslim women engaging in lively happy activities: wearing headphones; laughing, with a camera; wearing a tiara on top of a headscarf. She called the range Technicolor Muslimah and explains that it 'has a really bright spirit. It is confident, a little silly, and fun.' Even though her images are groundbreaking, Saba was conscious to challenge herself to ensure that her images, which aim to bring a diverse view of Muslims into the mainstream, were

5. Saba Taj created the 'Technicolor Muslimah' images range, describing it as having 'a really bright spirit. It is confident, a little silly, and fun.'

themselves diverse in their depiction of the variation within Muslim communities.

Shorthand visuals are often used to signify 'Muslim', and Generation M are fed up with the laziness of this. When Juan Williams, an American commentator for National Public Radio said: 'if I see people who are in Muslim garb and I think, you know, they are identifying themselves first and foremost as Muslims, I get worried. I get nervous', the response was the tumblr Muslims Wearing Things, to show how ordinary and varied the visual identity of Muslims is. The website Muslimah Media Watch was set up to discuss the problematic portrayal of Muslims, especially Muslim women, and the stereotypes that continue to persist.

Even photo libraries, with their vast resources and access, have limited and often one-dimensional portraits of Muslims, which then naturally filter into the mainstream media. In the USA, a new photo library that gives an alternative view of the 'Muslim experience' was launched. SalamStock aims to offer a broader range of imagery of Muslims and invites Muslims themselves to submit photos.

There's a more overlooked frustration that goes beyond the portrayals of 'Muslim woman = oppressed' or 'Muslim man = bearded and angry': the lack of intra-Muslim diversity that is depicted. Muslims are usually shown as Arab or South Asian, which is a source of contention for black Muslims, white Muslims, Chinese Muslims or anyone other than the man in long white thobe with ghutra or the woman in long black abaya and black veil.

The #BlackMuslimRamadan campaign was started by black Muslim American PhD candidate Donna Auston 'to increase visibility and exert a greater level of control over the American Muslim narrative, where black Muslims are rarely included.' What followed were pictures of black Muslims, depicting their presence, cultures, fashion, food and other cultural elements in order to assert that black Muslims are an integral part of Muslim communities but are by and large overlooked by mainstream portrayals of Muslims, and by Muslims themselves, who too often assume them to be converts. One image, entitled 'Black Muslim love', showed a line of black men and women side by side in a hall with a bride and groom leading a procession. Another showed five young men and women in glamorous clothing dressed up in their Eid 'swag'. Yet another was a montage of Eid festivities with black Muslims on stage, out shopping and eating at an outdoor café. One of those who took part in the campaign was Kameela Rashad, a therapist and Muslim chaplain:

> I was born and raised Muslim, however most people do not stop to consider that there are generations of Black Muslims who have resided in the US and grew up in vibrant communities. The assumption is that all Black Muslims are converts, ignoring the fact that Black Muslims have been pivotal in the establishment of Islam in America for over a century.

The lack of diversity in the visualisation of Muslims is being remedied using the resources of the digital ummah to push forward easily shared new imagery. After all, to be represented on their own terms is an important right which Generation M are not shy to assert.

This one-dimensionality of how Muslims are viewed and depicted – both from within the Muslim population and outside it – is particularly upsetting when Muslims feel that all they are seen as is terrorists. In 2013, the FBI ran an ad campaign on the side of buses in the city of Seattle. The 46 ads were part of a campaign on behalf of the State Department's 'Rewards for Justice' programme and featured 16 photos of wanted terrorists with the heading 'Faces of Global Terrorism'. Below the photos, the tagline read, 'Stop a Terrorist. Save Lives. Up to $25 Million Reward.' The photos were all Muslim and male. Jeff Siddiqui, the founder of American Muslims of Puget Sound, the area where the ads were run, said he had received phone calls from other Seattle Muslims concerned for their safety. He contended that a billboard ad posted by the government showing men from another ethnic group with the tagline 'The face of murderers in the United States' would be just as objectionable. 'It is affecting all kinds of people who have no experience with Muslims, who look at it and say, "Oh, Muslims are the face of global terrorism."' The ads were pulled after complaints from local Muslims like Jeff.

The images of Muslim women – by both non-Muslims and Muslims – can too often fall into stereotyping that all Muslim women wear hijabs and niqabs and without them they are not 'proper' Muslims. I write regularly for a major national UK newspaper. For some time, it didn't matter what subject I wrote about – sex, marriage, sports, royalty – the same picture would appear: black eyes set under a black headscarf, underscored with a black face veil. In fact, many Muslim women do not wear a veil of any sort, whether to cover their face or their hair. And our young Muslim generation are absolutely fine with that.

Even depictions of Muslims by those who are well meaning, like corporations or civic institutions, can far too easily fall into stereotypical images and icons. The reason is simple – there's ignorance about this forward-looking segment of Muslims. Those designing for Muslims therefore fall back on stereotypical images, believing this is the only way to attract their attention. Anything aimed at Muslims is therefore likely to feature a crescent moon, a bowl of dates or a rosary. The Muslims are likely to be in long plain clothing, with hats for the men and headscarves for the women. The imagery often feels very 'worthy' with no sense of irony, playfulness or humour. There may be a lot of dark green, as a reference to green as the colour of Islam. The Arabic lettering is classical in its font, up front and centre, particularly with halal logos. The depictions are unsubtle and simplistic.

Take the case of Ramadan, or in fact any advertising aimed at Muslim audiences. It is almost inevitable that it will feature a crescent moon. Burger King had a half-eaten bun as the crescent. McDonald's featured chips as fingers raised in prayer. This is definitely a powerful symbol to catch the eye of Muslims, but Generation M audiences complain that the moon is 'slapped on' sometimes when it is not even relevant to the product or service being advertised.

Islamic by Design

Vicky Bullen is the CEO of Coley Porter Bell, one of the world's leading design agencies, whose remit is to 'Make Brands Beautiful'. She says that the way that brands engage with Muslim audiences in Ramadan is 'how Christmas used to be in 1972'. She adds, 'Muslim consumers today are far more sophisticated.' Ramadan is the busiest period across the Muslim world for advertising.

The importance of design and branding applies as much for Generation M as for the wider consumer audience. In the same way that they are creating a language, culture and look for themselves through fashion and beauty, Generation M's visualisation of the world in print and video reflects their expectation that modern techniques and standards will be applied to bringing their faith to life. This is particularly evident in the area of advertising and branding, which Generation M consumers complain is filled with lazy design, treating them as though they were 40 years behind the wider global consumer community.

Ogilvy & Mather's CEO Miles Young says there is a huge chasm when it comes to engaging Muslim audiences from a holistic perspective that goes beyond just logos and lazy stereotypes:

> The reason it hasn't been done before is because it's viewed as legalistic and halal is viewed as a labelling exercise. One of the bugbears of Islamic branding is that the quality of design for

instance is very poor. The mind-set is that all you need is a label of halal and that passes by the whole world of design, modern architecture, marketing and so on, it's particularly design-deficient.

If you peruse the packaging of halal goods in supermarkets, much of it will be of poorer quality and design than non-halal counterparts, particularly in minority Muslim countries, although thankfully this is now starting to change. Retailers and manufacturers are relying on the halal logo to sell the product in spite of poor quality and substandard visuals. Traditional halal logos are deep green, the colour associated with Islam. The Arabic text is often basic. But more recent developments of halal logos show an increasing sophistication, with a broader palette of colours including brighter, fresher shades of green, or even pinks and blues. Some dispense with the word halal and instead use the name of the brand, which may refer to halal, or other visual cues such as a fork and a plate in the shape of a moon.

The visual cues that form part of Islamic heritage are also restyled for today's more modern designs. The geometry of traditional Islamic art may be layered into design and advertising, and this will inevitably catch the eye of Generation M, who are attuned to such cues. Sometimes it will be subtle, layered almost imperceptibly onto the design. Other times it may be a brighter, bolder revamp of the traditional look.

In the UK, the halal meat brand that coined the word Haloodies created a logo with a plate in the form of a roundel formed from an Islamic geometric pattern. None of the colours – bright fuschia, yellow, lime green and purple – is from a traditional Islamic colour palette, yet the green and yellow allude to some of the original hues of Islamic artwork, and the design is nonetheless pushing forward a Generation M-style visual culture.

When it comes to language and branding, we have already seen that Arabicised naming is a popular method for engaging with Generation M. The fonts used also often allude to Arabic typography, even where Arabic text itself is not used. Again, this is part of the expansive culture that Generation M is connected into.

Quality, however, is the key benchmark. Generation M are sophisticated. Anything rustled up in a back room or on an ailing computer is likely to generate dissatisfaction. They expect the same kind of global standards in visual expression as any consumer does.

Generation M are pushing cultural boundaries; brands and businesses reaching out to them with design, advertising and products must be conscious to do the same. Traditional Islamic cultural expression doesn't need to be abandoned, but branding and appeal need to take account of Generation M's future-facing attitude.

Expressing Identity through Fashion

'As a Muslim woman, when I look at fashion magazines, clothing stores and websites, or even generally walking down the street for inspiration, what I look for is something that represents my Islamic identity,' says Bangladeshi Naila, who lives in London. 'An identity that reflects cleanliness, tidiness and neatness. An identity that goes hand in hand with our inner nature. When both inner and outward appearance is reflecting this, then this makes up the true characteristics of a Muslim woman.'

Naila describes how the fashion industry can be a place for this identity to be fully and freely expressed, and where stereotypes can be overcome.

I would want the fashion industry to know that it isn't just burkas and black hijabs, which have been stereotypically linked to Muslim women. I would want them to look at the bigger picture and realise that, just like non-Muslim women, Islam encourages us to look good, to make an effort [...] and to look after our appearance.

When it comes to being fashionable, the key for Generation M Muslims like Naila is to enjoy trends but always remember the guiding faith principles in the way that they express themselves: 'The fashion industry needs to be made aware that we choose to be modest. That we actually enjoy maintaining our modesty and mixing it up with fashion.'

In Ramadan 2014, the American designer brand DKNY launched a 'Ramadan collection'. It was the first time a Western mainstream haute couture brand had engaged with Muslims during Ramadan. More than that, the collection was styled by two Middle Eastern women and featured a more modest approach to fashion with longer sleeves, lower hems and more flowing lines. In one of the UK's leading newspapers, Pakistani Muslim Bina Shah wrote: 'The result: outfits that are effortlessly chic, fresh and elegant, and inspirational for Muslim women looking for ways to be glam and modest at the same time.' For Bina, this was a sea-change:

> The fact that this collection has been styled by Muslim women who are professionals in the fashion industry is a brilliant move on the part of DKNY: these women aren't just experts in their field, but they know the context and requirements of the women the collections are aimed for. No fashion faux pas here: everything in the collection is beautiful – and halal.

While reaching out to Muslim consumers might leave their audience with a warm fuzzy feeling, there are financial incentives too. The global Muslim spend on apparel in 2014 was estimated at $230 billion and predicted to rise to $327 billion by 2020. The Muslim shopper for fashion is a force to be reckoned with. Most of the global industry outreach has so far happened during Ramadan, a time for new collections. International chains Mango and Zara have both tried out Ramadan campaigns.

However, things are changing. In 2015, Uniqlo in Singapore launched a line of clothing for Malaysia, Singapore and Indonesia designed by British-Japanese fashion blogger and designer Hana Tajima and modelled by pop star Yuna. Instead of using an Islamic religious name for the line, they highlighted its values, titling it LifeWear. The products included some specifics – hijabs and under-scarves. They also included items that would be suited to Muslim fashion but would also appeal to a wider audience, such as long flowing skirts, ankle-length trousers and long-sleeved tops, along with traditional clothing items like a kebaya or simple, long-length dresses.

We previously met Reina Lewis, professor at the London College of Fashion and author of the 2015 book *Muslim Fashion: Contemporary Style Cultures*. She asked if 2015 was 'The year the mainstream woke up to Muslim fashion'. She says that 'the needs of Muslim modest dressers were met initially by designers and creative entrepreneurs – often women – from within faith communities who realised they couldn't get what they or their daughters needed on the high street.'

She explains how the digital world that has shaped Generation M's identity so strongly has also had its part to play in the development of Muslim fashion:

> The advent of e-commerce online made start-ups easier and a niche market of modest fashion quickly developed, with a vibrant blogosphere emerging alongside. As social media has developed, and aided by the advent of affordable smart phones, designers and bloggers can become tastemakers on an international stage, with visually led platforms like Instagram transcending language barriers.

She laments how the fashion industry has been slow to see the potential of this sector and audience: 'For all the creativity displayed, for a long time women who want to dress modestly have felt neglected and disregarded by the mainstream: neither sought after as consumers nor recognised as style makers.'

It's not just the products themselves that are scarce. There's also a shortage of Muslim faces in mainstream fashion. Fortunately, we are seeing glimmers of change. The world's second-largest clothes retailer, H&M, featured Muslim fashion designer and Instagrammer Mariah Idrissi as part of a global corporate social responsibility campaign. Included in a video with approximately 60 other individuals, showing how fashion can break the rules, her presence attracted global media coverage. Each of the individuals and groups featured was voiced-over with an explanation of the received attitude they were breaking. For headscarf-wearing, modestly clothed Mariah, it was 'looking chic'.

The inclusion of Muslims in the visual identity of advertising is growing. Both Android and Apple have featured Muslim women wearing headscarves in their global advertising. During the American Superbowl, Coca-Cola featured a hijabi in its diverse line-up, set to the tune 'America the Beautiful'. This leads us naturally to ask, what does it mean to be beautiful, and how does Generation M define and apply the imperative for beauty?

Mariah's image as part of the global advert came to the UK at the same time that its most popular reality TV contest – *The Great British Bake Off* – was won by hijab-wearing, Bangladeshi-origin mother of three Nadiya Jamir Hussain. The final was the most watched TV programme of the year with 14.5 million viewers, and Nadiya was undeniably its most popular contestant ever, loved for her emotion, her quick wit and her immense baking talent. She became the nation's sweetheart. Having begun the series as a nervous candidate, she left the show as a national icon. Her victory speech left a nation in tears and encapsulates the Generation M attitude perfectly: 'I'm never gonna put boundaries on myself ever again. I'm never gonna say I can't do it. I'm never gonna say "maybe". I'm never gonna say, "I don't think I can." I can and I will.'

Reina Lewis comments on the power of such imagery:

> For a Muslim population accustomed to a welter of negative stereotypes in pop culture and news media, having two fabulous hijabis on the screen at once was unheard of. In a context where media and political attention often focuses on what Muslim wear on their heads rather than what they say or do, the fact that most of the press about the show focused more on Nadiya's cooking than her covering is undeniably a welcome change.

Generation M are using fashion and visual identity to position themselves as faithful modernists and make themselves more open to a world they are worried is nervous about embracing them. Reina Lewis notes: 'it may be that the mainstream fashion industry has heard the call from Muslim modest fashion designers and bloggers and is now ready to join with them in using style to combat stigma.'

Even Muslim men's beards have become fashionable as the hipster beard gains adherents all around the world from men who see growing their facial hair as reclaiming their manliness and a commitment to a lifestyle. It may have got non-Muslim men closer to the Muslim experience than they realise. When a group of bearded men gathered together in Sweden, the local police were called to investigate them as a secret gathering of a terrorist cell.

American company SnoreStop ran a billboard campaign featuring a soldier hugging a woman in niqab with the hashtag #BeTogether. It certainly gained attention, even if the connection of a Muslim woman in niqab to a snoring aid was tenuous. Muslim reactions were mixed – what did a niqabi have to do with snoring, and was it insensitive to have her hugging a military man (even though the image was supposedly based on a real-life couple)? Or was it great to see a Muslim woman in an advertising image that had nothing to do with her faith? Either way, SnoreStop says that the ad increased sales.

Muslim fashion has burst onto the scene globally but the mainstream fashion industry has been surprisingly slow to notice, although thankfully things are changing. In an industry that is quick to appropriate grassroots trends, this delay is astonishing but it could be explained by the same blind spot that fails to acknowledge the existence of Generation M: how are faith and modernity compatible? And how can fashion and its current obsession with body image and the superficial be compatible with modest dress? Generation M believe the two are not only compatible, but fashion can be used as an expression of faith.

Generation M believe that faith may have something to offer a fashion industry currently facing mounting criticism for crises about body image and sexualisation. Their approach is underscored by the fact that modest clothing is growing to encompass consumers beyond Muslims, from swimwear that offers more coverage than traditional swimsuits to long maxi dresses and pashmina shawls favoured by Muslim women and now widely available on high streets around the world. And it's no stretch of the imagination to think that the long hipster beards sported by trendy men in urban centres have connections with the beards of young Muslim menfolk.

The Business of Modesty

'You don't have to lose who you are to be in this business,' says Nailah Lymus. In 2012, after her exhibition at New York Fashion Week – the first Muslim fashion show as part of the wider week – Nailah, a Muslim of African-American origin, launched Muslim modelling agency Underwraps and immediately reached out for talent in the Gulf.

> Many people think women in Islam don't have any type of rights or think we're very docile and don't speak up, and we all wear black. But we're women, we like colours, we like makeup, we like wearing bright things, and shoes and heels and everything that women like. This is our religion, but we're just like regular people.

It's almost as though being fashionable is a duty for Generation M in order to dispel stereotypes that may be held about Muslims being oppressed, backward or simply out of touch with the modern world. Nailah argues that in order to model Muslim fashion and bring its values to life in the visual medium, models should be able to work in the modelling industry whilst maintaining their values.

Muslim fashion has sparked the growth of a whole industry, including models, magazines, videos and celebrity stylists. There is controversy about how fashion should be portrayed if it is to adhere to Islamic modesty guidelines. Conservative norms outline that faces should not be shown, so many fashion businesses and websites display garments on mannequins with no faces, or show real models and crop out the heads. Or there are concerns about how models should pose to avoid being alluring or ostentatious. But the visual language of Generation M is developing, constantly pushing to be much bolder and drawing inspiration from the wider fashion industry.

Singapore-based *Aquila Style* magazine is a striking example of this new balance. Its glossy pages feature women in haute couture poses, the colours vivid, the typography and look on a par with *Vogue* and *Elle*. Style is accompanied by political, business and lifestyle content, with the strapline 'Modern Muslim living'.

With the lack of mainstream fashion guidance aimed at Generation M, blogs and YouTube tutorials offer hints on creating a look, how to wear the hijab and how to 'hijabise' what you can find in the retail stores, as well as videos on how to wear your headscarf in a fashionable style. There are even shows where Generation M women gather to see the latest fashions. In the UK the Urban Muslim Woman show, which first started in 2008, showcases over a dozen global labels on a glamorous catwalk, to an audience of several hundred women keen to tap into the latest Muslim fashion trends.

A whole new Muslim fashion industry is sparking a wave of entrepreneurship, particularly among women. As described in our chapter on the internet, they are turning to online retail as a way to reach out and market products. As a result they are turning into global celebrities among Generation M.

Best known under her YouTube name, 'Amenakin' started out with YouTube tutorials to show fellow hijab wearers how to wear the headscarf and how to create stylish modest looks. She has since gone on to set up her own business, Pearl Daisy.

Dina Toki-O has also made her name as a fashion video blogger, designer and hijab-wearing style icon. Her Instagram account has over 800,000 followers and she has a truly international fanbase – from Indonesia to Canada to Dubai. She launched her own line in 2015.

Sarah Elanany is a British designer who creates a more striking urban streetwear look. Her designs sport graffiti-like leitmotifs and her colours include bold neons. When she describes her look for hip Muslim women she wants them to say 'I get it', because this is about identity, and Generation M expressing itself.

Taking a broader industry perspective, Alia Khan set up the Islamic Fashion and Design Council in Dubai in 2014 to focus the fashion world to better serve the needs of Muslim consumers. She explains:

Over recent years, the potential of the global Islamic fashion market has piqued the interest of a number of established mainstream designers and retailers, keen to access the loyal consumer following that this market yields. However, mainstream designers' efforts in accessing these consumers have been somewhat of a hit-and-miss scenario given the reviews from consumers and the actual clothing items offered. Key factors and requirements in the design of fashion that would appeal to the Muslim/modest consumer have been overlooked. Thus, instead of endearing themselves to what would be a very loyal customer base, designers and retailers have actually ended up in alienating these consumers by showing a lack of understanding and due diligence.

Pakistani-born, raised in Canada and the USA, Alia believes that the biggest misconception about Islamic fashion is that it

oppresses women. If it oppresses women, that begs the question: Why are so many women wearing it? Oppression is done by force, when choice is removed, which is the opposite of the growing movement of Muslim women under 30 who are choosing to wear the hijab. They're wearing Islamic fashion in an extremely stylish way – evidence of which you can see everywhere from New York to London to Doha to Mumbai.

Muslim swimwear is a huge market, pioneered by the Australian brand Ahiida which coined the word 'burqini' and set free a generation of young Muslim women who see sports and health as their right, but are not willing to compromise their outward appearance. The broader sportswear market is also being tackled. In Botswana, Muslim sportswear brand Friniggi says it aims to 'enable Muslim women to participate in sports without compromising her faith'. By taking away the worry about suitably modest clothing, the brand says it 'frees' women to focus on 'performance'. This sense of freedom through the products it creates is core to Generation M.

For the broader market, portals are springing up to start to aggregate the growing number of brand labels catering for the Generation M 'look'. In Indonesia HijUp is the most well known and in Turkey Modanisa is growing in popularity. Both are attempting to nurture a global target market.

Indonesia also has an Islamic Fashion consortium, whose chairwoman hopes to establish Indonesia as a global centre for Islamic fashion. Dian Pelangi is an Indonesian fashion designer and an example of the growing global Muslim fashion celebrity. Still only in her twenties, she is a rising star of the Indonesian Islamic Fashion initiative sponsored by the government. In 2016 she showed her collection at London Fashion Week. Her clothes and imagery are bright, effusive and cutting edge. The headscarf and modest clothing are central pillars of her look. She writes about 'street style', and one of her best-known fashion forays was a trip to Europe where she juxtaposed her cool global Generation M style with urban British and French backdrops. She includes local Indonesian fabrics, prints and techniques into her collections, balancing her global modest look with her own origins.

Under the patronage of Malaysia's first lady, the Islamic Fashion Festival has already visited Abu Dhabi, Astana, Dubai, Jakarta, Monte Carlo, New York, Singapore, Bandung and London. Dubai's Fashion Week aims to combine tradition with modernity. Muslim women are looking for echoes of their culture and religion in their fashion and in Dubai this means including the traditional abaya – the long black cloak beloved of women of the Gulf region which has become popular with Muslim women around the world.

The abaya has attracted haute couture interest from designers like Galliano and Ferretti, who showcased their custom designs at Saks in New York. Harrods stocked a line by a Qatari designer whose creations had Muslim women flocking to purchase items costing as much as $20,000. Raya Al Khalifa captures the essence of the balance that Muslim fashion aims to strike, whether it be high street or haute couture, Arab style or any other culture variation: 'Glamour is achieved, modesty is secured, and self-esteem is upheld.' In 2016, Dolce & Gabbana launched a range of abayas and shaylas (long scarves) aimed at the Middle Eastern market.

Haute Elan is taking premium matters into its own hands and describes its online portal as the 'Premier destination for luxury modest wear', offering a solution to 'a very real problem for modest fashion dressers' and has launched the Modest Fashion Awards. But it sees its role extending beyond fashion to develop 'a platform from which to create dialogue and break down national and faith barriers'. It states that £1 of every purchase at Haute Elan will be put towards establishing a World Women's Ventures Fund offering access to capital, mentoring and support to women bringing new technology and ideas to market, thus inspiring and supporting the growth of more female entrepreneurs.

This expression of modest but fashionable identity is a global affair; the principles are the same everywhere, but there is local variation: for example, in the way that the headscarf is worn, or the colours and prints that are used – these are underpinned by shared values, whether in America, Turkey, Indonesia or Abu Dhabi.

All the way from celebrities to the ordinary street dresser, the Generation M look is quite different to that of traditionalist Muslims. Their aim is to look 'cool', to blend in and to express their embrace of modernity through their appearance. To paraphrase the famous song, there is no need to seek her here, or seek him there. They are ready and waiting to be served: the dedicated – and faithful – followers of fashion.

The Paradoxes of Muslim Fashion

Ala is worried about traps that Muslim fashion could fall into. She's thinking about the 'lollipops and flies meme, pearls in a shell'. These are images used to depict how Muslim women ought to be covered up – to avoid attracting flies or becoming impure – and are a point of visceral contention for many Generation M women. 'I don't want the marketing to be anything like the way Muslim men market the hijab as I find that incredibly offensive. I would like to see them understand Muslim women [as] strong, intelligent and free-thinking,' says Ala.

In a bid to escape the stereotyping of Muslim women by what they wear, the assertion of identity through what they wear is undoubtedly a paradox. With Muslim women excluded or at best policed in traditional spaces of religiosity, fashion has offered them an open field in which to explore their religion and how they wish to express it.

Another paradox is that on the one hand modest dress is an important expression of faith. On the other, there are concerns about whether such fashion really adheres to the modest and humble aspects of Islamic dress. Does it lead Muslims into the same consumerist and image-conscious domain that women globally are increasingly fighting, and which modest dress is supposed to combat? Is it tayyab to wear clothes produced in a sweatshop? And does the increasing consumption demanded by the fashion industry go against the very grain of modesty and measured consumption?

Muslim Beauty: Rights, Responsibility and Pleasure

'When I visit London, I'll dress like the people there, just maybe wearing clothes a bit looser and a bit longer, but still very fashionable and I'll fit right in,' says 22-year-old Ayesha from Dhaka. 'The important thing is that I'm not taking the influences from the West, or from the TV or from my parents. I'm taking the influence from what's important to me, and that's me, and my God.'

Being beautiful is important from an Islamic perspective. Whenever I asked our target group what beauty meant to them, the answer was invariably to quote the well-known Islamic tradition, 'Allah is beautiful and loves beauty.'

They explain how beauty encompasses cleanliness, hygiene and good, tidy appearance, and it means presenting your best possible face to society. They see personal care as a form of respect for others and a fulfilment of a responsibility towards God. Beauty is also a pleasure for Muslim women and is a particularly social experience, frequently conducted in a female-only context, often across generations. For both husbands and wives, beauty is seen as a duty to ensure their spouse finds them attractive.

One anonymous Muslim woman writing for advice regarding the religiously inspired goal of looking good for her spouse asks: 'I want to make myself beautiful for my husband, for example make my hair nice, put make-up on, wear fancy clothes.' She notes, however, that there are practical considerations which make this challenging, both with regards to lifestyle and the way personal care products do not take into account Muslim religious rituals. 'I know I will have to go and pray, so then I would have to remove my make-up [to do wudhu, the washing of face, arms and feet required for prayer], and put hijab on, which will be very time consuming.'

Beauty is a right for both men and women. They are keen to do away with the misconception that there is a religious prohibition on beauty, when in fact Islam in their eyes encourages good grooming and aesthetics. Across Muslim markets there is high involvement in the beauty category, which suggests that Muslim women are just as concerned about beauty as their non-Muslim peers; it's just that Generation M's understanding of beauty and how to care for it and practise it are different. If anything, beauty is a responsibility and as long as it is practised within the bounds of modesty it is a Muslim's duty to preserve and enhance their physical beauty, as it affects everyone around them. Most noticeable in the discussion of Muslim beauty is that there is a recognition of inner as well as outer beauty and Muslims must be conscious of both.

This is clear in the way the agony aunt responded to our anonymous woman's query about instituting a beauty regime. After offering three practical points of advice (remember you are valuable, nurture your feminine energy and remember it increases your husband's love for you), she recommends a prayer for the woman to recite in order to focus her ideas on beauty: 'Oh Allah, as you have perfected my creation, so too perfect my character.'

Muslim consumers globally spent $54 billion on cosmetics and personal care in 2014, and this is expected to grow to $80 billion by 2020. The cosmetics and personal care industries aimed at Muslim consumers are built on two foundations: the use of halal ingredients, often with a focus on natural and recommended ingredients, and creating a proposition and a look that encompasses religious values and modest principles.

Indonesian business Wardah pioneered a 'beauty concept', believing cosmetics products are for 'the body and soul'. They 'encourage women to feel good about themselves and care for others. Some people see it as inspiring, others see it as beauty, we call it inspiring beauty.' Wardah's original celebrity face was Inneke Koesherawati, an Indonesian film star who underwent a very public move to a practising Muslim identity. The look of the adverts is soft, pure, elegant and modest, in pastel colours, but with the clear faces of the models, a modern picture of Muslim beauty.

Generation M are keen to revive Islamic traditions of recommended ingredients, naming their businesses to reflect their ethos. UK start-up Sunnah Skin Care describes itself as 'organic skin care with principles', alluding to the ingredients it uses as well as the emphasis on its business protocols following Islamic ethics. It highlights Islamically recommended ingredients like olive oil, honey and blackseed oil.

Putri Emma in Malaysia says: 'Habbatus Sauda is Black Seed Oil. Damn, that stuff is amazing.' She's writing in reference to the Malaysian beauty brand Good Virtues Co., which contains the ingredient in its hair and face products. 'The shampoo is halal, free from SLES, ALES, Parabens and free from animal testing!' she raves. The inner and outer dimensions that are important to Muslim beauty are made explicit by the marketing of this brand:

> We believe there is more to beauty than what the world sees on the outside. When you do good by your body, the joy, confidence and beauty will show. Good Virtues Co. wants you to be and feel beautiful without compromising your values.

That's the concept taken care of, but it then goes on to highlight that the contents are in line with beauty ideals:

> We do this by placing a strong focus on the integrity and purity of our ingredients. We are committed to creating halal products with high standards of quality and safety for you, and we only use ingredients that are safe and respectful to the environment.

The product's overall positioning is: 'Choose your own definition of beauty. Celebrate your noor' ('noor' is the inner beauty or light that is said to radiate from the true Muslim believer). The website offers 'celebrators' the chance to tell their stories as Muslim women demonstrating their inner beauty, and offers articles to 'inspire your noor', and the stories are quite moving.

One features Muzdalifah, who spent most of her working life in uniform in the Singapore armed forces, surrounded by men who saw her as one of them. She never saw herself as a beautiful person. It is only through a deeper understanding of her faith, and her efforts to achieve physical, mental and spiritual wellness that she has gained more confidence in herself. She organised a health movement amongst Muslim women in Singapore, launching Pearls of Paradise, Women of Wellness (POPWOW), which encourages Muslim women to care for the well-being of their body, mind and spirit. As part of this initiative, it organises an annual 5-kilometre WOW! run. She learned that many Muslim women were uncomfortable with exercising and sweating in public without the company of friends and thought a run specially for Muslim women would ease them into a healthier lifestyle and at the same time tackle the issue of obesity in Singapore's Malay-Muslim community. Muzdalifah says:

> It is important that people see beauty as far more than a matter of physical appearance. Inner beauty is the most important quality and it can be achieved by changing your lifestyle and having wellness in body, mind and spirit [...] I know now that I'm perfectly beautiful, the way I'm supposed to be.

Unexpected Beauty Innovations

'I'm not ashamed to admit that discovering O2M Breathable [nail] polishes constitutes the entire sum of my current happiness,' wrote Maria Kari in a blog for Pakistan's *Express Tribune*.

The Islamic daily prayer requires each individual to complete an ablution which touches all parts of the face, lower arms and feet, and this includes nails. So what is a hip, fashionable woman to do if she wants to wear nail polish? Either she has to spend time removing it before each ablution and reapplying afterwards, or she can explore innovative new options such as 'breathable' nail polish. Polish brand Inglot Cosmetics developed such a product, called O2M, for those wanting to offer a breathable option to their nails, and found a surprising market in Muslim women, many of whom believe that its water-permeable characteristics mean that it can be worn and the ablution carried out over it without any problems. There are mixed views on whether this is really the case, but it does give one obvious insight into Generation M: they are looking for innovation that will help them care for their looks without compromising their faith. Twitter user @MarwaSammi expressed her delight: 'Halal nailpolish. Bismillah and mashallah and all other holy words, this is exciting.'

Unilever's Sunsilk shampoo was one of the first to identify that the hair needs of women who cover their heads are quite different. Hair becomes lank and greasy. Their product was aimed directly at these problems. Their adverts too were groundbreaking. Unlike every other shampoo advert, Sunsilk ads featured no hair whatsoever. The clear-skinned, bright-eyed, feisty women wear headscarves. They work, they have fun, they play football, some of them even date. But their commitment to their Islamic principle to cover their hair is the core of the message.

What About Men?

'I had done manicures before, but not a pedicure. It was the first and the last. I can't believe women do it regularly,' said Mr Al Shehhi, who was 23 when he got married. The *National* newspaper in the UAE was reporting on a trend for male salons where Emirati men go to receive a 'groom treatment' before their weddings. 'We already take care of our hygiene and make sure we are clean as it is part of our religion and culture to smell nice and be presentable at prayers and to society,' Mr Al Shehhi said. 'But for weddings, we go the extra mile of torture to look good.'

Muslim men also care how they look, because grooming is important to both genders according to Islamic teachings, with equal emphasis on husbands and wives. However, Muslim fashion for men is not on the same scale as women's fashion, as is the case for fashion generally. There are pockets of interest. Shukr, the online modest clothing company, offers a good range of clothing for men. And, whilst the burqini has captured the hearts of Generation M's women, Muslim men are increasingly concerned about modest swimwear too, with brands like ModestKini, 'Europe's first modest swimwear shop', offering a range.

There is also a growing market for male grooming products. For example, Nielsen reported that Indonesian household spending on male grooming products grew 29 per cent in 2010 to reach $130 million. The order of importance is: smell, hair and skin.

'Muslim men are becoming more open to the idea of "men's grooming",' says Abrar Mirza, one of the founders of the London Beard Company. The company was founded in 2014 to tap into the growing global trend for beards and started selling its wares in the uber-cool Spitalfields Market in East London. The brand describes itself as 'urbavintage', and its advertising, featuring its dark dropper bottles photographed in front of vintage suitcases and leather globes, offers a contemporary take on a bygone era of shaving brushes, when men were men. It oozes style. Abrar says,

> Our faith was a big part of the inspiration for the business. As Muslims, taking care of your appearance and maintaining good hygiene is highly encouraged. It's also encouraged in the Sunnah to take care of your hair including the beard!

A Fragrant Side Note

'Even though women are socialised to care more about their appearance, personal grooming should be a gender-neutral territory to be embraced by both Muslim men and women,' says Fatimah Jackson-Best. Having completed her PhD in Toronto, she moved to Barbados to connect with her Caribbean heritage. She relates her memories of self-care, and in particular the role of fragrance.

> I can vividly remember my first lessons in personal grooming and beauty techniques. My glamorous older cousin introduced me to kohl when I was 12 and black-lined eyes became the foundation of my slightly overdone (but meticulous) make-up routine. And my mom's trademark white musk perfume has become one of my favourite scents – the clean smell reminds me of watching her get ready for work, looking her best.

The Prophet Muhammad talked of perfume as something that was never extravagant, something you could never get enough of. Muslims are advised always to smell good, especially at prayer time and definitely during Friday prayers. From a religious and a cultural perspective, perfume is equally important for men and women.

Mainstream brands are waking up to this lucrative market. The challenge for the perfume industry, like cosmetics, is that the marketing concepts and the ingredients in many cases contravene the idea of beauty and the halal ingredient requirement. Modern perfumes contain alcohol, which for many Muslims is problematic. To tackle the problem, perfume house Aramis launched a perfume called Calligraphy, a fragrance for both men and women that draws on the cultural heritage of Muslims of the Middle East by combining traditional and Islamic visuals with an updated and contemporary look. Although named Calligraphy in English, it also has a clear Arabic name: Al Khat Al Arabi.

In Ramadan 2015, Indonesia's leading fabric conditioner Molto ran a campaign highlighting how fragrancing your hijab can create positive effects on those around you. One cute advert featured a young husband collecting his wife after a long day of Ramadan. Fasting is well known to be a cause of bad breath, but between this newlywed couple, it was the fragrance from her headscarf that renewed his love for her. The campaign, which featured hijab designers and bloggers also talking about the importance of fragrance after a long day, was a huge hit.

Visual images are generally seen as a way of tackling stereotypes, and asserting beauty is one strategy. Eighteen-year-old Muslim American Abrar Shahin was awarded best-dressed student by her high school. She said:

> As a young Muslim-American woman, I just want to let every girl out there know that they should not be afraid to express themselves through their style! Growing up in this society can be difficult, but the only way to advance and break stereotypes is to stay true to ourselves and beliefs [...] [Winning this award] certainly shows that the younger generation is accepting and open-minded [...] I am glad that my story has reached places all around the world and has changed many misconceptions of young, American-Muslim women.

Mark Gonzales, Muslim artist and poet, summarises how visual identity and beauty are central to Muslim thinking, and particularly important at a time they are in the spotlight and stereotyped as terrorists. In his book *In Times of Terror, Wage Beauty*, he writes: 'What better way is there to shift a paradigm than by speaking in ways that encourage dreams, laughter and imagination. For those acts of creativity are not luxury, short sighted or simplistic, they are essential.'

9 WHAM! BAM! THANK YOU ISLAM!

Superheroes, Villains and Ethically Conscious Content

Once, the average comic book superhero was male, white and wore his pants on the outside of his trousers. We've been thrown some female heroines along the way: Wonder Woman, Lara Croft and Ms Marvel. And other ethnicities and faiths have made the occasional appearance, including Jewish, Latino and even transgender characters. But in 2013 Marvel Comics announced that a 16-year-old Pakistani-American Muslim girl from New Jersey would become one of their lead characters. She was to be called Kamala Khan and this new incarnation of Ms Marvel would be the first headlining Muslim superhero.

In October 2014, *Ms Marvel Volume 1: No Normal* was the bestselling graphic novel. By November of that year, it reached number two on the *New York Times* bestseller list of paperback graphic books. The popularity of the character has meant Kamala is the very first Marvel hero to get her own graphic audio adaptation. She's already debuted in a video game. She's also about to be introduced into the Avengers series. And there are rumours of her own TV series in the footsteps of Captain Marvel.

The series editor at Marvel, Sana Amanat, said the series was inspired by a 'desire to explore the Muslim-American diaspora from an authentic perspective'. Khan can grow and shrink her limbs and her body and ultimately, she'll be able to shape shift into other forms. Like all superheroes she has a backstory, and the series deals with how familial and religious edicts mesh with superheroics, and involve some rule-breaking.

Kamala is everything that Generation M see in themselves: a modern identity, religion and a fight to make the world a better place, someone who deserves to be seen as ordinary but finds themselves depicted as confused, marginalised and abnormal. Her popularity and mainstream crossover appeal is a hint of the growing presence of Generation M in pop culture, either from the trends their very existence is setting, or from them pushing for these expressions through their own work. The ambition is to challenge the stereotypes and villainous depictions of Muslims they believe are far too commonplace in modern global culture through mainstream cultural mechanisms.

'Kamala Khan is the greatest thing that has ever happened to me,' says blogger Maryam Jameela. The 23-year-old describes herself as an 'intersectional feminist'. 'I have a tendency towards hyperbole, but, disclaimer: I mean it. In this [blog] post, I mean it all.'

We've discussed how, on screen and in print, Generation M feel that stereotyping is replicated ad nauseam. So this nascent culture subverting these stereotypes is having a dramatic effect. Maryam explains:

> It's a shock to see yourself represented, it's a shock to see a character having a carbon copy of a conversation you're continuously having with people and it's certainly a shock to see yourself represented in a resoundingly positive manner [...] If you are Muslim, and an immigrant, or a second-generation immigrant, or brown, or a woman, or anything else that isn't typically considered normative – it needs to be communicated in some way to you that you are valid and that you are seen. That is exactly why representation matters, so you can become visible.

The writer for Kamala Khan, G. Willow Wilson, knows this struggle only too well. The Muslim American convert and award-winning author says, 'I wanted to make a story in which the Muslim woman narrates her own life.' Again and again, we hear about the need to tell stories on their own terms, whether Muslim man or woman. Gaining control of the narrative of their own lives is vital.

Instead of exploring what it means to be a young Muslim today through the prism of politics – the usual lens by which Muslims are surveyed, and which Muslims complain is limited and negative – G. Willow Wilson contextualises our female Muslim into the world of superheroes, offering a new backdrop for 'normalisation'. Notably, Khan does not wear a headscarf; and her creator says this is because most Muslim women in America, where the story is set, don't either. The significance is not the 'look' but the action.

Although Kamala is the first globally recognised character to have her own series, there are several other Muslim comic superheroes, both male and female, who have been created by mainstream publishers. Simon Baz is a fictional comic superhero appearing in books published by DC Comics, usually in those starring the Green Lantern Corps, an extra-terrestrial police force of which Simon is a member. Simon Baz was a Lebanese-American child living in Dearborn, Michigan during the events of the 11 September attacks in 2001. The Arabic on his arm reads 'COURAGE'. Dust, whose real name is Sooraya Qadir, is a fictional character in Marvel Comics' X-Men-related comic books.

Cynics argue that with comic sales declining, young minority demographics, especially Muslims, are looking to pop culture to counteract their absence in mainstream media. The introduction of minority and Muslim characters to appeal to a growing global Muslim population is an obvious market-development strategy. But the sales figures of the Kamala Khan series prove that Muslim characters appeal to a wide audience. Generation M do not feel exploited by this, rather they see it as a double win – a mainstream depiction that reflects their position as both faithful and modern, and a demonstration of their increasing influence and consumer power which until recently have not been recognised.

Introducing Muslim characters, authored in great part by Muslims, creates an opportunity to explore in safe and well-worn comic book tropes the relationship between Muslims and power – who can have access to power, and who has the right to be powerful. Do Muslims have the right to be powerful in a post-9/11 world of being on the defensive, they wonder?

A forerunner of this movement was the graphic novel and film *Persepolis*, written by Iranian-American Marjane Satrapi about her struggles with identity, and how she attempted to make sense of their complexities. The cartoon *Burka Avenger* debuted Pakistan's first female superhero in 2013, who wears a burqa as a disguise to conceal her identity while fighting villains. Her alter ego is Jiya, an 'inspirational teacher' at a girls' school. Jiya fights corrupt politicians and vengeful mercenaries who attempt to shut down girls' schools. She does this by using 'Takht Kabadi', a martial art taught to her by a spiritual master which requires her to rely on her own wits and involves throwing books and pens, and acrobatics. Subjects covered range from the ban on girls going to school, to child labour abuses, to environmental degradation. The programme, and associated games and music videos, was created and directed by Aaron Haroon Rashid, a multimillion-record-selling music artist whose songs were the first Pakistani videos to be aired on MTV Asia.

He was appalled at the Taliban closing down girls' schools in Pakistan, a country which already had low rates of female literacy. In a country where children's entertainment is in short supply, he believes his series offers 'a great role model to the kids of Pakistan and the show's women empowerment themes and importance of education for girls are essential'. In true Generation M style it's important that 'The show imparts these great messages and morals without being preachy.' And the tools he highlights in the fight against violent extremism further echo Generation M values: 'Her weapons are books and pens. Literally she clonks the bad guys over the head with books. Her motto is "Justice, peace and education for all".'

The series received much acclaim and, like Kamala Khan, Jiya's characterisation has opened up a dialogue about whether the Muslim contribution has something to add to more general popular culture. One *Washington Post* blogger wrote:

> Pakistan's new superhero makes the hoop-skirted, Prince Charming-obsessed Disney princesses look downright antiquated. She was not born into royalty. She does not obsess about her beauty. And she definitely does not want or need to be whisked off on some white horse or magic carpet. No,

the Burka Avenger is too busy defending women's rights and education for all. Her weapon of choice against corrupt politicians and Taliban fundamentalists who try to stop her (note: not gnarled witches or giant sea urchins)? Books and pens. Now that's what I call a role model for girls.

Being true to the superhero art form, as well as injecting local flavour, was key to characterising Jiya with her burqa disguise. Haroon says:

We wanted to hide her identity the way superheroes do. She doesn't wear the burqa during the day – she doesn't even wear a headscarf, or a hijab or anything like that; she goes about her business as a normal teacher would. And so she chooses to wear the burqa only as a disguise, she's not oppressed.

Like the reviewer at the *Washington Post,* Haroon wants to push forward the discussion about female superheroes, who are often criticised by women themselves for being dressed more to titillate than thwart villains. 'On the other end of the spectrum, a lot of female superheroes in the West are objectified, and sort of sexualized in their costumes, like Catwoman and Wonder Woman, and that certainly would not work here.' His social message extended off-screen too through investment in the local community. He chose not to outsource production and set up his own animation and production company in Islamabad, which also gave him control over the final product.

Haroon won a Peabody Award for his efforts, part of an awards programme, originally set up in 1941, to recognise when storytelling is done well in electronic media. In his acceptance speech he got to the rub of why characters like the Burka Avenger and Kamala Khan speak to both Muslim and wider audiences, and what can happen when Muslims grab opportunities to express themselves directly to the world in authentic ways. 'She is a fictional character yet she represents something very real in terms of the dreams and aspirations of the people of Pakistan, and' – he adds crucially – 'many around the world.'

Comics and Cartoons Reaching across the Divide

'I can hear the sound of misogynistic trash!' says Qahera. 'My super-hearing can't handle this nonsense.' The Muslim Egyptian comic superhero was created by Egyptian blogger Deena Mohamed as a way for Muslim women to deal with challenges within and without the Muslim communities. Sketched in black and white, the character is dressed in a traditional long black abaya. She swoops in to sort out oppressive husbands in typical superhero comeuppance. She then tackles Femen, an anti-Muslim-women 'feminist' organisation and finally takes street harassers to task.

The mainstream depiction of Muslim characters is welcomed, but Generation M are pushing for more: the creation of a culture that is modern but built upon Islamic values and Muslim perspectives. Two Indian brothers, inspired by their love of comics, created the brand Sufi Comics, using comic parameters to illustrate famous Islamic stories and sayings. They are now available globally, bringing wisdom through the comic format, summoning this new creative Islamic culture that Generation M yearn for. Another company, Split Moon Arts, created the Muslim character Buraaq, the name evoking the famous flying horse of Islamic history.

The best-known of these cartoon creations that aim to define the world on Generation M's terms is The 99, created by Kuwait-based Teshkeel Media.

These Islamic cartoon heroes were created in the wake of 9/11 by Dr Naif Al Mutawa, inspired by principles within his faith to offer new superheroes born of Islamic archetypes. The series follows 99 superheroes whose powers are based on the 99 Virtues of Allah: strength, courage and wisdom among them. But here's how this new wave of culture creation is different: The 99 was intended always to be universal and rooted in Islamic teachings. 'It doesn't matter what culture you're from, it can still resonate. What The 99 does is say: "Hey, our values, they're the same as yours; they're the same as the rest of the world. Let's just focus on the positives of this,"' says Naif. The comic books were turned into cartoons, all available in 70 countries. And now there are even amusement parks.

In France, *The Muslim Show* illustrates the everyday life and religious practice of a Muslim. Directed by Norédine Allam, the comics can be read on Facebook as well as on smartphone apps. The first comic was released in 2009 and on the back of this Bdouin Studios was launched in 2010, Europe's first publisher of Islamic comic books.

Norédine says the purpose of the series was 'telling the daily life of Muslim people with humour,' adding, 'It talks about Muslim people, their doubts, their fears, their desires, their hopes and their contradictions.' The comic is available in more than 30 countries and is already translated into ten languages, with more on the way. Behind the humour is a dismantling of the dichotomy that pits Islam in opposition to the West, to build universal bridges. Norédine reinforces the notion of faithful modernity as a lived reality for many Muslims around the world:

> Our subjects are universal and timeless. Beyond feelings, we talk about what I consider to be the real clash of cultures: the opposition between 'modernity' and 'tradition'. Wearing the veil or a beard, modesty, and respect are considered outdated. We want to tell Muslims that they can be proud of their practices and that these are modern.

The Problem with Cartoons

Mention Muslims and cartoons, and you may bring up far more contentious issues. The Danish cartoons published in *Jyllands Posten* in 2005 and later in *Charlie Hebdo*, and the attacks on the latter's offices and staff, created global shockwaves. This is not the place for a lengthy discourse on the varieties of reaction to such events, the motivations or the rights and wrongs. Even the frustration at double standards, the intricacies of how and when to exercise freedom of speech, the disparities of power relations and the responsibilities of social cohesion are best discussed in a separate book. However, it can be simply said that if and when cartoons set out deliberately to cause offence in the belief that Muslims are not 'modern', 'Westernised' or 'democratic', and that they need to learn 'our values', it is entirely expected that Generation M in particular will respond with vigour, but absolutely not with violence.

Of his own cartoons in *The Muslim Show*, French cartoonist Norédine Allam says:

> Sometimes, there is a misunderstanding with the media and the public: the comic was not created to give a good image of Islam and promote interfaith dialogue. However, it allows people from other religions to catch a glimpse of a daily life that they may not be familiar with. Some readers write to tell us that they recognize themselves in values such as mutual assistance, solidarity, modesty and the fight against materialism.

He adds pointedly, 'The goal is to make people think, to hold up a mirror; to offend would be counterproductive.'

Brought up in a world where their Muslim identity is in the spotlight, Generation M feel they are held collectively accountable. They are fierce in their response: defending their faith as well as demanding that people see Islam and Muslims as who they are rather than as exemplified by the violent extremists. 'As a Pakistani Muslim I condemn this attack, my religion is not under threat from cartoons #Notinmyname #CharlieHebdo' said @akhwandk succinctly in the Twittersphere.

The horror that Generation M felt about the killings at the *Charlie Hebdo* offices in Paris went side by side with their anger at the misrepresentation of their faith. They are consistent in refuting that there is a dichotomy between Western and Islamic teachings. As @rafstuf explained, 'As a Muslim, I can be appalled at the #CharlieHebdo murders, and still be offended by those cartoons. They are not mutually exclusive.' These young Muslims situate themselves in both the ummah and the wider global community. This is summed up by @Almis310: 'as a #Muslim I am offended by those images created by #CharlieHebdo But I am a million times more offended by the killings of innocent lives.'

From Playing Villains for Others to Being the Heroes of Their Own Lives

Kamala Khan's series producer Sana Amanat explains the challenges in creating characters that are Muslim:

> This book isn't preaching about religion or the Islamic faith in particular. It's about what happens when you struggle with the labels imposed on you, and how that forms your sense of self. It's a struggle we've all faced in one form or another, and isn't just particular to Kamala because she's Muslim. Her religion is just one aspect of the many ways she defines herself.

Muslim voices and characters struggle to make it in the media, in literature and on screen, beyond stereotypes and one-dimensional characters. Hollywood's baddies, who were once Russian Cold War enemies, are now replaced by Arabs and Muslims: foreigners attacking 'us' or fifth columnists from 'within'. Either way, if you're a Muslim on the silver screen, the portrayal is unlikely to be favourable.

Generation M are attempting to redress this balance. Despite Muslim advisory boards to the film industry, change is slow, and so Generation M are instead developing their own content that offers more scope to depict the world as they see it. This transformation from villain to hero was beautifully illustrated in the subversive activities of three graffiti artists on the set of the global hit TV series *Homeland*. *Homeland* follows the exploits of the American intelligence services in rooting out 'Islamic terrorists', primarily through the character of white, blonde, American agent Carrie Mathison in the face of a myriad of Muslim figures, all of whom pose an existential and evil threat to the US, notching up a raft of racial, cultural and religious inaccuracies along the way. It has been described in the *Washington Post* as 'the most bigoted show on television'. But its gripping narrative has sucked in a global audience of millions.

According to the three graffiti artists who staged the intervention, 'for four seasons, and entering its fifth, "Homeland" has maintained the dichotomy of the photogenic, mainly white, mostly American protector versus the evil and backwards Muslim threat.' They explain that the problem is that 'a show like "Homeland" plays a role in laying the groundwork for stereotyping. It frames current political issues with egregious mistakes by sloppily mixing fact with fiction in ways that rewrite contemporary narratives.'

Heba Amin, Caram Kapp and Don Karl, aka 'Stone', were contacted by *Homeland*'s production company when it was seeking people to add authenticity to the set of a refugee camp supposedly situated on the Syrian–Lebanese border but filmed on the outskirts of Berlin. They were asked to add graffiti to the walls that might typically be found in such a setting. The three, who call themselves the Arabian Street Artists, wrote subsequently:

> Given the series' reputation, we were not easily convinced, until we considered what a moment of intervention could relay about our own and many others' political discontent with the series. It was our moment to make our point by subverting the message using the show itself.

They say that when they met the production team they were handed images of 'pro-Assad graffiti – apparently natural in a Syrian refugee camp'. Instead of copying these, they wrote messages including: 'Homeland is racist', 'There is no homeland', 'Homeland is a joke, and it didn't make us laugh', 'The situation is not to be trusted' and '#blacklivesmatter'. They say,

> One of the more absurd graffiti tags we painted on the set walls was the phrase 'Homeland is watermelon', which spawned the popular #homelandiswatermelon. Watermelon, a vernacular term for 'nonsense' in parts of the Arab world, has caused both curiosity and amusement, proving that laughter as a tactic of resistance brings people together.

The subversive graffiti, mocking the programme on its own set and highlighting the artists' point in the most profound way possible, created global news coverage. The Arab Street Artists say the producers didn't check what was written, didn't even notice:

The content of what was written on the walls, however, was of no concern. In their eyes, Arabic script is merely a sup-plementary visual that completes the horror-fantasy of the Middle East, a poster image dehumanizing an entire region to human-less figures in black burkas and moreover, this season, to refugees.

The painting of the graffiti was the moment where the supposed villains of the fictional story became heroes in real life. 'It vindicates our instinct to take action. Many, including us, are standing up to reclaim our image.'

See you in Halalywood

Actor Omar Regan was fed up with the stereotyping of Muslim characters in Hollywood. After his own appearance in hits like *Rush Hour*, he set out to make a film. 'There are 1 billion Muslims around the world and there is nobody catering for us and our stories. So I left Hollywood and I'm going Halalywood!' He crowdfunded his first film, a comedy action film about rogue government officials using Islamophobia to maintain power:

> *American Sharia* is a Hollywood motion picture that sets out to use comedy to reverse the prejudices held against Islam and help promote the religion in a more positive way. [...] It is not a 'tit for tat' view. It is a Muslim telling the story for a change from a Muslim point of view.

What many Generation M content producers emphasise in their work is that they are aiming not just to create a counter-narrative, but in fact to produce a new kind of socially conscious content. Omar says:

> Here is our mission: we are going to provide halal entertain-ment, that's entertainment we [Muslims] can relate to. Secondly, we want to re-educate the masses about Muslims and Islam. Thirdly, it will provide a platform for young Muslim

writers, actors and directors, where they can go and get their stories made and they won't be turned away. It's an alternative form of entertainment, during a time where we are surrounded and exposed to increasing negativity and profanity.

Heroes Like Us

The same principles apply to the creation of video games. Generation M is increasingly complaining that Muslims (which includes characters who are Arab and Pakistani) are depicted as the villains and as bad guys. The global hit game *Prince of Persia*, which has a fantasy Middle Eastern backdrop, when it was first launched, pitted a blond hero against the bad Arabs. There are attempts to 'acculture' video games for Muslim sensibilities by removing references to alcohol and skimpy clothing, but Muslims realise that they can and should get more.

'How do we make video games that can move you towards deeper considerations?' asks Hamish Todd, creator of an Islamic-art-inspired puzzle game. 'There are very few games that you could describe as sublime.' Other developers are taking a more direct approach to culturejacking the video games industry. Afkar Media creates video games that are rooted in local culture, specifically the Palestine conflict. The founder says that children were paying for the games, in a region where pirating is common. He explains that they were 'paying for the idea', because it was different to the mainstream industry.

On the Small Screen

In Canada, comedy sitcom *Little Mosque on the Prairie* made it onto TV in 2007. It centred on a mosque, following the lives of characters in the local Muslim community in the town of Mercy, Saskatchewan. It featured an imam as a key character and the mosque was rented from Mercy's local church. The series ran for six seasons with a total of 90 episodes. In 2013 it aired in the USA.

The creator, Zarqa Nawaz, based much of the show on her personal experiences. Many of the characters are partially inspired by her family and friends. Zarqa herself has stated that the show's primary agenda is to be funny, not to be a political platform. She also says that she views comedy as one of the most valuable and powerful ways to break down barriers and to encourage dialogue and understanding between cultures.

The US series premiere gained 2.1 million viewers, on a par with other popular American series, and even at the end of the season was still attracting over 1 million viewers.

In the UK, the BBC aired the sitcom *Citizen Khan* in 2012. It is set in Birmingham, which has a high Muslim population, and centres on self-proclaimed 'community leader' Mr Khan, and his long-suffering family. It was the first time in the UK that a mainstream show had featured a Muslim family. Reactions were mixed. Some Muslims were happy simply that they were depicted on screen. Others, like the *Independent* newspaper's Arifa Akbar, commented negatively on its many clichéd jokes and character traits, drawing comparisons with 1970s-style sitcoms.

Simply being present in a non-hostile format is not enough; it must be done with the same subtlety, sophistication and modernity granted to other groups. These two sitcoms demonstrate Generation M's desire and efforts to fill the gap in mainstream depictions of Muslims beyond outdated racist stereotypes.

What makes for 'Islamic' content is also a point of discussion. For example, Al Jazeera, a news station that doesn't overtly pro-claim any 'Muslim' credentials, highlights its strapline 'the other view' in some of its shows, which is something that appeals to Generation M. Al Jazeera has been congratulated for playing a crucial role in televising the Arab Spring revolutions and thereby being part of the chain reaction of the spread of political change. As of writing this, Al Jazeera is still seen to be fighting the fight that Generation M promotes of transparency and freedom of expression by supporting its journalists who are imprisoned in Egypt.

Other global Islamic TV channels are quickly growing. UK-based Islam Channel is watched globally and is probably one of the oldest entirely Muslim-focused channels. It is more attuned to a traditionalist audience, but in recognition of the power of Generation M is attempting to create better-quality content. Other more recent channels include British Muslim TV, American

Muslim TV, Safeer TV and Ahlulbayt TV, all of which have a strong religious focus but are attempting to produce the kind of world-class content that Generation M expect. Some producers understand that serious straight-up religious content is not always attractive to Generation M, who are seeking quality as well as education. Plus Generation M don't want only 'serious' material, they want entertainment too.

In Malaysia, pop culture had a surprising encounter with religion when in 2010 the reality TV series *Imam Muda*, meaning 'Young Imam', was first aired, to find the best imam in Malaysia. Like global reality TV competitions *American Idol* and *X-Factor*, this was a televised popularity contest with audiences able to vote for the winners. Contestants recited from the Qur'an, counselled couples and carried out the rites of death. *Der Spiegel* described the competitors: 'They are young and proud to be Muslims, and to be part of a big and important community. They fear God, but they also believe in the power of money.' So popular was the show that in 2011 it opened entry to surrounding countries. The aim, according to the TV network, was to show Islam in a new light. This truly was religious pop culture at its most popular and populist.

Soap operas are becoming popular across the Middle East, particularly during Ramadan when TV stations compete to become the most watched stations. But it is Turkey's exports that have become the game-changer, especially for the Muslim women of the Middle East. Turkish series often tackle sensitive subjects such as rape, forced marriage, divorce and extramarital affairs, and as a result are inspiring female audiences to assert themselves. The number of reported rape cases has grown, women are increasingly asserting their right to divorce in unhappy marriages, and, on a less serious note, travel to Turkey is on the up. Muslim viewers want to rediscover their Muslim ummah and their shared Muslim heritage.

Nina-Maria Paschalidou created the documentary film *Kismet* to chart the popularity of Turkish soaps. She says about the huge popularity of such soap operas among Middle Eastern viewers: 'What they see is a woman like themselves, who is Muslim, who is religious, who is traditional, but on the other hand is modern and I think this is who they want to be, who they aspire to be.'

Ethically Conscious Content

'Alchemiya is a cultural experience,' explains Navid Akhtar. 'We promote and celebrate the cultural impact of Islam on the world.' A journalist, film and TV producer with over 20 years' experience, he's been working to set up an on-demand streaming platform that will provide a global home for Muslim documentaries, lifestyle programmes and feature films. With a subscription model and digitally driven international reach, it's been compared to Netflix. But Navid has a different way of thinking about what the company is trying to achieve. 'Alchemiya is targeting the global urban Muslim: the professionals, the highly educated, English speaking, digitally connected who buy cars and go on holidays. But they also practise and care about the image of Islam,' he adds.

Alchemiya – Arabic for chemistry – is about transformation: 'We want people watching our programmes to be stimulated in their thinking.' The next generation 'don't want to see green domes and gold stars in the branding', according to Navid. 'Whatever we deliver', he says, 'has to be as good as the mainstream.' He elaborates: 'Take a beautiful geometric tile panel in Morocco for instance; the people who designed and put that together did so because it's an expression of their love of God. And our aim is simple: to share what we love.'

Mainstream pop culture is under attack for being superficial, offering empty violence and being ever more sexualised. Mothers are asking for positive messages for their daughters in children's films. Women's rights activists are pushing for better roles for women, beyond romcoms and teen flicks. Generation M culture creators feel they have something to offer as an alternative. They want to create culture inspired by Islamic values to bring betterment to a global audience across religions and ethnicities. This is part of a wider trend discussing the possibility of ethically and socially conscious content. For Generation M, these ethics come from their faith as Muslims, reaching out to make the world better for everyone.

'We show hope and don't show people oppressed. There are plenty of other platforms where you can see that,' Navid says. 'We're doing things that make you proud to be a Muslim.'

New Literature and Magazines

'It's frustrating to see our religion being discussed so widely and narrowly by people who have little to no expertise about the religion of Islam,' says designer and artist Sofia Niazi. Together with two collaborators, she set up the 'zine' *One of My Kind* (*OOMK*). The publication describes itself as 'highly visual, handcrafted', and its content 'pivots upon the imaginations, creativity and spirituality of women. Each issue centres around a different creative theme, with more general content exploring topics of faith, activism and identity.' It has an open contribution policy 'from women of diverse ethnic and spiritual backgrounds' but says it is 'especially keen to be inclusive of Muslim women'.

The quirky publication is far from the narrative and counter-narrative that are so familiar to many discussions about Muslims and terrorism. Sofia says,

> I feel like one of the main dangers of this constant scrutiny and misrepresentation is that we could easily just spend all our energies defending ourselves to people who are going to have a problem with us no matter what instead of just being ourselves and growing as people.

The zine offers contributors a space to tell stories in the way that they want to tell them. 'Presumptions about who Muslims can and cannot be come from a single story that has been perpetuated through the media,' Sofia says.

> One of the reasons that we were so keen to start *OOMK* was so that we could start writing and drawing our stories and concern ourselves with the subjects that were important to us instead of getting tangled in other people's ideas.

This is far from a religious publication. The founders talk about a much broader space, one where women can get involved and express their concerns and identities. They are conscious they don't want the label 'feminist' hanging over their heads.

6. *The 'zine'* One Of My Kind *aims to tackle the presumptions about Muslims that come from a single story in the media.*

The liberation from mainstream structures that the internet has offered has affected literature too. The Muslim blogging scene exploded in the early 2000s as writers who would otherwise never have been given space in the print media could share their thoughts, globally, growing into journalists and authors and gathering large popular followings.

Slowly, literature is beginning to recognise writing that Muslims want to engage in – not the terrorist or liberal escapee dichotomy that most literature paints Muslims with. Award-winning Leila Aboulela, of Egyptian-Sudanese heritage, writes about the exploration of faith identity in her books. In *Minaret* her heroine falls from being a high-society woman in Sudan to become a mere shadow as she flees to Britain. *Lyrics Alley* follows a love story set against the backdrop of the end of British rule in Sudan and the effect on identity and faith. *The Translator* tells the tale of a young Sudanese widow who falls in love with a Scottish academic while working as an Arabic translator at a British university, charting a story of love that is both human and divine.

Leila says that she believes that the media portrayal of Islam is 'getting more sophisticated and more diverse', and she 'aims to make Islam more familiar to the reader', adding,

> I'm consciously presenting it as a faith. Islam isn't just part of the culture in my fiction, it's not a social norm or something like that, it's to do with the individual and their faith and their own belief and what they want to do. Maybe this is what makes my writing different from that of other writers, who see the sharia solely as part of society and part of culture, rather than belonging to the individual herself.

Writers like Leila are increasingly using the arts to explore the nuances of this modern faithful identity, again pushing discussions beyond the political and theological and the simple terror narrative. Leila says:

> I wanted to explore the lives of Muslims who aren't passionate about politics. I wanted to write about faith itself and how spiritual development is a need that is as valid and as urgent as love and career. I wanted to write about the average, devout Muslim and the dilemmas and challenges he or she faces.

The spaces for this kind of writing, whether fiction, non-fiction or news, are growing. Book festivals in the Muslim world are increasingly popular, including those held in Cairo, Beirut, Sharjah, Dubai and Abu Dhabi. Muslim publishing houses that cater for more Islamic content are also being set up. In Indonesia, Mizan Publishing follows global publication rules about copyright and royalties and aims to create a list that offers perspectives that are both modern and Islamic. In the UK, the Muslim Writers Awards were set up to encourage young British Muslims to write, and secure them contracts with mainstream publishing houses in order to bring their voices to the fore. In the USA in 2016, publishers Simon & Schuster launched Salaam Reads as a new imprint focusing on Muslim characters and stories.

Emel magazine was launched in 2004 but closed following its hundredth edition. Editor Sarah Joseph, a British Muslim convert, set an editorial line which she believed was infused with Muslim values and how Generation M readers wanted to see everyday lifestyle questions tackled. Other lifestyle magazines aimed at Muslims have sprung up around the world. *Muallim* launched in 2014 in India. *Hiba* is based in Pakistan. *Umma* is a Finnish-language publication. Although South Asia's *Aquila Style* magazine is a fashion magazine, it covers a huge range of lifestyle features. Featuring more thought-pieces, *Islamic Monthly* (USA), *Critical Muslim* (UK) and *Islam-Interactive* (India) are all publications aimed at furthering the discourse of the Muslim ummah.

Children's Culture

The development of culture is as much for Generation M's own benefit as for the needs they understand their children face. Having worked hard on both faith and modernity they are now looking to create cultural materials that normalise this balance for their children. They suffered poor-quality cobbled-together ideas from badly translated or misguided materials. For their children they want content – whether books, TV, film or cartoons – to be of the highest quality and to use the most pioneering of technologies. Some of the most frenetic cultural activity is therefore around children's content.

Children's Islamic books that share directly Islamic concepts and teachings are of increasingly high standards. In the UK, self-publisher Sufiya Ahmed created the series of books for children set in the 'Khadija Academy', a Muslim Malory Towers. She refused to hand over editorial control as she wanted to employ Islamic phrases, something that potential publishers were not willing to agree to. Sufiya held firm that this was important for Muslim children's culture, and her books are now staple reading among school-aged children, both Muslim and otherwise.

Young adult fiction is being developed as a way to engage broadly with Muslim children. Naima B. Robert, who lives between South Africa and the UK, is the author of several young adult books including *From My Sisters' Lips*, which looks at what it is like to grow up as a Somali Muslim woman in the UK.

Aliya Husain is the American author of *Neither This Nor That*, exploring the struggles of a Muslim American girl living in the USA. The story follows Fatima, whose parents immigrated to the USA from India in the 1970s. Although she was born in the USA, Fatima isn't quite sure if she completely belongs. Her traditional upbringing, combined with her Islamic morals, seems to be at odds with everything around her. The underlying aim of the book is to offer young Muslim readers a way to make sense of their identities and build confidence and pride in being Muslim.

New toys and games that reflect modern Muslim identity are also in development. Some of the most familiar are the Aamina and Yousuf dolls that recite Islamic phrases and verses of the Qur'an. They were created by UK Muslim entrepreneur and mother Farzana Rahman who, like many Generation M entrepreneurs, found there was nothing suitable for her children – and then promptly created it herself. Her small but very successful company Desi Doll now ships the dolls, along with other Islamic and educational toys and books, all over the world.

The Fulla doll is considered an alternative to Barbie. Fulla's colouring is darker than Barbie's and in some countries she comes with a veil, abaya and headscarf. Fulla's popularity demonstrates that consumers generally are looking for products that better relate to them and reflect their own lifestyles.

In 2016, Barbie announced a new range of dolls in varying shades and sizes. Nigerian Haneefah Adam created her own version as a response: 'Hijarbie', an Instagram account of Barbie meets the hijab, sporting a collection of stylish modest outfits that she had created. Teen Vogue dubbed it the 'best doll that Barbie forgot' and Haneefah explained that her aim was 'improving self-esteem by giving children toys that adopt your religion and culture, and show them in your own likeness'.

The merest hint of this was demonstrated by Crayola, a US company that makes crayons, coloured markers and coloured dough. Its focus is on creativity. To help the sales of its products it often provides additional materials, such as colouring pages that parents can print out. In 2013 it released a series of colouring pages for the month of Ramadan which included mosques, prayer mats and the pillars of faith.

*

Of course, creating new cultures, whether it be dismantling villains and stereotypes, paving the way for ethically conscious content or developing high-quality products for children, is something that a future-facing generation feels passionately about. It is part of Generation M's *raison d'être*. Their mission is to maintain the Islamic values they hold dear, even if it's against the weight of tradition and traditionalists, in contravention of their parents and communities or counter to what has always gone before. They believe unwaveringly in being modern, worldly, faithful Muslims.

In one Ms Marvel episode, Kamala Khan is not sure how to handle her superpowers. She can't reveal her powers to her father, but, worried for her, he sends her to religious scholar Sheikh Abdullah for a 'talk' and she assumes that the Sheikh will lecture her about boys and advise her to stop lying to her parents. Instead, he says, 'If you insist on pursuing this thing you will not tell me about, do it with the qualities befitting an upright young woman. Courage, strength, honesty, compassion and self-respect.' This sums up the faith-inspired values that Generation M want to inject into the new cultures that they are creating, in print and on screen, in order to tell their own stories.

10 UMMAH-TASTIC

From Individual to Global Community

Abdelaziz Aouragh runs an online sex shop for Muslims. 'We don't sell products that simply enhance the love life between man and woman,' he explains. 'All of our products provide a deeper meaning to sexuality, sensuality and even spirituality.' His company, El Asira, based in the Netherlands, offers products like 'sensual silicone' and 'glamour lotion'. All of his products are halal. 'The majority of our customers are women,' he says. 'With men there is too much bravado.'

According to Islamic law, sex is limited to between those who are married. But when it comes to exactly what you can do, and how sex is generally discussed, Islam itself is quite open. Sex is for procreation, but it's also for pleasure. Islam has always been extremely open about sexual pleasure, and in particular women's pleasure. There are stories about how Prophet Muhammad would be approached in the mosque by women and men asking open questions about sexuality. In one famous tale, a woman came to see him on her wedding night, to complain that her husband was too busy praying and hadn't come near her. The Prophet went to see the husband, admonished him for being too engrossed in religious prayer and instructed him to pay more attention to his bride.

Generation M complain that this openness has been lost over time, and discussions about sex have become taboo. Islam's approach to sex has always been free of guilt, even if Muslim societies more latterly may not have been. However, things are slowly changing. Wedad Lootah is a UAE marriage counsellor who published an Arabic sex guide, *Top Secret: Sexual Guidance for Married Couples*, on how to achieve sexual intimacy with your partner, claiming that couples needed the advice. Her book was blessed by the mufti of the UAE but she received intense criticism from traditionalist voices.

Jenny is an Irish Muslim, warm with sparkling eyes and a mischievous air. She is organising a two-part seminar for young Muslim women in Dublin: the first on marriage, the second on intimacy. It's not a sex instruction class that she'll be hosting. 'We're not telling them what goes where!' laughs Jenny. 'But these girls need to know their rights in the bedroom.'

A chick-lit novel published in Australia by Randa Abdel-Fattah, called *No Sex in the City*, features a Muslim heroine. And in the USA, an anthology of true courtship stories written by Muslim women was published, delightfully entitled *Love, InshAllah*. Amongst the narratives were some that were sexually explicit and spoke about sex both inside and outside marriage. The book itself was extremely popular, and its comparatively graphic nature drew positive feedback as well as criticism. It was followed by an anthology of Muslim male stories, *Salaam, Love*.

Sexuality, its role in forming a modern Muslim faithful identity, and the fears and aspirations that go along with it, are hot topics. The place and role of LGBTQ groups is part of the mix. The horrific shootings in Orlando in a gay nightclub by a Muslim American have further heightened discussions that were already happening about Islam and sexuality, pushing for greater openness and understanding. The highly sexualised global environment also puts immense pressures on those Muslims who want to live a chaste life – especially in environments where virginity is often seen as freakish.

There's a pivotal reason why we need to talk about Generation M's approach to sex, alongside the fact that they are telling us it is important to them. It illustrates the tension between their individuality and their societies, between the parts of modernity that they want to embrace and the parts of tradition to hold onto. It also vividly demonstrates the thread that runs from the most intimate inner self of Generation M individuals outward to marriage, family, community and ummah.

For these individuals, self-determination is non-negotiable. And so they seek to find methods to engage in sex, marriage, family and community spheres on their own individual terms, but in ways that they deem to be in line with their understanding of Islam. Despite their embrace of individualism, they are keen to uphold marriage, family and ummah. They want to be the heroes of their own lives, but also to make sure their spouses, families and communities are all the better for it.

Ummah in the Generation M Psyche

Islam as a religion has a strong emphasis on the congregation, whether that be in communal prayers, hajj, social responsibility or relationships with families and neighbours. And so Muslim societies have by tradition been collectivist in nature. There is an emphasis on a 'we' consciousness. Individuals are connected together, and through this togetherness gain an identity.

British Muslim convert Stephanie finds a sense of belonging within the ummah.

As Muslims, we can be under scrutiny because of how the media and such presents us. Every time I put on my hijab, I'm expressing my pride in belonging to a group of people, who despite facing such negativity, continue to show the true qualities of Muslims. I've seen so much kindness, compassion, generosity, and wonderful acts of charity, from our brothers and sisters. Mashallah!

Whilst this generation are more individualist than either their predecessors or traditionalist counterparts, their existence in relation to others is still an important part of their identity – as mothers, fathers, children, in-laws, friends and, of course, as members of the ummah. The emotional power of being connected to any other Muslim anywhere in the world, thereby satisfying the human need for a sense of belonging, is immense. Any mosque is home, any Muslim is family. That's why travel to Muslim countries is described as feeling like home.

The app Umma Spot was created, a kind of Airbnb for Muslims, to tap into this exact feeling. The strapline is 'Feel at home wherever you go'. The aim is to connect Muslim homeowners with travellers who want short-term stays, knowing it will be halal and their beliefs will be respected. The growing individualism of the protagonists of our stories is balanced by a strengthened desire to make the ummah a better place. The unknown faces, names and locations of the millions that make up the ummah are now palpable. The internet has made them real. No longer is the brief period of hajj the only place they can meet. The digital ummah has energised the ummah itself.

Malaysian investment company Ummah Catalyst says that it dreams 'of an Ummah that is progressive and at the forefront of development'. Through its efforts investing in start-up businesses, it believes it can harness the power of 'collective effort': 'All of us need to work together to catalyse the change within the Ummah.' Ultimately, what they want is to 'give back' by contributing to 'uplifting the Ummah'.

When we talk to Generation M we should know that we talk to the whole ummah. They carry upon themselves a duty to divulge important information, to care through charity, to congregate through prayer, to visit family, to travel to see their shared history, to champion their causes, to correct their wrongs. Their high levels of connectivity and the importance they attribute to their own individual role in improving the ummah mean they are proactive influencers.

In global political discourse, the question is often posed: why do Muslims *here* care so much about Muslims over *there*? The simple answer is: the weight of religious duty to care about the ummah is heavy. This is a group of people who see their behaviours and attitudes as global, that people far away are just as much like them as those who are near. The shared values of this global community of purpose lead people in one location to feel intimately connected to those far away. Shared vision, shared beliefs, shared aspirations and shared rituals all lead to a shared identity which in turn creates a powerful sense that what happens to 'them' is actually happening to 'me'.

Hufsa, a respondent, says:

I feel as if I'm in this secret – but actually not so secret – international club. Being part of the ummah, you know that wherever you go there will nearly always be people around who believe in the same simple truth that you do and that they will be there to help you out if need be. Even a simple smile in a foreign land from a passing brother or sister goes a long way. Even on social media, you can rely on strangers to make du'aa for you simply because you're their sister or brother in faith.

It is imperative therefore that organisations who wish to communicate to this group ensure that their messaging is consistent across geographies, languages and cultures.

For all the emphasis on shared identity within the ummah, it is important to add that its diversity is increasingly highlighted as a key factor that gives it strength but also raises challenges. Theological viewpoints, scholarly interpretations, customs and cultures and political relationships all vary hugely. Negotiating these variations is a source of tension that the abundance of online material has heightened.

A further tension Generation M complain about facing is the collective guilt poured on them when a terrorist action takes place. Unhappy with the stereotyping that all Muslims are to blame for the actions of a few, many will feel that the burden to denounce is unfair and will voice their discontent.

One of the many unsavoury aspects of violent extremist organisations has been an attempt to subvert this desire for a global Muslim community by promoting their cause as the only ummah, rejecting the diversity of ummah. Journalist Nabeelah Jaffer spent months talking to British and American 'sisters', before and after they travelled to Syria. She tells the tale of one woman who had left the UK to join the 'Islamic state'.

Umm Umar had travelled to Syria because she wanted to join a perfect Islamic state. Like the other women, she painted a picture of an Islamic utopia. This was for the sake of propaganda and, I suspected, to reassure themselves that they had made the right decision in going over. To all these women, ISIS was simply dawla [state], as if no other country existed or mattered.

The idea of joining the perfect Islamic state is the pull factor. But there are also push factors which largely go unremarked.

Filmmaker Deeyah Khan, who produced *Jihad: A British Story*, explains that for such women, 'Islamic State presents a route of escape', and they are using religion – in an entirely misguided way – to flee both wider society and prohibitive family structures through the language of religion, which they see as the only way they can rightfully oppose their parents. Deeyah explains: 'Some who seek to counter parental controls may turn to scripture, to use a language that carries weight within their households.' But the real push into the arms of the self-described Islamic utopia, which in fact is nothing but anti-Islamic hell, is that,

> A great deal of racist violence is also directed at Muslim women, who are more visible than men. This can leave women isolated and fearful; hyper-aware of their identity, which marks them out for hostility. There are many reasons why a person might become interested in more radical interpretations, from spiritual curiosity, an awakened political awareness or a wish for a more 'authentic' identity. Each journey has its own beginning, but each is a quest – for meaning, identity, community; for answers.

A similar story might be told for the young men who join Daesh too.

For Generation M the key point is that diversity of opinion is not to be suppressed, and violence is absolutely not permitted in enforcing any notion of ummah. Judgementalism – and especially its extreme religious form known as 'takfirism', which is to pronounce another Muslim as a 'kafir' (unbeliever) – is thoroughly rejected. Islamic teachings and Muslim cultures put strong emphasis on social relations, on the idea that relationships with neighbours, citizens and nations – within or outside the faith – are to be maintained. Growing interfaith and intrafaith movements in both minority and majority Muslim countries are testament to the weight given to good community relations.

'After personally examining my faith, I now feel I am better able to serve society,' says Maguid Maruhom, executive director for Ummah Fi Salam, a development and peace-building initiative in Mindanao, the Philippines. He connects his own individual faith with the betterment of Muslim communities and then extends that to wider society:

My own approach to development is both social and spiritual, therefore. I give a lot of importance to my spirituality because it offers me deep values and righteousness, including commitment, accountability, service, love, kindness, and honesty, that I put to action every day in my development work.

The real power emerges when his individual efforts connect with wider communities. 'The solutions to common problems faced by people of different faiths are similar and interfaith dialogue is inspiring us to find what is common among us.' Faith is central in his view to social transformation:

There is a need for faith to be involved in a quest for solutions to our social and economic development needs. Faith-inspired organizations have demonstrated successes in solving local issues, discrimination, human rights, etc. through interfaith dialogue. If this can be enacted and replicated all over, surely the world will succeed in its quest for social change and peace.

They Lived Happily Ever After

'I fell in love with my husband after I married him,' writes Javaria Akbar.

We met only twice before we walked up the aisle, after being introduced by a mutual family friend. Neither of us had been in a relationship before and we didn't live together before our wedding day. And, although the odds were stacked against us, we've been happily married for almost five years. It was the quickest and the best decision I ever made.

She notes that her choice is one that can be confusing and is constantly questioned by those not familiar with arranged marriages. It is a decision that 'I will probably never stop having to field questions about as long as I'm alive. The one that triggers knee-jerk judgement in strangers.' Javaria describes her 'back-to-front love story' but categorically adds: 'arranged marriage isn't backward at all.' She says, 'For me, marriage was the route *towards* love, rather than a tangible marker of its presence. It was about security, friendship and adventure with a person who shared my values.'

Javaria explains, 'It's hard for people to reconcile that a woman like me can still call herself a feminist. But I am, unequivocally.'

When it comes to love, there is an expectation of something more than staid traditional notions of toleration but somewhere short of a Hollywood romance. Generation M get riled by what they see as proscriptions on the expressions of love. In Malaysia, for example, a campaign was launched to ban Valentine's Day. In the Middle East, influential leaders have criticised celebrations of Valentine's Day as importing traditions that are alien to the area, being against Islam and making love into a consumerist product. The only argument that Generation M as a whole have truck with is that love is perhaps being 'sold' with such traditions. In this they are aligned with broader consumer movements that worry about commercialisation.

Independent, autonomous choice is crucial when it comes to marriage. There is a clear difference between an arranged marriage and a forced marriage; conflating the two is a cause of great consternation. Forced marriage is absolutely not an option.

The boundaries of the search were once tight: the family, the tribe, the village, the ethnicity, the school of thought. But now in the global Muslim village, spousal choices no longer rest solely on family tradition but on finding someone who embodies the same values they hold dear: faith and modernity. So even though arranged marriage is still common, it is not as a family duty, but rather to fulfil faith requirements.

Some may be quite content to have family involvement in finding prospective partners and introducing them. The traditional matchmaker also still has a role to play, but increasingly marriage is something that Generation M are not willing to abandon to fate or family forces, ensuring they are an active or leading part of the search and selection. This might take place over the course of daily life. But matrimonial websites are also opening opportunities for marriage with those of different backgrounds. Speed-dating has become commonplace too.

This is bringing new challenges as Generation M may be choosing to marry outside their traditional family circle, outside their social class or even – especially in minority Muslim countries where ethnic and sectarian groups may be more diverse – to Muslims of totally different backgrounds. Some may even choose to marry those who are not Muslim. Naturally, these trends affect the traditional cultural fabric of communities. There may be opposition from family elders, but the response from Generation M is simple: they are establishing the ummah on Islamic values rather than ethnic, cultural or traditional ones. Samia Rahman writes in the *Critical Muslim*'s 'Love and Death' issue that there has been an increase in mixed-ethnicity marriage among second-generation Muslims 'with parents sometimes just relieved that their over-thirties children are marrying at all!'

With marriage holding such importance, weddings are a central pillar of an individual's and the community's life cycle. The nikah is the Islamic religious ceremony, usually conducted by an imam, and often takes place in a mosque. Consent must be freely given by both the bride and the groom. Other than the key Islamic contract of nikah and mahr, there is huge variation in wedding traditions.

7. *Salaam Swipe offers a modern digital solution to Muslims seeking life partners via the internet.*

Because of their size, and because of the many cultural customs accompanying weddings, the event can be extremely costly. In the UAE some estimates put weddings as expensive as $100,000. For the nikah ceremony to be valid, the groom must give the bride a gift known as 'mahr', which can be any gift that the bride selects, but usually takes the form of money. Whilst the amount of mahr is at the bride's discretion, cultural norms often dictate that this can be even in the tens of thousands of dollars. If they cannot afford such mahrs, young men may delay marriage.

Divorce rates are also rising in Muslim communities, a trend that is causing great consternation. One study found that in Saudi Arabia up to 70 per cent of new marriages were ending in divorce.

Whilst the family is set to remain at the heart of Generation M's life, changing gender dynamics, more dispersed families and a heightened sense of individuality within the bounds of the family are likely to herald changes of structure and emphasis in the coming years.

Influencing the Influencers: A New Kind of Celebrity Leadership

'I decided it was time to speak out,' said Kristiane Backer when her autobiography *From MTV to Mecca: How Islam Inspired My Life* was published in 2009.

> I wanted to show that Islam is a beautiful religion which helps you become a better person and is a benefit to society [...] how Islam is very much compatible with life in the West. I overcame my prejudices and found my peace and happiness in Islam.

At the height of her fame, Kristiane was awarded Germany's most prestigious TV Award, the Golden Camera, and two Golden Ottos, for her television work. At MTV, she hosted the *Coca-Cola Report* and the MTV European Top 20, among other programmes. She has used her fame to promote high-profile social and charitable causes. Since her conversion to Islam, she has been nominated Global Ambassador for the Exploring Islam Foundation and has become one of the faces of the 'Inspired by Muhammad' media campaign.

Islam is currently the fasting growing religion in the world, and women are the most rapidly increasing segment within it. Bringing with them their own heritage and local culture, converts often act as catalysts in creating new facets to the faithful modern identity. They bring with them the opportunity to taste new foods, or newly created halal variants of them. They insert new linguistic terms and artistic trends into the dialogue. It is no coincidence that many singers, writers and artists who are particularly influential among Generation M were professionals in those fields before they came to Islam. They have travelled their own journeys on the path from modern-world expectations to the fusion of Islamic values. The conversion story as a genre of motivation and identity creation is very popular with Generation M. And those in the public eye often carry huge weight as influencers.

At the other end of the spectrum, some converts are saddened that they are not always seen as 'real' Muslims, as they were not born into the faith. Many often feel a sense of social isolation.

The most respected celebrities are those who have stood by their faith – or sometimes adopted faith – despite their fame. In the Sunsilk advert mentioned earlier, Unilever used Wardina Safiyyah, a Malaysian actress and model who wears a headscarf. She caused a public ruckus when at the peak of her celebrity in 2000 she started wearing the headscarf. She is now a role model for Malay Muslim girls.

Generation M celebrities come from all walks of life: sports, business, politics, fashion, music and business, as well as scholarship. Two-time world boxing champion Amir Khan, born and brought up in the north of England, wears his Muslim faith as part of his public identity. In July 2005, just days after the attacks in London, he stepped into the ring for his first professional fight, wearing Union Jack shorts. Later that year he visited a school in Pakistan where over 100 children had been killed in an extremist attack.

He believes his celebrity is something he needs to use to counter violent extremist voices.

Kids don't grow up thinking about going out and killing innocent people. It's why I go to schools and tell them: 'Look, you want to follow the right path. You want to represent your country in a good way. You want to build a name for yourself and your families.' I stand up all the time and say this. Obviously innocent people shouldn't be killed. Obviously this is wrong.

We've seen how music stars like Maher Zain and Sami Yusuf are acting as charitable ambassadors. Fashion icons like Wardina Safiyyah and Dina Toki-O have become voices for a young, urbanised segment of Muslim women who want to see their views reflected back at them. The media and digital space are giving platforms to 'on the ground' voices. One such voice is Muna AbuSulayman, who is a Saudi female activist and entrepreneur. She hosted the first women's TV chat show in Saudi Arabia and has a huge Twitter following.

There is also a growing phenomenon of celebrity scholars.

'R-O-C-K-S-T-A-R, is what I thought when I first saw Sheikh Hamza Yusuf speak at a[n] Islamic Society of North America (ISNA) conference in Chicago,' says Nadia S. Mohammad.

I was in awe, not just of his words, but by the size of the crowd. This was not your average local *halaqah* [gathering] – this was a crowd of thousands who had traveled from all over the United States to attend the conference and to see Yusuf. […] After the lecture they were there to stand in line to ask him to autograph their copy of his book and maybe, if they were lucky, to get a photo with him.

The esteem in which scholars are held stems from the spiritual revival and sense of gratitude their fans find in their guidance. It's a global phenomenon. Nadia explains:

They were there to catch a glimpse of the face behind the voice from lectures played on car stereos on their way to school or work. They were there because his calm demeanor and smooth rhetoric inspired them to be better Muslims and better Americans.

Such religious celebrity culture is 'most prevalent in the social media realm where Muslim scholars maintain carefully crafted public profiles on sites like Facebook and Twitter,' writes Safia Latif in *Islamic Monthly*. 'These scholars diligently offer 140-character snippets of religious wisdom. They also post personal anecdotes, self-help advice, and the occasional political grievance. Sometimes, they even share scholarly "selfies".' Latif goes on to say that the response from 'thousands of followers' is to 'evince gushing admiration through "likes", "favorites", and "retweets". The lionization of scholars for their down-to-earth religious swag is reminiscent of the devotion of millions of followers to popular personalities like Oprah or the Kardashians.'

Since Islam is supposed to be about self-effacement, and our Generation M individuals aspire towards modesty and humility, the almost cultish popularity of religious scholars can be confusing. 'We love our Muslims scholars so much so that we jump at the first chance to follow their lives and they indubitably mean well in their efforts to reach and relate to a tech-savvy generation,' concludes Safia. 'But we must question the psychological and sociological impact of this culture on our collective Muslim ethos.'

Paradoxically, the democratisation of religious knowledge has given individuals a sense of equality with scholars. Finding the balance between respect for scholarship in an age of celebrity and belief in one's own high level of acquired knowledge is a tension that is yet to be resolved.

The Institutions of Muslim Life

Muslim spiritual life is traditionally centred on the mosque. Daily congregational prayers, Friday prayers, Eid congregation and Ramadan are central pillars, and community and pastoral events may also take place at the mosque. However, there is growing disgruntlement about whether mosques in their current state are really fit for the modern Generation M world.

Traditional mosques were the preserve of older men who wield family and social authority, and for whom open discussion was seen as disrespectful or taboo. The exclusion resulting from this has been felt particularly acutely by women and younger individuals. In many mosques, there simply were no spaces for women, who thus missed out on the sense of congregation and knowledge acquisition. Muslim American activist Hind Makki set up the Side Entrance tumblr to allow women to document this experience, which is too often denied by male management committees. Women post photos of the poor entrances and facilities they face in a bid to share experiences and confront denials of their complaints. Now better educated, often working, and connected via the internet, Generation M's women are no longer willing to tolerate such exclusion and are either forcing mosques to create space or are creating their own.

In 2015, the Bradford Muslim Women's Council in the UK announced a consultation for a project to develop the UK's first centre of excellence in promoting Islamic education and scholarship for Muslim women. Bana Gora, the CEO, explains:

> The alienation that women feel has profound consequences for younger generations who are taught that Islam treats both men and women as spiritual equals yet the practice within mosques contradicts the principles. In an era in which many young people feel that their faith is no longer relevant, or are going to extremes, we want to be able to provide a safe space for them to question, learn and grow whilst having an appreciation of their heritage as well as the opportunity to make informed choices relevant to the 21st century.

In 2016 a similar initiative was announced in Denmark. For younger members, an alternative is online spaces which offer the freedom to raise issues barred in the mosque, to speak out without fear of social reprisal and even to benefit from the cloak of anonymity to raise difficult issues. In the USA, PBS documentary 'UnMosqued' followed this new generation. The filmmakers describe the growing need for reform in many mosques in America and explore why young Muslims feel disconnected, unwelcome or disenfranchised. It begs the question, what does the future look like for mosques? The makers of the documentary explain:

> As Muslims become integrated within American society and grow up in a diverse multi-racial environment, it becomes

increasingly uncomfortable to enter a mosque that is predominated by a certain culture. Millennials and Generation Xers do not have as strong of a relationship with their parents' country of origin which exacerbates the discomfort they feel when entering ethnic-based masajid.

Many feel estranged from traditional mosques because they feel their global and modern understanding of Muslim values of togetherness, diversity and ummah is not reflected there. It is obvious, then, that the role of the mosque as a venue for cultivating violent extremist ideas is overstated. Rather, youngsters do not frequent these institutions and are immersed online.

Despite political cynicism about governments, Generation M as a collective still trust national authorities and religious bodies with activities like halal certification. Businesses and brands are also custodians of authority and trust. As consumption has established itself as a key marker of identity, and as brands need to demonstrate transparency and accountability, they can have great sway on opinion, knowledge and trust. It's a surprise that big brands are not stepping into this role, but it does require care and attention to both the brand's own business values and to the way it communicates with this audience.

The significant role of the ummah comes up in almost every aspect of our story. But what should also be coming through is that Generation M are characterised by a robust tension in asserting their individuality within a framework of maintaining family and community relationships. The nature of these relationships and how they are being created and maintained is being re-evaluated. Who gets to hold authority, influence and leadership, and where are they held? The ummah is still working through the answers to these questions.

11 SUPERSIZING CELEBRATIONS

Ensuring the Rites of the Islamic Calendar
Don't Go Wrong

In Indonesia, the celebration of Halal Bihalal follows Ramadan. Muslim Indonesians visit their elders, the extended family, the neighbourhood or their work to show respect to them, during and immediately after the festivities of Eid ul Fitr. It's an occasion of mutual forgiveness, a time to seek reconciliation and to preserve or restore harmonious relations. New clothes are worn, usually in white, to symbolise the wiping clean of the slate and a new start. While Halal Bihalal is unique to Indonesia, the post-Ramadan spirit of renewal it symbolises is common around the Muslim world. It's a similar pattern for all the events of the Islamic calendar: while traditions may vary from culture to culture, the core rituals and their meaning are consistent.

Two questions that arise again and again in proposing the idea of Generation M are whether there is any such thing as a global Muslim (consumer), and whether Muslims across such diverse cultures, geographies and languages can be united through shared characteristics. These questions are answered when we look at the events and rituals of the Islamic calendar. The core is the same, the values are the same, the religious rituals are the same, it is just the expression that is different.

Eid, for example, is a day that marks new beginnings, after a spiritual cleansing of 30 days of fasting. New clothes are a consistent feature for Muslims celebrating Eid, marking the day as one of joy. The core religious ritual – visiting the mosque for Eid prayers – is the same the world over. Getting together to share food, exchanging gifts, paying respect to elders, giving charity and visiting cemeteries to remember those who have passed show remarkable consistency around the world. What may vary is what Muslims wear, what they eat, and how many days are spent in celebration. This balance between universal religious rites and local cultures encapsulates why we can assert with confidence that there is a universal Muslim experience.

There are a multitude of dimensions beyond this global–local scale that further underpin Generation M attitudes and behaviours towards the events that punctuate Muslim life.

With the emphasis on new clothes for Halal Bihalal in Indonesia, it should come as no surprise that the Indonesia Islamic Fashion Fair was organised to coincide with this period. Dian Pelangi, one of the designers featured, moved away from her signature bright colours to invoke the spirit of Eid. 'White symbolizes a clean slate at Idul Fitri [*sic.*],' Dian told the *Jakarta Globe*. 'That's why people wear white garments on the holiday.' Describing her collection, she epitomises the Generation M approach to the events of the Muslim calendar and life cycle: 'I wanted to follow the tradition and also create something that was different.'

Tradition versus modernity, individual versus family and community, consumption versus commercialisation, brand development versus religious authenticity, unity versus difference. We see the tensions which lie at the heart of Generation M life visible again in marking the rites of the Islamic calendar. They appear at the new year, Ramadan, hajj or the two eids, or in life events that have specific religious rituals: birth, marriage and death. No story told about Generation M can be complete without looking at how Generation M experience them and the tensions they face.

Some Quick Facts

The Islamic calendar is lunar and so the new year and each month begin when the new moon is sighted. The new year is not a significant time for Muslims, except in South Asia where Maal Hijrah is marked, or for Shi'a Muslims, for whom it coincides with a time of mourning as it is the period for commemorating the massacre of the grandson of the Prophet Muhammad and his family.

Ramadan is a month of fasting from dawn until dusk, refraining from all physical input, which includes food, drink, sex and smoking as well as medical intervention where possible. Some people are exempt from fasting due to health reasons, such as the old and sick, but also travellers as well as pregnant and breastfeeding women.

Hajj is the mandatory once-in-a-lifetime pilgrimage to Makkah for all those who have the financial resources to pay for the journey and the health to undertake it. It involves rituals in Makkah as well as in nearby locations in Mina and Muzdalifah which lie within a few miles of Makkah. Anywhere up to 3 million pilgrims take part each year from over 180 countries.

Ramadan is immediately followed by Eid ul Fitr, which marks the end of fasting and celebrates a new slate after sins have been wiped clean in Ramadan. Hajj includes within its ritual Eid ul Adha, the Festival of Sacrifice, which is celebrated by both pilgrims and those who remain at home. It denotes the erasing of sins by those carrying out the hajj, but is also a commemoration of Abraham preparing to sacrifice his son to fulfil God's command. For Muslims, this son was Ishmael, not Isaac, as in Judeo-Christian teachings. Instead of Ishmael being sacrificed, a sheep took his place. As a result, Eid ul Adha usually involves the slaughter of an animal, and the meat is shared between family, friends and the poor as a form of charity. It symbolises each person sacrificing something in their lives important to them.

That Muslim Feeling

'I can feel a different atmosphere in Ramadan,' says Safeenah from Indonesia. She sighs, 'Alhamdulillah! I feel peace and close to Allah. I feel somehow it's just a month that I don't want to lose forever. So wonderful I feel, I don't know why!'

That Muslim feeling flourishes in Ramadan as individual spirituality gets a boost, while the sense of community is enhanced as people come together for the religious and social rituals. This feeling is built on a combination of inner meaning and outer identity. Each event in the Muslim calendar highlights both aspects, and that Muslim feeling is what keeps drawing Generation M back to the Muslim cycle of life.

In Ramadan, the suspension of 'normal' life in lieu of fasting alongside all other Muslim friends and family means that the volume is turned up on Muslim identity. That sense of unity may come from visiting the mosque for extra prayers, spending time in religious congregation, sitting with family and eating traditional foods at suhoor, inviting guests to share iftar or giving charity to pay for iftar for those who cannot afford it for themselves.

The traditional foods of Ramadan therefore take on a heightened meaning and act as lightning rod for that feeling. Dates are the recommended food for breaking fast and become ubiquitous during the month. They appear alongside the omnipresent crescent imagery on visual communications. The date meme is a popular point of humour: 'Ramadan: the only month when I have a date every night' and 'Date every night and doesn't cost much. Only #Ramadan.' Dates are everywhere: date syrup, date sparkling drinks, date ice cream, even date mocha frappuccinos.

That Muslim feeling, for Generation M, also comes from com-mercially inspired experiences. Sameera is a young Omani fashion designer. As she lays out the feast for iftar to break fast she describes the traditional spread of food: 'Luqaimat, sambosas, dates, Omani coffee, laban, Vimto and water were basics for any Omani Iftar.'

Wait – Vimto? The purple nectar invented in Britain in 1908 is a staple of Ramadan in the Middle East. No table is complete without it. The drink has an annual spike of sales during the month of fasting and inspires devotion from its fans. Saudi artist Alaa Wardi created a 96-second video tribute to the drink, the music composed purely from sounds made by Vimto bottles (it's surprisingly tuneful). Vimto is so closely tied to Ramadan that it makes 70 per cent of its sales in the holy month. It sold more than 25 million bottles in the Gulf and other parts of the Middle East in 2010. 'We got used to it being a Ramadan regular in our tender age,' says one consumer. So woven into the fabric of Ramadan is Vimto that when some supermarkets restricted sales to consumers, there was shock that 'only two bottles were allowed'.

Rooh Afza generates similar emotions in the subcontinent. In Pakistan, Tang wants to break into this market, so its ad campaign connects the product to childhood. One of their ads features a girl on her first fast – an event which merits its own celebration in Pakistan, where it is called Roza Kushai – who can think of nothing better than to break her fast with Tang and insists that her guests are treated with the drink too.

Generation M want to share that Muslim feeling with everyone, especially as they feel that their own voices are too often blocked from the global conversation. In 2015, pilgrims to Makkah were able to stream their experiences live on the twenty-seventh night of Ramadan, which is one of the 'nights of power' when Muslims engage in devotion all night. Snapchat created a live story after Muslims lobbied for coverage, opening up the city for the world to see. More than a million people tweeted about Mecca_live, which received effusive responses from non-Muslims and from Muslims, who were joyful to see a different part of their faith portrayed. As @zee_e said, 'Thank you #snapchat #meccalive'.

Like Ramadan, that Muslim feeling during hajj is a heady cocktail of performing the rites, along with a sense of togetherness, celebrating diversity and difference, bringing to fruition a heartfelt spiritual aspiration.

For every hajji, or pilgrim, there's a hajj story. The experiences and feelings they recount are all remarkably similar: anticipation, anxiety, being overwhelmed, emotional breakdown, spiritual epiphany, rebirth, connection to the ummah, return. Hajj is one of the defining events of the global Muslim community, an aspiration Muslims hold almost as soon as they are old enough to appreciate being Muslim. Islam is the only religion where it's compulsory to undertake a pilgrimage at a specific time, in a specific place, with specific rituals so that it's in unison with others of the faith. It's a deeply collective experience from start to finish. Pilgrims will be waved off by the whole community, who will also come to receive them on their return, often with flower garlands. In some Muslim countries, even ministers will make a trip to the airport to lead the welcoming committee.

'My favourite memory is going around the Ka'ba seven times, then between Safa and Marwa seven times, then drinking the sacred water Zamzam,' says Papa Djibril from Dakar, reflecting on his experience of the pilgrimage. 'When I was there I felt like I was born a second time, surrounded by brothers and sisters from all around the world, all of us wearing our white robes.' Pilgrims wear white clothing to erase all trace of worldly existence. In a world dominated by commercial messages, it's a space of clear thinking, uncluttered by the advertising and media noise. 'All of us pure, so grateful, so happy, all of us one voice, one heart for Allah. My biggest dream is to go back to Mecca inshallah one day again,' he says.

When the pilgrims make their way back home, they travel with mounting expectations of major life changes. Their new honorific of Hajji or Hajja gives them an elevated status, one that each pilgrim must live up to with newfound piety. More important than what others expect is what the pilgrims themselves anticipate – a real change in their own actions and lives after their pilgrimage. Completing the hajj is seen as a moment of epiphany. 'I felt really different, the same as if all the bad things that I had done in my life had gone,' says Ahmad from Fujairah. 'I felt I was a new person, without any mistakes in my life.' That's the ultimate feeling that Generation M are chasing.

Navigating Difference

'Praying with other Muslims of every tribe and creed from all over the world' is what Kehinde from Lagos recounts as being the emotional high of hajj. 'We were all dressed in the same simple clothing, all equal in worship. There was no reference to Sunni or Shi'a or any other sect, sex or station. It was the Islamic brotherhood.' It's a utopia that fills the Muslim heart, but in reality differences are something that are still to be resolved.

With an ummah of 1.6 billion Muslims, even with a shared calendar and rituals, there is difference of opinion and disagreement. This is where Generation M's love of unity and shared identity is tested to the maximum and the questions of what it means to be diverse and how to accept and even celebrate diversity are debated. Despite their claims to a modern, faithful identity that is focused on building a unified ummah, they are aware that this is one aspect that demands solutions for difficult questions.

Sighting the new moon is a communal enterprise, and the crescent brings with it a mix of excitement, anticipation and community bonding, tying the emotional and functional parts of faith together. That's why the moon is such a powerful visual symbol – and used so excessively. The difficulty is that the new moon is visible on different dates, depending on where you are. So there is rarely agreement on when it has been seen. As a result the #MoonWars hashtag is now a staple of Muslim digital life. One tweet jokes: 'Wishing you early/on-time/late eid Mubarak depending on which country's moon you prefer.'

So all the excitement of Eid, for example, can turn to frustration; @farazz yelled on the Twittersphere: 'There's literally zero logic behind doing Eid in the UK based on moon sightings in Saudi, do you do namaz [prayer] based on the sun's position in Saudi too?' Not everyone agrees with this way of deciding moonsighting.

It's a challenge to the core Generation M identity because behind it lies the debate about upholding traditional Islamic teachings versus following modern science. It's about making decisions based on individual knowledge versus the unity and togetherness of everyone celebrating on the same day.

While the new year passes quietly for most Sunni Muslims, for Shi'a Muslims it's a time of mourning as the commemorations of Ashura fall on the tenth of Muharram, the first month of the Islamic calendar, and Arba'een follows 40 days later. These mark the occasion of the killing of Husain, the grandson of the Prophet Muhammad, by the Caliph Yazid for opposing his despotic rule. It's a time of strong emotion, with participants wearing black, reciting mournful eulogies, gathering together every night and engaging in public commemorations as well as in community work.

It can be a contentious event, as Sunni–Shi'a sectarian tensions have flared up in recent years due to the conflict in Syria and the popularity of Salafi doctrine, which often brands Shi'a Muslims (to their intense frustration) as outside the pale of Islam. Daesh in particular has a publicly avowed intent to kill all Shi'a Muslims.

Clearly, if the flames are fanned, such differences undermine the sense of unity within the ummah and can be fatal for those branded as being outside Islam. There's an imperative as a result to resolve differences, and education is seen as fundamental.

Our new generation of Shi'a Muslims are working hard to explain Ashura to those unaware of its meaning, to create bridges to their Generation M peers whom they feel are being unduly influenced by hostility towards them. One such initiative is the annual 'Who is Hussain?' campaign which describes itself as:

> a campaign created to let the world know about one of the most important men in history; what he stood for and what he died for. Hussain is a universal figure of inspiration and it is our objective to share his message with everyone. This campaign has no religious, political, or monetary aspirations: it simply aims to inspire you to become a better person, using the timeless example of Hussain.

The campaign included train station adverts, handing out branded bottles of water, social media videos and greeting cards. The people behind it went on to launch the campaign #TeamGiveBack, which saw acts of compassion of all flavours across the globe: blood donations, homeless initiatives, water bottle handouts, awareness and interfaith events. And, although the message behind the campaign is incredibly serious, there's clearly a sense of humour behind the message of unity: they started handing out bottles at an India versus Pakistan cricket match.

The Mawlid is another event evoking strong, emotional differences of opinion. It marks the birth of the Prophet Muhammad. It is a joyful celebration held around the world, sometimes with processions, floats, singing and prayers. However, some believe that the occasion is forbidden as birthdays should not be marked. Further, disagreements rage as to whether birthdays in general should be celebrated, with some parents refusing to send their children to birthday parties or mark their own special days. As with the 'moon wars', the disagreements continue. The question is whether Generation M can find a way for such fundamental religious and social issues to be accommodated by the practice of everyday life if they are to live up to their claims of togetherness and diversity.

Tradition versus Modernity

Nerina grew up in Bosnia but now lives in Chicago. Whenever she thinks of Ramadan it makes her nostalgic.

> Ramadan brings the memories of childhood when I would run up the street to wait for the lights on the mosque to be lit […] it was the most amazing moment for me. Before that I would run to the bakery and get somun [a special bread made during Ramadan] and all the streets had the scent of freshly baked goods. Bosnia during Ramadan was just a joyous place as I would be dressed up as a doll and would go to the mosque with my grandmother.

The dilemma is whether to look backwards to remember tradition or look forward to create new traditions. Nerina explains:

> This Ramadan I have made a decision to go on a cultural exploration of the vibrant and colourful world of Islam. I have visited an Arabic, Indian, Pakistani, Turkish and a Bosnian mosque. I was welcomed with a delicious, sweet tea at the Pakistani mosque. In an Indian mosque an eleven year old had tried to set me up with her cousin, with all the seriousness of an adult woman that I could not help but laugh. And at the Arabic mosque the men were so kind and generous.

But ultimately it's about togetherness, the theme we keep coming back to. Nerina says:

> There is something sacred in the notion of brotherhood and sisterhood that comes with the Islamic way of life, that I cannot help but feel privileged and honoured to be part of billions of people who turn to Makkah every day.

For Generation M, the dilemma in Ramadan is the same dilemma they face all the year round, in whatever milestone of Muslim life: should they look forwards or backwards? Should their emphasis be on upholding tradition or on inventing modernity?

Traditional Cultures Build Communities

Nostalgia is a potent force for Generation M to reaffirm the rhythm of Muslim family life and reinforce the community. This is not tradition for tradition's sake, but to keep family strong and as a result give succour to Generation M's identity.

Older traditions are the backstory to this new modern identity and its new traditions. In Egypt, for example, the 'fanoos' lantern is the sign of Ramadan. Another tradition is 'al-mesarahaty', the 'night caller'. He takes the task of walking around the village or city waking people in time for suhoor. In some small villages he may even stand in front of each home and call each inhabitant by their name in order to wake them. In larger places he may stand on each street and bang his drum to wake people. Whilst these remain more of a novelty, or stories recounted from older to younger generations, nevertheless they are important in Generation M's self-understanding as part of a long-standing culture. Traditional celebrations of individual events reinforce family and community relations.

Baby Zakariyah has his own YouTube video documenting his aqiqah party, the feast that celebrates a newborn. In his subcontinental-style aqiqah held in the USA, he's dressed in a smart little suit, almost a mini-me version of his father, who is carrying him, also wearing a suit and tie. His mother, dressed in a sparkling emerald and gold outfit, turns to her baby and says: 'We want to wish him a very happy, blessed life.' But of course this is a community event, one that ties the individual to the ummah, so she adds: 'We are very happy to be sharing this with our family and friends. And now I will welcome the guests.' Many Muslim cultures will also send out sweets, part of the tradition of gifting in order to build community ties. Traditionally, the baby is named on the seventh day after birth.

In Malaysia, the cukur jambul ceremony is similar: the baby's aqiqah day is held at the house of an elder, where all come to meet her. One of her locks is trimmed, and family and friends share a meal. In the background, prayers and Islamic devotions are recited.

Feasts – known as 'walima' – are religiously recommended, and are embedded in cultural traditions. They are held at birth, marriage and on return from hajj. The meals clearly entrench community togetherness. But they keep returning us to the deeper goal of spiritual renewal. After marriage, a Muslim is considered to have completed 'half their faith' and their prayers are worth 70 times what they were worth before – pointing to the weight placed on moving into a state of marriage. And, of course, after the completion of the hajj, a Muslim's record is said to be wiped clean, allowing them a fresh start. In some Muslim cultures, even circumcision becomes a reason for communal celebration.

These events also emphasise the importance of giving to charity. For the baby's aqiqah, hair is cut or often shaved, then weighed, and then the equivalent value in gold or silver is donated to charity. The meat that comes from animals usually slaughtered for the birth, marriage or hajj is shared between friends and family and also given to the poor.

Changing Habits

Despite soft-focus memories of happy Muslim pasts, traditions are changing, driven by digital technologies, globalisation and the greater emphasis that Generation M place on the individual's experience even while community and family remain central.

Take TV and online activities during Ramadan. In the Middle East, a whole raft of new TV dramas – a business in itself – are aired in the evenings. Many are imported, particularly from Turkey and Egypt, but there is a growing desire for home-grown programming. In the UAE, a series of Emirati-made and -themed programmes will be broadcast for the first time during Ramadan. TV scheduling encourages people to spend the entire evening at home in order to stay up to date with the soaps, dramatically changing normal viewing habits. TV advertising thus becomes a popular, if expensive, choice for brands.

The change in usage occurs on the internet and social media too. The Online Project in the Middle East found that positive engagement on Facebook and Twitter increased during Ramadan, and this positive feeling actually continued after the end of the month. Facebook noted 47.6 million posts about Ramadan and Eid in the Middle East and North African (MENA) region alone by over 14 million people. Twice as many posts carried photos as normal. Hashflags were used by Twitter to introduce a crescent in posts to do with Ramadan. Snapchat carried live stories of Ramadan from five cities in the region. Google and YouTube launched a Ramadan Companion to curate local content, including recipes and even traffic updates. The traffic is more important than you might first think, because everyone is rushing to get home at exactly the same time. Punctuality is crucial – traffic jams wreak havoc on the streets and tensions run high. With people stuck on the road and the Islamic injunction to feed people the iftar, charitable organisations often hand out food on the street.

In Indonesia, daily patterns shift to an 'eat, pray, shop shop shop' model. People go online earlier, at 4 a.m. to coincide with eating at suhoor, and browse online as well as shopping before praying the morning prayer. There is more shopping at lunchtime, suggesting that Indonesian Muslims are turning to e-commerce and retail consumption instead of going to lunch. At around 6 p.m. shopping drops as people hurry to eat iftar, and then it picks up again before midnight. In a similar pattern change, in Saudi Arabia internet usage peaks between 3 a.m. and 6 a.m. just before suhoor, reflecting the way people stay up and use the web for entertainment and connectivity. An online shopping portal in Malaysia succinctly puts it: 'Ramadan is a season of spirituality and togetherness; precious moments that should be spent with family and friends instead of being stuck in traffic and fighting crowds in shopping malls.'

This is where the advantages of modern life really come to the fore for Generation M. They are turning to technology to offer clever ways to improve their spiritual experience. Ramadan apps, Ramadan portals and SMS reminders of the time to break fast all support the spiritual aspect of Muslim rites. These are all excellent examples of how brands collaborating with Muslims can actually be a support rather than a form of commercial exploitation.

Travel habits are changing too. For the travel industry, business was traditionally quiet as people treat themselves and take advantage of the long office closures, sometimes up to ten days, following the end of Ramadan. Religious tourism to Makkah and Madinah is naturally popular, and Turkish Airlines, for example, is promoting 'Ramadan in Turkey'. Ramadan packages to traditional holiday destinations such as Thailand are also appearing, with the menu for the all-inclusive deals served at night and kitchens open for the pre-dawn meal. Instead of staying home for the big community occasions, Generation M are putting their own individual experiences first.

A Woman's Work is Never Done

Instead of women having the burden of cooking huge feasts, families are starting to go out to eat for Eid, although this means that some traditional elements of society are complaining that Eid is no longer a family-oriented festival. These transitions are a facet of the impact of Generation M, who believe in maintaining the religious values of Eid, but not imposing a burden, especially on women, and who want to try out new ways of celebration.

'When I think of Ramadan, I think of many things, but the first is almost always my mother,' says Noha from Montreal. '[She was] up before the rest of us an hour and a half before dawn to prepare the food we would sleepily consume in the last half hour before the fast began.' It certainly sounds as though Noha's mother was full of energy and devotion for her family, fasting all day, cooking the iftar and then preparing suhoor too.

My mother would wake us up with home-cooked French fries, still sizzling on the plate. Into our bedroom she would sweep, singing 'wake up, wake up, your food has come to you' in a jolly voice, and as I rolled over on the top bunk to face her, I would find a handful of hot, salty fries stuffed into my mouth before my eyes were even open. It certainly was an effective tactic.

It's a common childhood story throughout the world, of Muslim mothers cooking until the adhaan sounds for iftar while the rest of the family waits, tired and hungry. One study in the Middle East found that wives spend twice as long cooking during Ramadan than the rest of the year.

Like in many cultures, Generation M women are struggling to play the role they remember their own mothers playing, of creating powerful (religious) experiences for their children. Playing mother is important because tradition and nostalgia are such an important role in their own lives. But Generation M women are asserting their own right to participate in the spiritual and public aspects of Ramadan. We are likely to see a growing trend to help them address this challenge.

Commercialisation Versus the 'Real' Meaning

As I get older I've come to see that Ramadan is a lot like a reset button. The one time of the year where you truly get to reflect on your relationship with not only food but with your family, your friends, your community and most importantly your relationship with God.

Radwan, aged 24, who moved to Canada when he was five, explains that Ramadan is:

How new year's should be, but with a lot more will power to meet all your resolutions. This Ramadan has reconfirmed to me that Islam is the only thing that can help you realize the simplicity of life and explain the complexity of death.

Some might claim that with the increasing commercialisation of Islamic religious events, this is a rose-tinted view of how Generation M really experiences the calendar.

Food shopping begins several weeks before Ramadan, for example, and brands in Muslim countries plan weeks, even months, in advance. Stockpiling, product shortages and price hikes are commonplace. Basic commodities can become unaffordable, forcing governments to step in to protect the consumer.

In Pakistan, Vital Tea ran a Ramadan TV campaign showcasing a middle-class couple with the wife asking her husband the prices of various items upon his return from the grocery store. She exclaims in shock each time he tells her the cost. She finally picks out a bag of Vital Tea and smiles at the reasonable price. She expresses a Ramadan dilemma: 'On the one hand, there is the joy of Ramadan, on the other hand, there is the pain of everything being expensive.' The ad ends with her requesting companies to 'At least respect the sanctity of Ramadan' and urges them not to exploit consumers. One Muslim group in the UK chides Muslims themselves for over-indulging and encourages 'fasting not feasting'. This perfectly captures the tension between moderate consumption and extravagance which many members of Generation M believe is leading to the loss of meaning of Ramadan and other rituals.

In some countries, particularly where there is a significant urban/rural divide, returning to the family home in the countryside is an important element of eid traditions. It is seen as connecting to roots and capturing a sense of authenticity. In Indonesia this is known as 'mudik'. But once again commercialisation is competing with meaning. Some city folks take out loans to buy themselves new clothes and objects to show off their success as they 'bling up' to go home. There are complaints about one-upmanship during mudik about who can bring home the best gifts.

Ramadan is a noisy time in terms of commercial activity, and advertising is cluttered. Brands are constantly trying to capture the meaning and lived experience of Ramadan, but are too often felt to teeter on the edge of tacking on Ramadan-related iconography in a cynical bid to generate sales. Far too many adverts have crescents and dates pasted into them, or are decorated with lanterns and rosaries for no apparent reason. Generation M can get very agitated about obvious selling, which can easily be interpreted as 'exploiting' Ramadan. Instead, they warm to brands that help Muslims achieve their personal, community and spiritual goals during this month. This tension between a spiritual focus and an increase in consumption is one that troubles Generation M, acutely aware of the paradox that they live during Ramadan.

The challenge is to move past glib generalisations about Ramadan to deeper insights into consumer behaviour and aspiration. For example, it's trite to point out that Muslims are hungry, and it's insensitive to advertise food during the day. But Nando's managed to create a humorous ad about counting down to iftar time. A young man holds a chicken leg poised by his lips as he watches the sun slowly setting.

Despite the ethos of Ramadan being one of restraint in consumption, iftar meals tend to veer towards indulging in rich heavy foods. This leads to the paradox of Ramadan: despite the emphasis on empathy with those who have less, and on withholding the physical in favour of the spiritual, weight gain during the holy month is a widespread and increasingly worrying social phenomenon. In 2014, Qatar reported that 100 people were hospitalised on the first night of Ramadan for having eaten too much.

In spite of the utopian dreaming about Ramadan, it is tough to uphold the 'real meaning', and Generation M recognise their own human frailty as they attempt to live up to their high aspirations. There are plenty of jokes about the bad breath that accompanies fasting, and there are serious complaints about dehydration and fatigue. Productivity becomes a challenge. The ProductiveMuslim.com website offers its 1 million visitors guidance on being more Islamic with their time by ensuring greater productivity. For Ramadan, it gives guidance on how best to deal with fatigue, dehydration, headaches, anger and other obstacles that fasting places in front of the idealistic spirituality promised. In 2015, it titled its articles 'Aiming for an Awesome Ramadan Series: It's Time to Change Your Life.' It offers tips from life coaches, links to apps, doodles and worksheets to help maximise output during the month. It helps you to address your iman, your goals and even your kitchen.

Hajj is facing the ultimate challenge of becoming commercialised. It's not cheap to go for hajj, and it's becoming more expensive every year. Muslims start saving as soon as they can afford it. Some governments support hajj savings schemes or set up investment funds. In other areas, wealthy benefactors will sponsor pilgrims as a way to gain reward for themselves. In 1963 the Malaysian parliament launched the Malaysian pilgrim's management fund as a response to unscrupulous operators who were targeting potential pilgrims, an ongoing scourge around the world. The fund now has 5 million members and at 23 billion Malaysian ringgit it's the world's largest Islamic savings institution. It even bailed out large Malaysian corporations during the financial crisis. Faith helps out finance.

The preference for more expensive premium hotels for hajj has led to a proliferation of global-name, high-rise hotels surrounding the holy sites, encouraged by a Saudi government initiative to bulldoze and rebuild the area with a city of skyscrapers. The result is that accommodation and facilities for less well-off pilgrims are pushed further out. Worse, the local authorities have admitted to destroying heritage sites in order to make space for the growing number of pilgrims.

It's ironic that it may be Generation M's own tastes for a premium hajj experience that are amplifying the poor–rich divide and undermining the egalitarian spirit of hajj. Further, when banks like the Sharjah Islamic Bank in the UAE offer fee-free 12-month interest-free loans to prospective pilgrims it is seen as walking a fine line between supporting the pilgrimage aspiration and crossing over into debt encouragement.

The 'greening' of the hajj is a movement that is gaining momentum, and this concern goes side by side with saving the Islamic heritage in the area, which is being destroyed. In London, Hawra reflects on her experiences in Madinah:

> I was amazed by the beauty of the green dome. But once inside the masjid, it seemed like a luxury venue and nothing of it made me experience how it could have been during the time of the Prophet. I searched for my Prophet's grave from one room to another but nothing was found. Tears started shedding in a desperate call to find my beloved's tomb, pulpit, rawdha [grave] and house but nothing was there. Instead, massive dividers were placed to prevent me from visiting my beloved's

rawdha, women were only allowed twice a day to see part of one wall covered with Qur'ans after hours of wait. I did not get a sight of the Prophet's pulpit, nor all the historical part and my excitement was transformed to sadness and anger.

Throughout the Islamic year, the sense of Muslim identity is periodically heightened for Generation M, as they attempt to live the most enjoyable, modern life they can, appreciating every aspect of their Muslim practice. On each occasion, spiritual renewal goes hand in hand with community affirmation. But the tensions erupt at each flashpoint, as they determine how to create balance between fun and religious obligation. When does enjoyment turn into commercialisation?

Their worry is that the Islamic festivals go the way of Christmas, Easter and even Valentine's Day – all tinsel, baubles and chocolates, but robbed of meaning. If anything, comparisons with Yuletide make them even more determined not to lose the real meaning. Since Islamic festivals are tied to spiritual salvation and the existence of a global ummah, it's no wonder that remaining authentic is at the forefront of their minds.

12 'FORGOT TO BE OPPRESSED, TOO BUSY BEING AWESOME'

Generation M Women at the Forefront of Faith and Modernity

Being a hijabi is tough. It really is. There are days I wish for nothing more than to take it off. Days when I just want to be like everyone else. I don't want to stick out like a sore thumb. I don't want to be different.

Ethar is fed up of her existence being defined by her hijab, fed up of having a war fought over her Muslim woman's body, at pains to point out that there is so much more to her than her clothing.

I'm tired of being the token 'omg-look-such-an-articulate-awesome-non-stereotypical hijabi!'
[…] I realized being thought of as 'amazing' was actually insulting.
Because the assumption was that being veiled meant I was stupid and very non-amazing.

But mostly, she's tired of the hijab discussion.

I'm tired of hijab taking up so much space in my life.
I'm tired of speaking about it.

I'm tired of explaining it.
I'm tired of defending it.
I'm tired of being treated differently.
I'm tired of having to prove I'm normal.
I'm tired of being thought stupid and backwards.
I'm tired of the judgments – from both sides.
I'm tired of the opportunities denied.
I'm tired of expectations.
I'm tired of hijab.

It's not just the media that is stereotyping hijabis into anonymous, homogenous oppressed ghosts. There's a war going on over Muslim women's bodies, battlegrounds of the supposed dichotomy which Generation M oppose, of Islam versus the West. Muslim women are frustrated that their status is defined as silent obedience and opposition to the West, rather than on their own terms – even by Muslims. They are told 'good Muslim women' wear veils, 'good Muslim women' defend honour, are obedient, are not Westernised.

The outcome is that Muslim women become objects, reduced to what they wear and how they look; they are defined by others, spoken about or dismissed when speaking for themselves. As Ethar writes: 'Hijab is so personal / And yet it's so public.'

Despite the obsession with veils, and how Ethar and her peers are often at pains to dissipate or ignore this obsession, it is here that we need to begin, precisely because so much of the discussion facing faithful, modern Muslim women is about what they wear and how they look. We need to get to the bottom of what they feel about it.

Women are possibly experiencing the most rapid changes, with increasing levels of education, with greater empowerment in education, employment, marriage and childbearing and with more active public participation. If we were to pick a face that captures the global pace of change in the coming decades, it would most likely be a Muslim woman – she is part of the largest population, in the nations where change is happening fastest and in the segment where change is most potent. In short, Muslim women are where it's happening.

Obsessed with Veils

'We don't care what's on your head, we care what's in it' said the Canadian advertisement. The image was of a female doctor, stethoscope around her neck, headscarf around her hair. The Lakeridge Health Authority in Quebec was aiming to recruit more Muslim doctors to its staff. The advert was first run in a newspaper, and then published on Facebook. It was a simple straightforward strapline, a sentiment often expressed by Muslim women themselves. Lakeridge received nearly 80 applications within three days of the advertisement being published. It was not only a breath of fresh air for Generation M's educated Muslim women, eager to get involved in society and the workplace, it also established the centre as open to cultures and diversity, something that undoubtedly earned it the affection of staff, potential employees and potential patients. It was a particularly bold move by the authority as it was published against a backdrop of Quebec debating whether to ban the niqab.

A quick Google search on 'I'm not an oppressed Muslim woman' (or other similar variations) will bring up pages and pages of hits from Muslim women around the world. In one of them, 20-year-old Azra is angry and sarcastic:

> I'm a young Muslim woman. I am not oppressed by my hijab, I'm liberated by it. If you don't understand that that's completely fine, you don't need to. However if you're going to launch a campaign against something, it's best to consult the women you're 'fighting' for. No one can throw the idea of being oppressed and expect me to lie down and take it, as though 'hey maybe because YOU think I'm suffering I'm going to abandon my religious beliefs thank you so much for enlightening me I didn't understand before, that I need to be free from something I wasn't sure I was chained in!' The emotion you're seeing in my eyes is not a plea to 'help me' but one for you to take your self-righteous bullshit and shove it up your arse.

Yes, Muslim women swear too.

The International Museum of Women is an online museum for social change that amplifies the voices of women worldwide through global online exhibitions and arts and cultural programmes. In 2013 it launched 'Muslima: Muslim Women's Art & Voices', in order to counter stereotypes of Muslim women by giving Muslim women themselves space to express their stories through words and imagery.

'What does it mean to you to be a Muslim woman today?' asked the organisation. A picture from young Bahraini artist Tamadher al Fahal's tongue-in-cheek zine captures her frustrations at the injustices and inequality she feels as a Muslim woman. On the left-hand side the cartoon shows her seated in front of a backdrop of Qur'anic text, a blindfold held over her eyes, a hand over her mouth. The caption reads: 'What society wants me to do as a Muslim.' On the right-hand side she sits on a throne. The hands this time are placing a regal robe on her shoulders and a crown on her head. She smiles and behind her is a bright yellow star backdrop, as though out of a superhero cartoon. This time the caption says, 'How Islam

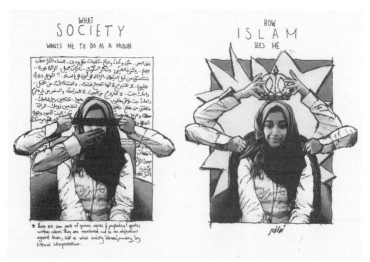

8. *Bahraini artist Tamadher al Fahal discusses how Muslim women are seen and see themselves in her 'zine' 'Diary of a Mad Arabian Woman'.*

sees me.' It's the difference between how Generation M women see themselves and how they feel they are stereotyped.

The curator of the Muslima exhibition, artist and Muslim activist Samina Ali, explains that 'the rich diversity of opinions, appearance, spectrums of faith, occupations, cultures and even languages that exist among Muslim women is wiped clean to instead mass-produce a distorted image that is meant to sell copy and perhaps even governmental politics.' The result is what the Muslima exhibition describes as 'appearance overload' which is a fixation with the way Muslim women look and what they wear rather than what they are doing.

To address this, the International Museum of Women teamed up with Miss Representation to create an infographic on how the media – and by extension politics and public discourse – packages Muslim women. They found there were three common ways: veiled, oppressed and homogenous.

The visual images used to accompany stories about Muslims invariably feature Muslim women in niqabs and abayas, even if the story has nothing to do with Muslim women, head coverings or cloaks. Equally uncreative is the way Muslim women are headlined, usually with some pun about veiling.

Noorain Khan offers the 'Complete Guide to Bad Burqa Puns' with gems such as 'Unveiling the truth', 'Veiled threats' and 'Behind the veil'. She feels that 'these puns perpetuate the idea that Islam (metaphorically) or Muslim women (literally), are things that ought to be unveiled'. And, directly relevant to our point about removing agency from Muslim women, she adds: 'Notice how often others unveil Muslim-y things, it's not painted as an autonomous act.' Her advice is: 'if news outlets are committed to their puns, perhaps they can at least be a bit more creative.'

Even the reputable Pew Research Center, which does excellent work on religion and public life, fell foul of this obsession with visuals of Muslim women. In January 2014 it published its findings to the question 'How do people in Muslim countries prefer women to dress in public?' Bizarrely, it explained that 'An important issue in the Muslim world is how women should dress in public.' Generation M women fighting issues of access, equality, misrepresentation, work rights, maternity care, personal law and much else are likely to disagree. It gets worse. To identify the preferred dress code, each respondent was given a card with six headshots showing different styles of headcovering and asked to choose the woman 'most appropriately outfitted for a public place'. The reduction of women to these six 'looks' failed to take into account that many of these are cultural. Neither did it look at how Muslim women themselves prefer to dress, rather asking what others thought appropriate.

Muslim women were none too impressed. Maureen Ahmed put it simply: 'Why we don't need another survey reinforcing stereotypes of Muslim women', explaining that it was perpetuating 'a reductive idea of the Muslim world, and that empowerment can somehow be measured based on how covered – or uncovered – women are'. She added that this being

> yet another study in which Muslim women are discussed rather than listened to helps reinforce the concept of needing to save Muslim women. If Muslim women are being forced to cover in public spaces, and they can't speak up, they must need our help, right?

Muslim women being given a platform as long as they are 'always the victim' is the second pillar of the Muslima infographic on stereotyping. The 'misery memoir' literary genre, with books like Jean Sasson's 'Princess' series or *Not Without My Daughter*, is testament to this being one permitted – encouraged even – expression of Muslim womanhood. Muslim women are depicted as 'voiceless, submissive, passive, oppressed victims instead of the powerful creative leaders that they are', explains the commentary, adding, 'there is a lack of focus on the achievements of Muslim women especially those who do not fit a veiled and victimised stereotype.'

The same problems of objectification, reduction to what they wear and assumptions of lack of voice or proactivity appear in discourses by Muslims too, which young Muslim women are rejecting. Umm Abdillah from South Africa discusses in her article 'Pearls in Oysters (and Other Patronising Hijab Analogies)' how such descriptions reduce Muslim women to pretty, passive objects whose existence is defined simply by the fact that they tempt men. It's also offensive to men, she says, to be compared to flies.

Just as Muslim women say that the one-dimensional stereotypes of Muslim women as oppressed and weak take away their agency, the same problem arises when lollipop-type analogies are applied by Muslims to Muslim women (there's plenty of them: pearls in oysters, gift wrapping, bubble wrap, even ipad covers – I'm not joking here). According to Umm Abdillah these 'patronising depictions of hijabified Muslim women' all have one intent: 'These analogies are invented and maintained to express relations of power.'

It's a double bind: objectified by stereotypes, but equally objectified by parts of Muslim discourse too. As one Facebook poster, Aisha Sch, responded to the lollipop analogy, 'Hijab is supposed to exempt us from objectivization and yet, every argument I find uses an analogy where we are either a diamond (in the best cases), an ipad or a lollipop (in the worst cases).'

Politically, it can turn into a battle over Muslim women's bodies, with events like the war in Afghanistan predicated on 'saving' the women there. Equally, Muslim women have been directed to reject 'rights' because they are 'Westernised'.

Amidst this battle, Fazeela in Stockholm believes the essence of modest dress and especially the hijab as Muslim women see it has been lost:

> Wearing the hijab is an act of worship for those who believe in it and choose to wear it, first and foremost. Yet it has become and is increasingly being marketed by ourselves as an act of political battle above all in times of wide discrimination and persecution of hijab-wearing women.

Creating Spaces on Their Own Terms

'Man, I look so photogenic in my hijab!' says Safa Siddiqui, 26, a freelance writer in Mumbai who had never seen her mother or sister in a veil. 'I was a hijabi at 22 and warned I may not find a media job. I faced rejection and my hijab was a reason they cited.' Before her next interview, she sent out an alert. 'I'm a hijabi and it doesn't come in my way.' She landed her first assignment and it's been four years since.

Fashion is one of the means by which these young women are asserting their self-expression and identity. Part of the motivation is to overtly demonstrate that they are 'normal' like everyone else, that they are not oppressed or anonymised. Equally, it is an expression of Islamic identity against a backdrop of some Muslim ideas that do not offer space for women (literally in the case of some Islamic institutions and social structures). It is also a fierce rejection that women's presence should be erased from Muslim discourse. No wonder that these young Muslims like Safa are happy to be part of the selfie generation or that hijabi fashion and make-up bloggers are celebrities.

The sharing of photos by hijabis around the world like Safa is one strand of the activities of #WorldHijabDay, which is an initiative to reclaim the hijab. It began in 2013, created by Bangladeshi-born Nazma Khan who moved to New York when she was eleven years old, who says that: 'Modesty is part of our Islamic faith. No one should be discriminated [against] for following their faith.' The aim is to 'build empathy for this perspective and to encourage non-Muslims, and Muslims who don't normally wear a hijab, to try it out.' Since 2015, #WorldHijabDay has trended on the day.

Global Pink Hijab Day was founded in Missouri to remove stereotypes about Muslim women by engaging in dialogue about breast cancer awareness and join in walking groups by wearing pink headscarves.

Miss World Muslimah is an annual competition held in Indonesia to find Muslim women who show dedication, reputation and concern for Islamic values and community development. Although it has been dubbed a Muslim beauty pageant, the organisers say that contestants are required to demonstrate religious piety, to be positive role models and show a life of Muslim spirituality. They take part in events designed to test their qualities and the winner is picked by a group of 100 orphans at a selected orphanage, based on her actions and character. It includes a catwalk show of the participants who all must wear hijab.

The proactive adoption of hijab and modest wear offers a sense of belonging. In Indonesia, chapters of the Hijabers Community have already been established in three of the country's main cities.

The group describes itself as covering 'From fashion to Islamic studies, from hijab style to learning Islam, anything that will make us a better Muslimah insyaAllah. And it is hoped through this community, every Muslimah can meet new friends, get to know each other and learn from each other.' Tia, who is part of the Jakarta chapter, says: 'I can sense that this friendship is real and solid. It's a crazy world full of temptations out there, but Hijabers Community perfectly balances worldly and godly ways. I love them. This is my second home.'

In India, Daud Sharifa Khanam has been working towards setting up the country's first women's mosque. While men will be able to pray there, the administration and governance will be conducted by women. She was fed up of women not having a place to express themselves, but more importantly, she was sick of women's lives being decided by male committees in mosques into which women

9. *Indonesia's Hijabers Community brings like-minded women together to enjoy 'From fashion to Islamic studies, from hijab style to learning Islam, anything that will make us a better Muslimah insyaAllah. And it is hoped through this community, every Muslimah can meet new friends, get to know each other and learn from each other.'*

are not allowed to enter. If a woman had a problem, her case would be heard and judgement passed without her presence. Her belief is that women need to challenge the power axis of the mosque community. But her approach – in true Generation M style – is to do it through her beliefs as a Muslim. For example, the mosque is still the centre. She has arranged for verses of the Qur'an which talk about women's rights to be translated into the local Tamil language. When India's male clerics criticised Indian tennis star Sania Mirza for wearing shorts – reducing Muslim women as ever to what they wear – she hit back by asking what they were doing to tackle deep problems of dowry, incest and alcoholism which are far more serious than what one girl wore to play sports.

In Iran and Saudi Arabia, female university graduates out-number their male peers. In Egypt, TV presenters fought and won a legal battle against television stations that took them off air when they chose to wear headscarves.

Greater education and freedom has brought increased partici-pation in the labour force and the economic independence that this brings. And later marriage brings freedom and self-determination, all of which are being enhanced by global connectivity among Muslim women's groups which allows sharing of experiences and the creation of solidarity. The internet has also opened up the business space for Generation M women. Social media have been bringing down physical barriers to influencers, resources and target markets, making female participation more immediate and more acceptable. These significant global trends affecting Muslim women are creating previously unimaginable spaces for innovative thought and activity. Politically, intellectually as well as commercially, women are both the producers and consumers of innovation.

Empowerment, Visibility and Voice

Only ten minutes after she was married in Bangladesh, Farzana Yasmin had demands put to her by her new husband that she pay him a dowry. Dowries from the bride to the groom are illegal in Bangladesh and have no standing in Islamic teachings. But in some regions the tradition persists, and if the bride's family cannot pay up, the bride is too often subjected to torment. Farzana decided on the spot to divorce her new husband. 'The dowry has become a cancer of our society. I have read this in newspapers and always wondered why people should put up with it,' the master's graduate said. 'When I found myself getting caught up with this, I thought I have to protest […] at least I have taken a stand.'

Women's rights activist Sultana Kamal called her a 'heroine'. But there was backlash: 'Already she is facing recriminations with several parties trying to defame her and portray her as a loose woman.' What is remarkable about Farzana is how she demonstrated her beliefs through her actions – a trait of Generation M women – in order to create a change in society for everyone's benefit.

Modern ideas of women's empowerment rightly emphasise economic liberation, an end to violence and freedom from discrimination. But for fulfilment in all spheres, we must include the right to be active in the search for companionship and love. As we've seen in several other chapters, women are keen to gain an education and engage in employment, and marriage ages are rising. Marriages by choice, across ethnicities, families and cultures, are growing more commonplace, and Generation M women are asserting their right to do so through religion. Islamic values encourage women to be proactive in marriage. It's not shameless, lewd or impertinent for a woman to express her interest in being married.

A 2013 study published in India looked at the rising trend among Muslims to use online matrimony sites. It found that profiles conformed to gender stereotypes prevalent in Indian society: family had a stronger role in a woman's search for marriage than a man's, around 75 per cent of female profiles claimed to be posted by someone other than the candidate. One interpretation is that putting oneself forward for marriage is considered inappropriate for a woman, as it is 'unconventional' for Indian women 'to initiate their matrimony'. The only occasions where this might be acceptable is if the woman is older or divorced, reinforcing the attitude that this is not something young, innocent, nice girls do. Overall, women claimed to be more religious than men. A woman using a progressive or 'forward' technology might be afraid of emphasis on her credentials as too modern, and find herself forced to employ a greater number of markers of religiosity to compensate.

The internet and social media have affected Generation M in more spheres than that of marriage, and have had a disproportionately positive impact on women. In many Muslim cultures, the digital age has broken down the physical barriers to knowledge, allowing women access to information, resources and people that are empowering them to fight cultural prejudice, to build Islamic blueprints for the changes they are pushing for and to establish themselves in business. The digital realm is also helping them to gain solidarity with other women fighting the same cause.

In 2011 two notable internet-based campaigns were set up to assert the rights of women in the Middle East. In Egypt, HarassMap was established as an online portal for women to document where they had suffered abuse. Mapping the locations of hotspots was finally a tangible way for harassment to be quantified, located and presented as fact. Organisers then printed out the maps and took them to the localities to show residents the problems women were facing in the area. In Saudi Arabia, the Women2Drive campaign hosted videos of women driving in contravention to the social prohibition on women behind the wheel.

Late in 2011, to explore the relationship between social media and women's empowerment, the Dubai School of Government published a study on 'The Role of Social Media in Arab Women's Empowerment'. There is a gender gap, with Arab women using the internet and social media less than Arab men, and less than the global female average. Respondents felt this was because, in a region where family and reputation are important, there were still concerns for women's privacy. Societal and cultural limitations were cited as the main barrier.

Women used social media for information, news and advice more than men did. That makes sense in an environment where they may be excluded from access to influencers, bureaus and advice outlets. Women were also more likely to use social media for 'family and friends' networks as well as entertainment, again tying in with the restrictions women may face due to cultural norms on movement.

Where the study was most interesting was in how women themselves felt – more than men – that social media was helping them to change their own situations. Women were optimistic about social media, feeling that it makes it easier for Arab women to express themselves; social media can enhance Arab women's participation in civil society; it can empower women to be role models for change; it can provide economic and entrepreneurial opportunities and it can advance the cause of women's rights. One of the respondents further noted: '[Social media can help with] education for self-empowerment, recognition of women's rights, and benefiting from other experiences outside the Arab region.'

For Muslim women without recourse to physical communal spaces such as mosques, and often cowed down by claims that women's voices should not be heard, the virtual world has created safe spaces for identities to be explored, asserted and shared, creating the opportunity for solidarity across once-disparate groups, offering awareness of other movements around the world and creating a wave of Generation M women's energy.

Many traditional cultures view the expression of voice and visibility by women as contentious. Women are often told on Facebook to remove their photographs because they are immodest or because their photos are being used by unscrupulous men, even if they are modestly covered. A woman's voice is in some teachings classed as 'awrah', something that should be kept private. By extension, women's voices are often banished from the public space.

Generation M women don't accept this. As we've already seen, they are confident and proud to be visible. The rapid growth of Muslim fashion is one example of this. The growing number of Muslim women artists who are creating the soundtrack for Generation M's world are also tackling issues of expression. There are female Muslim stand-up comedians, TV presenters, YouTube stars and even scholars. The rise of Muslim female comic superheroes that we saw earlier gives us an insight into the way that Muslim women are asserting power. Of course we're still waiting for global films and film stars to feature faithful, modern Muslim women, including those who wear the hijab. It's a woefully overlooked opportunity.

Ultimately this is about Generation M women asserting their right to self-definition and self-determination. They want the power to set their own agenda and to do so for their own ambition, to gain their own rights and for the good of the whole community, both men and women, to be better Muslims. It is not about wresting power from others but about rights and justice.

Role Models and Trailblazers

'Islam is a religion that encourages freedoms and was based on the liberation of the bodies and the minds from slavery, oppression and fanaticism,' says Tawakkol Karman of Yemen, who won the Nobel Peace Prize. Her life demonstrates that it might be possible finally to demolish the myth that a practising Muslim woman cannot be a women's rights activist. Tawakkol wears her faith proudly. Her long history of activism challenges those who believe women of faith cannot contribute to women's empowerment. She says her strength and power are derived from her religion.

This is exactly what Generation M's women tell us – that it is their faith that empowers them to fight for justice, fair representation and equality. Using their power to 'normalise' Muslim women is something that Generation M women are keen to do. Sometimes it may be as simple as giving voice to their feelings. A Twitter campaign trended on #AsAMuslimWoman, offering mundane self-descriptions from Muslim women such as: 'Early mornings irritate me & I enjoy chocolate', 'I hate the District line in the morning. It's cramped. And it smells funny' and 'I'm running my business, enjoying motherhood and living my dreams.'

There has been a proliferation in recent years of Muslim women power lists right around the world: lists of extraordinary women, future leaders, current leaders and women from Islamic history. This all contributes towards Generation M's efforts to create a holistic narrative of their history, particularly for women, and therefore their future in a modern Islamic-values world.

Tawakkol symbolises the growing number of Muslim women who are making waves in the political arena. In the UK, in 2015, of 13 Muslims elected to parliament, eight were women. Hadia Tajik was the first Muslim member of the Norwegian parliament. In 2009 she was elected as an MP and three years later she was named minister of culture, the youngest ever Norwegian minister. Dunya Maumoon is the Muslim foreign minister of the Maldives.

In the broader cultural space, in Indonesia Sakdiyah Ma'ruf takes on traditional attitudes through her comedy. Detractors said she wouldn't succeed because she had too much of a message. But that's why she stands up: precisely so voices like hers can be heard. In

Kashmir, an all-female Muslim rock band created waves, but clerics condemned them. In Saudi Arabia, Haaifa Al Mansour was the country's first female film director with her film *Wadjda*. In the UK, newscaster and journalist Mishal Husain is one of the BBC's most popular faces, and recently became the first Muslim to anchor the BBC's flagship radio news programme *Today*. On rival Channel 4, Fatima Manji is the UK's first TV news anchor to wear a headscarf. In sports, Indian tennis pro Sania Mirza draws in the crowds, US fencer Ibtihaj Muhammad will be representing her country at the 2016 Olympics and Zahra Lari will represent the UAE in the ice skating at the 2018 Winter Olympics. Yasmin Mogahed is an Egyptian American whose book *Reclaim Your Heart* is a hit with Muslim women around the world looking for spiritual guidance on how to reconnect with the Divine. Lubna Olayan is a Saudi businesswoman, CEO of the $10-billion Olayan Financing Company, and named by Forbes as one of the world's most powerful women.

It's impossible to list the growing number of Muslim women across the globe who are breaking barriers, acting as role models and combining both their faith and their aspiration to make it big and change the world in a representative and all-encompassing way.

Balancing Family, Self and Workplace and the Shift in Gender Dynamics in the Home

A 2015 poll conducted by the *Guardian* newspaper and the think-tank Demos on British Muslims found that most young British-born Muslims reject the view that married women should stay at home while their husbands go to work, marking a shift in attitudes from older generations of Muslims in the UK. More than half of 16- to 24-year-olds disagreed with the statement 'A husband's job is to earn money, a wife's job is to look after the home and family.' Less than 24 per cent agreed. In contrast, 50 per cent of those respondents aged 55 or older agreed with the statement, while less than 17 per cent disagreed.

Women are becoming more educated and going to work, raising the average marriage age. In the UAE, this has risen from 18 to 24 in just ten years. In the marital home, the increased education, financial independence and worldliness of Generation M women are having an impact. Cooking patterns have started to change: working wives and mothers are cooking traditional foods – which can often be time consuming, and seen as a 'special' effort – only at weekends, whereas quick international foods are considered suitable during the week.

Recent years have seen the launch of several ready-made halal baby foods, pointing to the fact that no longer do Muslim women feel duty-bound to be slaving at the stove, but are in need of convenience foods to fit in with their busy lifestyles. Nasim Rizvi, a Norwegian Muslim mum, is the founder of Nasim's Halal Baby Food, which she started because there was little in the way of products to suit her baby:

> What I did was buy the baby food vegetable jars that were available in the market, I then boiled meat and chicken and added that to the mix. But it takes time. Being a mum, you are stressed and have a lot of other things to do – taking care of children, the home and other things.

She feels that the products offered to Muslim women are hugely behind the times.

> It was only 50 years ago that baby food was introduced to the western woman in Norway. But what is interesting is the amount of time it freed up for women, allowing them to work and do other things. It's a way of freedom.

The mother of five children adds, 'As a Muslim mum, I felt that all the other mothers had the opportunity to buy baby food on shelves but I could not.' Her range of products includes chicken, meat and fish and proudly sports halal logos. They are described as 'following the Quran's directions'. They are currently available in Norway and the UK, and Nasim has plans to expand to France and Germany. Housework around the world, including childcare, is disproportionately carried out by women, and Muslim households are no exception. However, we are starting to see change. In the UAE paternity leave is growing in importance. Rabea Ataya, founder and CEO of Bayt.com, said that following his own experience of taking a week of paid vacation after the birth of his first child, he introduced a week for his male employees. 'I realised when my wife delivered [our first child] I really needed to spend time with her and my newborn daughter. I couldn't imagine going back to the office the day after my wife had given birth.' And what if a male employee asked for six months of paternity leave? 'I've never been asked that question but I certainly hope that my answer would be "that's ok".'

This is in part being driven by a growing consciousness of Islamic duties. It's not just men being educated in their Islamic duties: wives are using their growing Islamic knowledge of their own rights. For instance, celebrity scholar Nouman Ali Khan has a series of video sermons on marriage responsibilities. His Facebook video 'What Are the Rights of the Wife?' has been shared over 43,000 times, and viewed nearly 1 million times.

In the travel industry, independent women travellers are increasingly coming onto the radar. With more money, marriage and child-bearing ages rising, and a fading away of taboos on Muslim women travelling alone, Generation M women are maximising the opportunities to travel, seek thrills and share time with friends. It's not unusual for Muslim women to head abroad and hire a private villa for a hen do. Women-only tours are arranged to Muslim heritage sites. And even when travelling with family, the requirements of women who want more privacy or facilities tailored specifically for women are pushing the hospitality industry to be more sensitive to the needs of the women in the group.

Knocking down traditional expectations of how Muslim women conduct themselves in society is at the very heart of what Generation M women expect. A 2010 study done by TNS in Saudi Arabia is a rare look at Muslim women's aspirations. According to Steve Hamilton-Clark, CEO of TNS MENA, in the 'Arab as a Consumer' study, 'women are motivated by technology, education and media. They are now demanding respect in all aspects of their lives, fuelled by external pressures and trends, including the growth of nuclear families and an increasing desire to expand social networks.'

'Figures show that 29 per cent of women feel that technology provides an avenue for self-expression, 32 per cent believe it provides the power from information and knowledge, and 30 per cent enjoy the community aspect of online communications,' he said. The findings revealed that key aspirations are freedom, fun, self-expression, respect, acceptance of overt beauty, as well as an increasing inclination to health and well-being. Steve Hamilton-Clark added, 'The boundaries of traditional husband and wife roles have been redefined, the expectations of marriage have changed, educated women want to work, and then find that being a working mother is challenging,' he said.

The survey also showed that 48 per cent of the participants felt that women in the workforce were an economic essential, and 44 per cent rated having a job as an important influence on confidence levels and self-esteem. Women worldwide face pressure in their home–work balance. Amina Jabbar, a Canadian doctor and activist, explores how this balance is framed through the lens of faith for Muslim women, and how these limits are 'implicit'.

> I grew up with a mother always insisting that I be an educated, professional woman. Her reasons were many, including that being a professional would help me retain a certain amount of flexibility and independence should crap hit the fan of life. I share the experience, not because it's the exception, but because it's common to the lives of many Muslimahs.

Some of these limits are professional:

> The stereotypes of hijabi women are, not surprisingly, often applied to all Muslim women: they are assumed to be meek, subservient and more interested in being married and starting a family. So, it's no surprise that Muslim women struggle with being hired and securing economic stability. In other words, the experience of the glass ceiling is different for Muslimahs.

There is often an assumption that a woman should be with the family:

Many Muslimahs have enormous domestic expectations. While my heart was set on Internal Medicine for a career, I'd be lying if I didn't tell you I thought twice about choosing this residency over Family Medicine, where schedules tend to be more flexible and the residency demands a bit more forgiving. The Muslim men I knew didn't talk about altering their career paths based on the pressures of getting married and having children. But Muslimahs have to 'balance' their careers with their families.

The most significant factor of all is how the balance is affected by traditionalist Islamic discourse. Generation M women are challenging this. 'Familial obligations are often discussed as religious obligations – as if Muslim women should really only be working if it doesn't interfere with raising children and maintaining life at home.' Other issues include the notion that the home is the 'natural' place for women and that there is something scary about independent women, a point always raised in discussions about the growing number of unmarried Muslim women. But Generation M women are themselves using Islamic teachings as a way to highlight that they can and should work and that shared responsibility for household duties is a must. What Amina is hoping for is a major change:

A real shift in media discourse on professional women, one that truly acknowledges the importance of women in Islam, would mean equitable sharing of gender roles within relationships based on principles of justice. Wrinkles of that impending change are evident in the blogosphere.

The work–life balance is just one of the many tensions facing Muslim women that are shared more generally with women around the world, although the framing may be different.

Another shared challenge is the objectification of women and increasingly sexualised imagery. Even women who veil experience this. Ask Google images about Muslim women and you'll get pages of the stereotypical black cloaks but there will also be pictures of nude women wearing nothing but a face veil. Or Lady Gaga in a gauzy neon pink burqa, Madonna with a bizarre niqab made of chain mail, or a Diesel ad of a naked tattooed woman and a denim burqa.

The female Muslim experience has something experimental to offer women in general. When so much of the feminist debate is dedicated to understanding what beauty, body and femininity mean when freed from the male gaze, these spaces already exist within the Muslim environment, where ubiquitous sexualisation of the female form is banished. There are women-only spaces created by Muslim women where a celebration of womanhood takes place beyond the male gaze. Weddings and parties are the most popular of these – often strictly women-only settings – where women can explore what it means to be beautiful and sexy for themselves. In this, say Muslim women, perhaps those industries concerned with how women look, or women's movements fed up with the body scrutiny, may find opportunities to explore how women themselves define who they are and their beauty.

'We have such a strong feminist tradition in Islam. I'm pretty tired of feminists not getting that,' says Sarah in San Francisco. Alaa in the UK echoes that frustration:

> So many Western feminists (white ones especially) suffer from tunnel vision when it comes to 'other' women's issues (despite claiming to fight for 'all' of us). I think, as a Muslim feminist, I have the advantage of bringing diversity and shedding light on issues that wouldn't normally get discussed by 'traditional' feminists. I believe Muslim feminists are advancing the movement and developing new feminist values that focus on the fact that women vary. We all define oppression/liberation based on our background and culture. [No] gender equality theory works for every single woman. The original wave of feminism lacked that. And that's what Islamic feminism brings to the table.

The really fascinating part of this growing assertion of freedom and rights is that it is being developed through their religion as Muslims. These young women are saying that they want equality and rights and that this is promoted by Islam. They are not abandoning their faith, as Western feminism demanded in its infancy (and continues to demand from Muslim women as both Alaa and

Sarah describe), they are entrenching themselves in their faith as the very means to secure their freedom. In fact, because many young Generation M women see faith as their primary motivator and framework for advancing women's empowerment, they are rejecting today's feminism because they feel it both excludes their viewpoint, and does not aspire to the greater blueprint of gender rights they feel is embedded within Islam.

These are some of the reasons that lie behind the horrific and bizarre allure for young women of organisations like Daesh. It is their very feminism, their belief that their faith empowers them, and their rejection of cultural traditions and norms that make them believe that the Caliphate is for them. However, this is a rare handful of women, and our Generation M women, who feel a strong sense of belonging within their societies and reject violence and hatred of the other, believe such women are misguided and have misinterpreted their faith.

Rejection of cultural norms in favour of religious ideals is motivating Muslim women to join the mainstream discussion about women's rights more generally. To support this, female religious scholarship and activism is on the rise, looking back at history to reclaim female role models and recontextualise the position and role models offered to Muslim societies today. There are translations of the Qur'an by women, and hadith studies reinterpreted from a feminist perspective. Of course, these are proving contentious but they are injecting female perspectives into conversations with traditionalists and traditional religious scholars. In Morocco, the female 'morchidat' are trained in religious and community matters and visit mosques and communities to offer guidance to women. In Singapore, the number of women on the mosque management boards that steer the mosques doubled in a decade from 63 in 2000 to 111 women in 2010. Of course, this is still hugely under-representative.

Two authors, J.E and Ismcdit, from the Project Silphium in Libya, write, 'I'm a Muslim and I'm a feminist', laying out their arguments about why Islam itself in both theology and history inspires them to support Muslim women's rights. First they address the idea that feminism is imposed by Western white saviours, advocating instead for 'Islamic feminism' which is grounded in an Islamic framework.

Then they refer to Islamic history and the prevalence of powerful female role models such as the wives of the Prophet. 'Many women believe they have to choose between being a Muslim and being a feminist but I believe I can be both. [...] I've never felt that my faith was at odds with being a feminist.'

Alaa, whom we met earlier, adds:

> Muslim feminists contribute to the wider movement by continuously trying to break the myth of 'Islamic patriarchy', which is patriarchy nonetheless. We stand up for our human rights from a pro faith perspective that differentiates our fights from white feminists, but at the same time, links us to them in terms of believing that men and women are made to be equal. And we have every right to believe in gender equality, because after all Islam is the first religion to actually give rights to women and view them as human beings.

Driving Innovation as Entrepreneurs and Consumers

'She knows what's important to her and that's all that matters,' explains the brand Friniggi. 'We're also not just about covering your body. We are well past that. Just like you are. We are about sports and your athletic experience. Just like you.' Most importantly: 'Compromising is a thing of the past.' The unwillingness to endure compromise is driving innovation.

Many Muslim women want to combine their aspiration to uphold their religious beliefs in wearing modest clothing with their desire for sports activities. Typical headscarves are not well suited for physical activity as they fall off, move around, the excess material can get caught, and the fabric is not comfortable when getting hot. Clothing too is a mismatch of non-sporting items which meet the modesty requirement but are not suited to sports. As a result, Muslim women who want modest clothing either find themselves exercising in inappropriate attire, which makes sports less enjoyable, or refraining from exercise totally, which leads to frustration.

In March 2014, FIFA authorised the wearing of the headscarf for Muslim women taking part in its official tournaments. In 2018,

Zahra Lari of the UAE will become the first Olympic figure skater to wear the headscarf.

> In my country women don't do much sport and even less figure skating. I want to encourage girls from the Emirates and the Gulf to achieve their dream too and not to let anyone tell them not to do sport, not only figure skating but all sports.

She said, 'I skate with the hijab, my costume is in line with Islamic tradition.' She chooses to dress modestly and to pursue her ambition. There is no compromise.

Women themselves are the drivers as well as the consumers of innovation, not content to wait to be given economic or social power, but grabbing it for themselves.

Aheda Zanetti, founder of the company Ahiida which we mentioned earlier as a producer of modest swimwear, introduced the word 'burqini'. She says,

> [I]f they did participate in sports with a veil, or whatever they wanted to wear, there really wasn't something suitable. The fabric was not right, the construction wasn't right.

She realised that there was a market for sportswear for Muslims when she saw her niece playing netball:

> When I was looking at her playing sport with a two-piece veil and a skivvy [long-sleeved, high-necked shirt] and the pants and then her netball jersey on top and then her skirt, I thought, 'Oh my God, there must be something better than this.'

Two halal organic cosmetics companies, One Pure Beauty and Saaf Skincare, were set up by women with cosmetics backgrounds, who became Muslim and found that there were no cosmetics products they believed genuinely met their religious aspirations as halal. So, they innovated, creating new products and businesses.

HiLo Soleha milk in Indonesia focuses on veil-wearing Muslim women's needs for Vitamin D and calcium due to reduced sunlight absorption. Again, it's a sharp insight into the lives of Muslim women.

When Muslim women see that their needs are not being met, they innovate. It's a sentiment that echoes throughout the activities and actions of the Generation M women who are empowering themselves through education, employment and their religion. They are determined to create something better for themselves, and for those around them. Ainee Fatima took a photo of herself with her leather jacket and aviator glasses. With the caption 'Forgot to be oppressed, too busy being awesome', her meme has gone viral. And that's no surprise, because it captures to a T the sentiment of our Generation M women.

13 SAMOSAS AND SU-SHI

Living as a Generation M Minority

It is Ramadan, and in North London Shazia Wahid, a UK Muslim food blogger, is excited to go into her local supermarket. She is enjoying seeing the large signs wishing shoppers Ramadan Mubarak, designed with traditional Islamic geometric patterns in shades of green, and the shelves of the long Ramadan aisle stacked with a mix of cooking basics and luxuries. 'The first Ramadan promotion I saw this year was at my local Tesco supermarket where they have an aisle specifically arranged with food aimed at Ramadan and mostly the Asian community,' she said. Of the company's 6,000 stores, in 2013, 315 carried the Ramadan promotion.

It's about more than shopping. 'It helps reinforce the feeling that I live in a country that accepts different people of different faiths,' according to Shazia.

Her excitement was tempered, though, by seeing that only foods from one or possibly two ethnic backgrounds were ranged, without reference to the diversity of Muslim heritages, nor to the growing sophistication of Muslim consumer palates. She was also disappointed in the absence of the innovation which other consumers are offered, the poor quality and the lack of healthy options.

The paradox of excitement at being recognised in the mainstream, while feeling that only second best is being served up, is a recurrent theme for Muslims who live as minorities around the world. They feel that they are not always recognised on a par with others, despite their own strong feelings of patriotism and belonging. Like Shazia, they are frustrated at being seen through a retrospective lens that focuses only on what their parents and grandparents were like, rather than what they themselves are like. Yes, British Muslims of South Asian origin might like a samosa or two, but they are also partial to all sorts of cuisine, from roast lamb to rendang, burgers to beef bacon, satay to sushi. And of course, British Muslims are a diverse bunch hailing from all around the world. Similar stories apply in other countries too.

By 2030 nearly 500 million Muslims will be living as minorities, and in South and South East Asia in particular, these minorities have long histories. India will have an estimated 249 million Muslims, the largest Muslim population in the world, outstripping Indonesia at 245 million and Pakistan with 230 million. Other notable minorities include China and Russia, which will reach 30 million and 17 million respectively. A whole raft of other countries, such as Thailand and Singapore, have sizeable, historical and influential Muslim minorities.

In the West, the USA will have over 5 million Muslims, France over 6 million and Europe's Muslim population as a whole will have grown from 43 million in 2010 to 57 million in 2030, and that is without even considering Turkey. Despite difficult political backdrops and tired arguments about clashes of civilisation, survey after survey finds that these Muslims see no conflict between faith and country, and are as patriotic – if not more so – than their peers. They are bringing their Muslim values – values which they translate as 'universal' – into the public domain. They are also opening doors to greater connectivity with their Muslim peers around the world. And with their rising numbers due to larger family sizes, and their improving educational and employment status, they have stronger spending power and are developing new companies and segments, particularly through the growth of halal.

This is a fascinating period of transition and cultural development that Generation M are at the heart of, taking a renaissance in Islamic consciousness and fusing it with several cultural heritages to create something new. The music, the look and the forms of expression are novel and fresh.

The Generation M protagonists find this process of identity creation is heightened for minorities precisely because of the limelight that is shone upon them. Paradoxically, the pressure from the wider culture, the tensions placed on immigrant populations and the focus the wider global Muslim population fixes on such well-documented minorities is creating a perfect storm for a new kind of Muslim culture.

It is just as much of a paradox that, whilst Muslims who were previously under the dominion of Western imperial powers want to turn towards their own growing global stature, they still watch carefully how those very same countries treat Muslims, and they follow the development of those minority Muslim populations. There are several notable historical Muslim minorities that show how local Muslim cultural variations take root in a country's own narrative. In South Africa Muslims have a history spanning more than 200 years and were a prominent part of the anti-apartheid movement. India's history is even deeper and longer, and there is great national introspection about the Mughal heritage and the place of today's Muslim population in the country's future, a point of tension with rising Hindu nationalism in India that seeks to exclude Muslim minorities.

The more scrutiny these minority Generation M populations face, the faster the cultural development, and in turn the greater their influence in driving wider Generation M development globally.

Local Islam Versus Global Islam, History Versus Future

'Not even many Indian Muslims know that we are the second largest Muslim population in the world,' says Shihab in Bangalore. The pride, power and substance of Muslim minorities is wildly underestimated in the global discourse, as is the variation in local Muslim cultures.

We have the second largest hajj quota after Indonesia. Waqf properties are the third largest landowners after defence and railways in India. Muslim businessman Azim Premji was the wealthiest Indian for ten years. We have Muslim personal law in India which grants us freedom to lead a life of our own choice as an Indian Muslim. Out of the 12 presidents of the Republic of India, three were Muslims. And though there is a ban on

beef slaughter in certain states in India we are still the largest
beef exporter in the world.

He smiles wryly. 'While there are issues that each and every country
faces, these are some of the insights to show how it feels to be an
Indian Muslim.'

There is no single way to be Muslim, and our global Muslims are
champions of diverse Muslim experiences. They feel themselves to
be firmly part of the ummah. Their values, attitudes and behaviours
are shared around the world, but they also have a strong sense of
local and national identity. In fact, they see themselves very firmly
as an important and vibrant part of their local culture.

Around the world core theology remains consistent, but its
application, culture and traditions show a natural variation as
a response to local conditions and history. So we have Muslim
Americans, Australian Muslims, South African Muslims and so
on. I can't emphasise enough how much in common Generation
M individuals have across all these local cultures, while also being
intimately tied into their local communities, countries and cultures.
They are proud of their diversity. One of their greatest achievements
is that they pull off this paradox with poise and aplomb. In fact,
their global values that echo with the distinct voice and culture of
their own countries is what defines Generation M: rooted in local
culture, united in global faith, aspiring to a better modernity.

One of their frustrations is asserting how significant their own
minority, such as the large Indian minority, is in the wider ummah.
Another is fighting the 'Arabisation' of the diverse ummah, a form
of assertion of their own local identity within the wider ummah.
'My frustration stems less from non-Muslim representation and
more from Muslim representation,' says Heather, in Columbia,
USA.

How often do you see Muslim pages posting pics/memes that
depict Muslims as anyone other than an Arab guy with beard
and white thobe and the woman wearing a black abaya and
hijab and niqab. Where is the representation of diversity? We
glorify Arab as ideal and everything from a culture that isn't
Arab as lesser!

Pride in local identity is important. 'We can wear our own culture's clothing and eat our food and all that stuff as long as those things meet Islamic standards. I want to see pictures of all the different ways we actually dress and eat as Muslims.'

Generation M want to ensure they are a firm part of their local community. They want to be included, not separate themselves. They believe that it is outrageous to think of them as a 'fifth column' rather than an integral part of society. Some of the ways in which their legitimacy is being asserted are through history and active community work, key means by which Generation M choose to engage with the wider world. We know that Generation M are proud of their heritage. They believe history is what gives a Muslim minority its local flavour. If they are built up of relatively new immigrant populations then they have strong cultural traditions which can differentiate them. Whilst they wish to uphold their cultural heritage, this is not how they wish to be defined in their entirety. The 'hyphenated identity' is a socio-cultural challenge which many young Muslims say they face.

Imran Garda, from Johannesburg, is a TV presenter and author. In his debut novel, *The Thunder that Roars*, his hero is Yusuf Carrim. In his description of Carrim, Imran could be describing himself, or any other Generation M individual:

> The young journalist has an exceptional grasp of world affairs, which he attributed to his hyphenated identity. He says, 'Well I sometimes wonder. Am I South African? Am I an Indian? Am I a Muslim? Rather, more wonderfully, am I all these things blended into one and created for a purpose? I have been obsessed with these issues, Middle Eastern politics, migration, social justice, for long as I remember. It could be all because I am a baby of the new South Africa. We were born into a miracle and an ideal, at the same time as our country reinvented itself and soothed the painful scars of racial oppression.

There's a pride in their complexity, and a strong sense of history.

Generation M want people to know about the history of Muslims in their own cultures. No wonder that Muslim Americans are looking back to see how and when Muslims arrived on the continent. Or why Australian Muslims want to showcase local Muslim history. Or why British Muslims talk about Britain's commercial trade with the Muslim world as early as the seventh century. The fluidity of exchange between Muslims and other nations and civilisations is something that minority Muslim populations in particular have promoted as a means of demonstrating a long tradition of positive interaction, into which they contextualise themselves.

These minority Muslim populations in Europe, North America and Australasia are generally a result of immigration over several centuries, and in particular the last half century, although there is a growing conversion story too. Identity is therefore being negotiated through a complex web of parental culture, their own new local culture and a global resurgence of faith. It is often their identity as Muslims that allows them to make sense of all these different elements.

This has some surprising consequences. Generation M may well appear to be more religious than their parents, whom they feel are 'cultural' Muslims, practising by virtue of inheritance from their previous majority Muslim cultures. As mentioned earlier, the growing phenomenon of young women wearing the hijab and niqab is often in contravention of their parents' wishes. Finding themselves in a minority situation, they have a thirst for religious learning which is not satisfied by the traditions taught by their parents, many of whom lack religious education for themselves.

It's the future that Generaton M are looking to: how they can contribute to their local communities, how their actions and traditions need changing, and their vision for where they live. Some of this is lived out through social change: marriages across ethnicities and theologies are increasingly common as young Muslims seek partners with shared values rather than ethnicities, seeing marriage as an individual choice rather than one that must be accepted due to tradition.

One of the great transitions that Generation M minorities are making is bridging the ethnic and theological divides that often spring up in the global Muslim ummah, some parts of which are unaware of other Muslims living as practising minorities. London-based Afshan reminisces about her travels:

When I was in Egypt, I was approached by a few people (which then turned into many interested parties!) [who asked] whether I was a Muslim despite my hijab and abaya, and if I could recite Qur'an? They promptly found a mushaf from which I read. There were gasps of amazement: a British-born, yet brown-skinned, non-Arab Muslimah in Cairo? I felt a bit like a celebrity.

Global Muslim connectivity is part of the power of minority Muslim populations if their countries learn to harness it properly, particularly in furthering national economic prosperity. When the UK prime minister David Cameron announced in 2013 that the UK would be working towards issuing £200 million in sukuk bonds it positioned London's stock exchange at the forefront of a growing global move towards Islamic finance. Due to the growing economies of majority Muslim nations, these bonds would allow the UK to access sovereign wealth funds and other financial instruments only open to Islamic finance. The relationship between the UK and countries which are championing Islamic finance, such as Malaysia and the GCC, is growing as a result.

The UK's Muslim population played an important role in securing such investment, thereby asserting their positive contribution to the nation. It has benefited them directly too with the government promising support for Islamic finance products in the consumer and investment spaces. The prime minister also said that 'no one should be denied access because of their faith.'

Countries like Australia, Spain and Japan are pushing hard to promote their Muslim-friendly credentials, showcasing their Muslim populations and history in order to tap into the growing Muslim tourism market. China's trade with the Muslim world has also grown in recent years. Again, the local Generation M are using their skills and location to the country's advantage. Often trained at religious madrassahs, they have learned to speak Arabic. Like Yang Jianyang, whom we met in Chapter 7, they act as the perfect cultural and language interpreters for Arab Muslim traders who come to China for business, enabling them to navigate linguistically as well as being properly supported in their food, accommodation and cultural needs.

Singapore has a well-established minority Muslim population, making up approximately 15 per cent of the country. It is well connected into the larger Muslim populations surrounding it in Malaysia and Indonesia. So well established is their position that the government even has a Ministry for Muslim Affairs, and halal food is regulated by MUIS, a government body. This reflects the small new nation's concern with harmony amongst the different populations. In recent years, the government enterprise body SPRING has been encouraging SMEs to develop the products, skills and branding to grow businesses aimed at Muslim audiences. The country's reputation for hygiene and technology, together with a Muslim minority that, albeit small in size, is well recognised and well connected regionally, have positioned it well to grow its halal credentials.

Feeling Loyal while Being Branded Disloyal

'Do you ever wish you were fully Aussie?' The Australian writer Randa Abdel-Fattah begins her essay with this question that has been posed to her. It is a sentiment familiar to our Generation M minorities, wherever they are in the world. In the essay 'Veils and Vegemite', published in the *Sydney Morning Herald*, she describes how the complex process of identity formation takes in history, multiple heritages and a social construction of values and ideals. She talks about her own struggles with faith, ethnicity and being Australian. 'One's past, whether ancestral or as a migrant, necessarily shapes one's present.'

Despite her own sense of being part of society, Randa feels exclusion is being imposed on her: 'Political rhetoric is spun, demands are made for citizenship tests, Australian values are invoked to justify an "us and them" mentality, some migrants are deemed less Australian.' She's blunt: 'Muslim and Australian are widely perceived as being mutually exclusive, as polar opposites. One does not need to adopt a victim complex to arrive at this rather obvious conclusion.'

It's the double standards that she believes are part of the problem:

The Australian-ness of a non-drinking Muslim bloke who steps out of work to go pray at lunchtime, or a woman at the bus stop with a suit and hijab on, is suspect. [...] Well, what about Orthodox Jewish women, I hear you protest. As a symbol of modesty, they cover their hair with a wig and expose their real hair only to their husbands. And what about nuns who also wear a veil? And Mormons, who have strict dress codes and also do not drink? So many similarities between Islam and other faiths and yet for every five or more documentaries a week about Muslims, Muslim women or the veil, there are virtually none about the almost identical principles of modesty found in Judaism, or Paul's admonition to women in Corinthians that their hair should be cut off if it is not covered.

There are legitimate wider questions to be asked about what it means to be a minority, one that minority Muslims are posing themselves. They believe they have duties to their nation, but equally the nation needs to invite them in and treat them like everyone else, just as Randa's description suggests.

In the spring of 2013 in Sri Lanka, serious violence broke out among local Buddhists when the government said it was considering a halal certification scheme. The scheme was aimed at the domestic Muslim community. As a bonus, it would help establish a place for the country's products in the growing world halal economy. The local body of Islamic clerics who proposed the scheme subsequently withdrew it in the interests of local harmony. Maintaining peace was the right thing to do, but a loss for local Muslims and a blow for Sri Lanka's share of 2020's forecast $2.6 trillion global Muslim consumer spend.

It's a common story: halal is all too often hijacked by political narratives, a political football for deeper ethnic and religious tensions. In 2014 in the UK, British Muslims felt the brunt of such discussions when halal meat processes came under scrutiny for allegedly being inhumane, even though after investigation it turned out that halal processes were on the whole extremely similar to non-halal processes.

In 2014 in France, Marine Le Pen, the leader of the far-right Front National party, stated that in areas where her party won local elections religious requirements would not be tolerated in school meals, and alternative non-pork meals would not be offered to children. In France, all children must eat the meals provided at school. The bottom line, reported via the media, was that her position was 'eat pork or starve'. It was a clear dig at France's huge Muslim population, and more fuel to the halal controversy in France which Le Pen has been stirring, in the process producing anti-Muslim hatred.

Of course, in spite of being aimed at Muslims, the ruling would also affect France's notable Jewish population requesting kosher food at school as well as vegetarians who also would have no alternative meals offered to them. This alliance between Muslims and Jews in minority countries over religious rituals such as food operates quietly but effectively. The discrimination that the two minorities face is also linked. According to the 2007 Gallup poll published in *Who Speaks for Islam?*, rising Islamophobia is directly correlated with rising anti-Semitism. When hatred towards one group rises, it shows an increase in hatred for the other group too; societies with Jewish and Muslim minorities ought to take note.

These controversies about the availability of halal meat in minority Muslim countries are a snapshot of the wider challenges facing minority Muslim populations who find themselves negotiating their faith with local cultures. With the global political climate concentrating since 9/11 on the 'War on Terror' and the current global villains being Muslims, it's easy to see how minority Muslims are the scapegoats for anger.

Yet the beliefs that such minority Muslim populations hold about their relationship with the countries where they live is consistent around the world: they are proud, patriotic and optimistic. In 2011, French halal ready-meal brand Isla Délice ran an advertising campaign with the strapline 'Fièrement halal' – proud to be halal. The imagery featured icons that are recognised as part of French cookery heritage, referencing the very French passion for good food. The panels were displayed in a main square in Paris and therefore would have attracted attention from non-Muslims as well as Muslims. 'Fièrement halal' is a direct and clear statement to its target audience that halal produce can be bought in the public space and goes hand in hand with their pride in being French.

Fighting Discrimination but Determined Not to Play the Victim Card

'The greatest challenge I personally have been struggling with for years is institutional racism. I have felt barriers in going for jobs, there are greater obstacles because of my dress,' says Saleem from Blackburn, in the north of England. 'I feel it is practically impossible to go beyond a certain level in most places in the public sector without hitting a glass ceiling, in particular for conspicuously practising Muslims.' And yet despite feeling powerfully dejected by his experiences of discrimination, he remains positive. You can almost hear his chest puffing out with pride. 'Besides this, overall, I feel proud living in Britain and believe there is no better alternative place for Muslims to live in the world.'

Saleem's sense of discrimination is not something that he is imagining. Muslims face the worst job discrimination of any minority group in Britain, according to research which found that they had the lowest chance of being in work or in a managerial role. Muslim men were up to 76 per cent less likely to have a job of any kind compared to white, male British Christians of the same age and with the same qualifications. And Muslim women were up to 65 per cent less likely to be employed than white Christian counterparts. Another study by UK think-tank Demos found that Muslims are half as likely to hold a professional or managerial job as the average Briton, and are substantially more likely to be unemployed, or living in poverty.

There's a similar story in France. According to Paris-based think-tank the Montaigne Institute, men who self-identify as Muslims are more than four times less likely to get a job interview in France than their Catholic counterparts, with only a 4.7 per cent chance of being asked to interview for a job, compared to a 17.9 per cent chance for a practising Catholic. Marie-Anne Valfort, a senior lecturer at Sorbonne University in Paris, who carried out the study, says that many French citizens associate Islam with religious extremism and the oppression of women. 'These two stereotypes feed a very strong discrimination, particularly regarding male Muslims. The recruiter perceives an increased risk of transgressive religious practice in the workplace and associates it with a risk of insubordination.'

No wonder Generation M in particular, having grown up with this backdrop, feel frustrated at the conflicting demands to 'prove' loyalty and integration, at the same time as feeling that they are denied the opportunities that the wider population has. They don't play the victim, but they do feel short-changed.

In 2006, CNN-IBN-Hindustan Times conducted a survey of 29 Indian states and concluded that Muslims suffered under a 'myth of extra-territorial loyalty', pointing to the fact that all but 2 per cent of Muslims said they were 'proud' or 'very proud' of being Indian. Levels of pride in being Indian were at almost identical levels between Hindus and Muslims.

In 2009, the Coexist Index published by the Coexist Foundation in conjunction with Gallup found that European Muslims show as much or more loyalty to their country as the wider public. Fully 86 per cent of British Muslims said they were loyal to the UK, compared with just 36 per cent of the wider population who saw themselves as loyal. French Muslims identify with France as much as the general French public (52 per cent versus 55 per cent). In Germany 40 per cent of Muslims identified with the country, as against 32 per cent of the wider public. If anything, they see their faith as making them better citizens, in the drive to be honest, loyal and law-abiding, as well as working to make their wider societies better for everyone.

A 2011 Gallup poll in the USA on religious groups paints a picture of Muslim American communities characterised by optimism while seeking acceptance by fellow citizens and suffering high levels of discrimination. Among Muslim Americans 93 per cent said they were loyal to America, and they were more hopeful about their lives than other groups. All this is despite the fact that 48 per cent of Muslim Americans report that they have experienced some kind of racial or religious discrimination, far more than Protestants, Catholics, Jews, Mormons or atheists.

'Living in the USA and being exposed to so many different Muslims from so many different countries and cultures made me realise that there are many faces to Islam,' says Samar, who lives, writes and teaches in Florida.

Instead of becoming distanced from the faith she grew up with in the Middle East, it was when she moved to the USA and started having to defend herself as a Muslim that her faith deepened.

Being Muslim in America has meant for me to be waiting to answer the next e-mail circulating, which could be describing how an American Muslim can never be a good citizen because we have to kill Christians and Jews. The more I received these e-mails, the more I learned about my faith and discovered that it also talks about embryology and geology, geography and astronomy.

Despite the hostility, she says that 'being Muslim in America makes me a better Muslim, one with more hope for the future.'

Minorities within Minorities

Within minority Muslim populations there is huge diversity. Whilst Generation M's defining characteristic is their shared faith and the importance of that faith in their lives, we must not mistakenly assume homogeneity among them. Generation M are deeply antagonistic to the notion that one ethnicity carries more importance than another. At the same time, one of the frustrations of Generation M is that Muslim populations themselves also hold stark prejudices about other groups within the wider Muslim community. Mosques in some countries will often be divided along ethnic lines, and cultures may vary between them too. Intra-Muslim racism is too often a taboo subject.

Negotiating the culture and politics of minority Muslim populations, in particular where they are predominantly also immigrants, is a challenge for the growing number of converts to Islam. Islam is the fastest growing religion in the West. But for converts – who are leaving behind faith, culture and often family too – whilst the religion itself may feel like coming home, the cultural experiences of Muslims can make them feel like outsiders.

Sadly, they may experience rejection from the more traditional elements of the Muslim population and complain of feeling isolated. They often feel frustration at being overlooked in mainstream discourse about Muslims.

There is a further hostility that converts have to deal with, which is anger from those who feel that they have created a betrayal through their conversion to Islam; this hostility can be quite vehement. Canadian convert Chelby says dealing with a majority non-Muslim population brings challenges. 'When people hear I'm a convert, they go, "you chose this? There's something wrong with you. What rational modern person chooses this religion?"' She adds, 'There's a suspicion of converts and what we actually believe.' Part of this is the media coverage of converts who have gone on to commit extreme atrocities, and who have attracted disproportionate attention for their convert status. She says: 'You do see good converts, you just don't notice them.'

What's frustrating for Chelby is that 'We're a double minority. We're not understood by the public community and we're not understood by Muslims either.' Because mosques are typically dominated by one ethnicity, she explains, 'Converts in many respects don't feel connected to existing, mosque-based Islamic communities.'

Across the mosques and Muslim communities in any minority Muslim country, there is diversity in school of thought as well as ethnicity, minorities within minorities. Shi'a Muslims often feel that their beliefs are seen as an afterthought and not included in mainstream Muslim traditions, or worse, actively excluded, even with hatred being fomented. Alongside some theological differences, Shi'a Muslims in particular mark two events, Ashura and Arba'een, which note the remembrance of the massacre of the grandson of the Prophet, Husain, his family and supporters.

Familiar imagery of these events is of groups of people dressed in black, visiting mosques, and many travelling to Iraq to visit the place where Husain is buried at Karbala. Whilst the new year for Muslims is a muted affair, for Shi'a Muslims it would therefore be considered an affront to create a festive or celebratory atmosphere during this period. Alongside visits to Makkah, Madinah and Jerusalem as holy cities, they would also visit Karbala, Najaf, Samarrah and Kufa in Iraq. Damascus was also amongst these destinations until the Syrian civil war began, and other destinations include Amman, Cairo, Mashad and Qum.

In order to recount their own experiences, perspectives and narratives as Shi'a Muslims, specific media is also being developed by Generation M Shi'a Muslims, including publishing houses and TV stations. Shi'a Muslims often live as minorities in majority (Sunni) Muslim nations, and global political events mean that tensions can rise between Muslims. Daesh proclaims the annihilation of Shi'a Muslims as one of its goals. Incidents like a massacre of Shi'a Muslims in a Pakistani snooker hall or employment discrimination in countries like Saudi Arabia and Bahrain remain very real challenges.

On a day-to-day level, their identity and culture is part of the Generation M landscape. But they feel they still need to reach out to build bridges. 'Living in the West means that you are interacting with people from different ethnic and religious backgrounds. Therefore we have ensured that our content is understandable to those groups,' says Amir Taki, director and executive producer of English-language Ahlulbayt TV, which aims to air programming inspired by the teachings of Shi'a Islam. He holds a first-class honours degree in television journalism. He sees the channel as a way to tackle hostility towards Muslims, and Shi'a Muslims in particular:

> As a broadcaster which reaches to all communities, our duty is to educate people about the basic tenets of Islam and try to alleviate the misconceptions and stereotypes which have been created against our faith. We believe that through education and engagement, more and more people will understand and accept us for who we are.

A natural consequence of Generation M's connectivity is inter-marriage, which theologically and ethnically proves challenging to the spouses and to their wider families more familiar with marriages between people sharing the same ethnicity and school of thought. These Sunni–Shi'a unions have even gained their own status, almost a symbol of pride, and also recognition of how they are increasingly common – they are called 'Su-Shi'.

Roshan, a Sunni from Pakistan, describes how marrying a Shi'a Muslim changed her understanding of the country's Shi'a Muslim minority as she spent more time with her husband's extended family. 'I was in the thick of it, yet not "one of them". At times I did feel I stuck out like a sore thumb. Over time, I realised that that is exactly how the Shi'as feel all the time [...], marginalised.' Whilst the theory of the Muslim ummah is a glowing testament to egalitarianism and unity, the reality of minorities is quite different. 'Sadly, we as a nation tend to single out our minorities and are not very tolerant of someone "different", the prejudice being based on ethnicity, religion, sect or anything that differentiates.'

In Indonesia, Muhammad is concerned about the growing number of attacks on Shi'a Muslims like him. He is married to Sunni Muslim Khadija. 'So far, my children have never been harassed by their friends at school,' he says, but here is the crux of worries for minorities: 'basically, no matter how small the differences you have with others, when you are in the minority, they can lead to conflict.' He says that the main thing he would tell his children is never to flaunt their differences to others. For them, unity is the most important thing. Both Muhammad and Khadijah involve themselves in as many community service activities as possible: 'We must show people that we just want to do good here and that we're not here as part of an exclusive group.'

Asserting Themselves Against Extremist Voices

Kübra Gümüşay received her first death threat at the age of 21. The daughter of Turkish immigrants, Kübra might well be Germany's first hijab-wearing Muslim columnist. She says that when she was given her bi-weekly column: 'I suddenly was expected to defend my religion and the millions of people who practise it.' This comes with a pressure, often self-imposed. She says, 'I was terrified. My editor said, "Write about you", but I only heard, "Write for the entire Muslim community."'

Germany's Turkish Muslim minority is 2.7 million strong. The rate of unemployment among Germans of immigrant descent is higher than those with non-immigrant backgrounds – 5.6 per cent versus 3.1 per cent. Kübra wants to help others express themselves and launched a social media campaign on Twitter under the hashtag #SchauHin for Germans to discuss the racism they encounter on a daily basis.

The man who sent her the death threat wanted to explain to her why he was more German than she was, and shared details with her of how he was going to kill her. Kübra's weapon of choice against extremist voices is storytelling. Four years after the threat, she wrote about her wedding. 'After I published [it], he wrote again, saying he realised I was "just another human being". The man ended up apologising.' It's a strategy that is deployed across minority Muslim populations, often effective, although sadly not always with such positive outcomes.

It's not just far-right or racist extremists that are being tackled. Raising their voices against violent Muslim extremism such as Daesh is of equal concern. In Germany in September 2014, when Daesh was rising in notoriety, thousands of German Muslims came together for a day of nationwide protests against the organisation in a 'Day of Peace'. Instead of yielding to Muslim extremist voices to isolate themselves from wider society, to do hijrah migration to Muslim lands or to the so-called Caliphate, Generation M are doing the opposite, reaching out across the divide and strengthening their community relations.

Following the murders at the *Charlie Hebdo* offices in January 2015, Mehdi in Berlin changed his status on Facebook to read: '1. I am aghast at the act of terror and my thoughts are with the families of those murdered. 2. Were the Prophet Muhammad alive today, he would surely have made clear: #notinmyname.' The 26-year-old law student immigrated to Germany from Lebanon. A Shi'a Muslim, he goes to the mosque regularly and fasts during Ramadan. He also goes to cafés with his friends, plays football, enjoys German poetry and hopes to get his PhD. He says that the Muhammad caricatures were tasteless and insulting, but the terrorists, he continues, did more to insult Islam than the caricaturists ever could. Despite this, he is worried. 'I am afraid that Paris could strengthen the extremists, particularly racists, for whom the attack represents an opportunity.'

Mehdi, like his peers, is constantly walking a fine line between extremists on all sides, rejecting the ideologies that they profess and which feed off each other. Generation M see themselves as the voices of balance and moderation, duty-bound to fight all extremism, but also to vociferously reject violent Muslim extremism as an abomination of their faith, in order to safeguard Muslims and instigate tolerance and harmony in the societies of which they are part.

The Business of Ordinary Day-to-Day Life: Inclusivity, Courage and Values

According to Adnan Durrani, the founder and CEO of American Halal Co. Inc., which wholly owns the halal ready-meal brand Saffron Road, most Muslim Americans are:

> uplifted by finally being validated, even if to date only nominally, as meaningful American consumers. At Saffron Road, we have received hundreds of letters from passionate Muslim consumers affectionately thanking us for providing halal options to a community of millions of Americans that hitherto had zero national availability of halal products.

He's right: almost 90 per cent of respondents in a study we carried out with Muslim Americans about their thoughts on brands' engagement in the mainstream felt that most American brands and businesses don't understand Muslim values. Adnan says, to illustrate this point,

> New York City ranks one in America in terms of the number of hotels and yet this Ramadan, I could not find one (out of 700!) that offered or supported the pre dawn 'suhoor' meal to its guests, let alone even understood what that was.

Our study showed that 86 per cent of Muslim American consumers believed that American companies 'need to make more of an effort to understand Muslim values', and 98 per cent felt that American brands 'don't actively reach out to Muslim consumers'. This is despite the fact that these consumers show the potential to be an extremely loyal customer base, with over 80 per cent saying that they would prefer to buy brands that support Muslim identity through promotion and celebration of religious festivals. Adnan adds: 'These consumers are still not at a point of walking in to a Hallmark or CVS and being able to buy an Eid or Ramadan greeting card.'

There is a clear expectation that they should be treated like anyone else going shopping and have their dollar carry equal importance as any other. Almost 75 per cent of respondents wanted brands to 'make Muslims feel like an integral part of the wider community, not a marginal group'. Muslims instead feel that the lack of recognition they perceive on high-street shelves is in itself a way to exclude them from the mainstream discourse.

Muslim Americans feel that brands have more successfully engaged with Muslim consumers outside the USA than within it. What is equally interesting is that our US Generation M Muslims were the tech-savviest among the Muslim population as a whole whom we asked about this; 63 per cent of them believed that commercial engagement with Muslims might be better outside the USA. Of their non-Generation-M counterparts, almost 50 per cent said they didn't know enough to judge, all of which points to the greater connectedness and more informed nature of our protagonists. Muslim American consumers feel a deep need for inclusion in the fabric of American life, especially in such troubled times, and believe that brands and the corporate world have a responsibility to promote inclusivity.

In 2011, Prudential became one of America's first brands to include a Muslim as part of its TV advertising campaign. The placement was to promote retirement planning. Hundreds of people across the USA were asked to photograph their first day of retirement. These photos and the accompanying documentaries were collated on a website displaying this user-generated content. As part of this creation of nationwide stories, Prudential developed a range of adverts looking in detail at several different individuals and their needs for retirement planning. One of these was a Muslim retiree called Mujahid Abdul Rashid. The story depicted his family life and the importance he placed on planning, in the same ordinary-American style of the entire series of documentaries. As with all the other documentaries, Abdul Rashid was a real person, not a character. And while a name like 'Mujahid' (a person who undertakes jihad) might ordinarily have sparked panic through misunderstanding, it was used in the commercial without any worry.

This was possibly the first mass-market product commercial where a person who is identifiably Muslim is depicted in an ordinary, everyday American setting. For Muslim consumers, this was incredibly powerful. The only disappointing note in this excellent engagement by Prudential is that it didn't step up and show pride in depicting an ordinary Muslim as part of its target consumer base. Of course the praise that the campaign has received may well encourage Prudential and other brands to deepen their engagement with Muslim consumers.

The presence of Muslims in advertising in minority Muslim countries is growing, as shown in the examples we mentioned earlier: DKNY, Zara, Mango, H&M, Uniqlo, Coca-Cola. Just like The Halal Guys we met from New York, whose street corner cuisine is set to go national in America, Generation M are very comfortable with – even demand – the fact that just like other parts of the population, their identity must be accepted as part of the mainstream.

These trends are replicated over and over across the minority Muslim world. Events like Ramadan, which are of course hugely significant to Muslims, once passed under the radar in minority Muslim countries, but now are growing in prominence. Of course it's worth noting that in countries like Singapore, India and other African nations where Muslim minorities have a longer history, those occasions are almost a feature of national life.

In 2013, one of the UK's leading broadcasters ran an entire series of programming dedicated to Ramadan, including the early morning call to prayer to signal the beginning of the fast. Navid Akhtar – who has gone on to found the TV channel Alchemiya – was the producer behind the adhaan video that has now become iconic, featuring a young British Muslim Qur'an reciter walking across the urban backdrop of London. He also created a series of two-minute reflections broadcast every night by British Muslims, discussing their faith and their place in the country. It was a ground-breaking move, the first time that Ramadan had been marked in the mainstream media in a consistent and fully committed way. Channel 4 noted that viewing of the channel at the approximate 3 a.m. slot when the morning call to prayer was broadcast grew, and the overall viewing figures for the month stood at an impressive 5.3 million, which included Muslims and non-Muslims alike.

Clearly, brands that show courage in reaching out to Muslim audiences despite hostile voices in the marketplace are amply rewarded with loyalty and praise. In 2009 US consumer electronics retailer Best Buy prompted a backlash when it referenced the Muslim festival of Eid in a holiday flyer. Best Buy stood by its decision, winning the support of Muslim consumers in the process. More recently, in 2011 a marketing campaign by health food supermarket chain Whole Foods to promote Saffron Road halal foods during the month of Ramadan also faced criticism. It too held firm, and sales of Saffron Road products went up 300 per cent and Whole Foods acquired a new segment of customers.

Later that year, TV channel TLC began airing an eight-part series called *All-American Muslim*, which followed the lives of five Muslim American families in Dearborn, Michigan. The pilot episode polled the second-highest ratings for the station's reality TV shows. Predictably, the show stirred controversy but TLC kept it on the air and it continued to gain ratings. From a brand perspective this kind of courage was proof that addressing Muslims can and does pay off, and that mainstream America is ready and willing to watch.

The fall-out from the show was fascinating. The far right pressured advertisers to pull their airtime, claiming that the show was trying to make terrorists look normal. One of the advertisers, Lowe's, capitulated. It turned out that it had given in to a pressure group consisting of just one person. In the mainstream press, by contrast, debate focused on how wrong Lowe's was; many Muslims as well as non-Muslims withdrew their custom, and a discussion was kicked off in the USA about the $170 billion spending power of Muslim Americans – and, more significantly, about their right to be treated like everyone else.

Finding the right language for dialogue with Generation M's Muslim minorities is vital. They want to be part of the mainstream debate, but are aware that – rightly or wrongly – any public discussion of their place in society must be handled with sensitivity, because some will refuse to hear them and instead react with hostility. A universal language of values is a central part of Generation M's global approach to reach across barriers and establish co-operation, mutuality and dialogue.

In the UK in 2012, a small Muslim charity launched a campaign called 'Inspired by Muhammad' to tackle some of the underlying prejudices about what Muslims believe, in particular about the Prophet Muhammad. It featured the faces of British Muslims, and a statement about how their lives were inspired by their faith and its Prophet. Sultana Tafadar, a human rights lawyer, appeared in the campaign, and accompanying her picture the strapline stated: 'I believe in women's rights. So did Muhammad.' Rupon Miah, a front-line worker at a homelessness charity declared, 'I believe in social justice. So did Muhammad.' The aim of the campaign was to find language that communicated the values of Islam, but framed in the language of contemporary social discourse to engage with the wider world.

Asil describes herself as having grown up in three different countries and five cities. After finishing her degree in Melbourne, Australia, she moved to Japan. She encapsulates the worry, the pride and the aspiration of Muslims who live as minorities.

> I understand that the current situation makes us feel unsafe, unwanted, and alienated. The current fear-mongering in Australia clearly demonstrates that the hysteria is in no one's benefit, whether you are Muslim or not. While the fear of being attacked or abused remains, the only thing Muslims can do now is to be the best and do the best that you can. You have to be the best person you can be, whether you are a mother, father, daughter, son, neighbour, professional, artist, teacher, scientist, student, or shop owner.

Despite the obstacles and challenges of living as a minority, the positivity remains. Fatema says:

> It's been seventeen years since I moved to Britain from Kenya, a country where although Muslims were in a minority, the culture and Islam was a huge part of the country and you would never feel different or out of place [...] Seventeen years on and even after being at the receiving end of three Islamophobic attacks – one major – I still feel very much at home. As a minority, yes I sometimes have to explain the what, how and why but it has made me more aware of the essence of Islam and rather than blindly following, it's made me profoundly reflect on the way of life Islam dictates that we follow. Hand on heart, the essence of what makes us human and the humanity I have found within most people in Britain makes me feel blessed to have come here.

14 BELIEF! COMMUNITY! ACTION!

*Generation M's Faith Means a
Better Future for Everyone*

A bedroom in your parents' home seems a good place to start an organisation that's going to change the world. Steve Jobs built his first 50 computers in such a bedroom, which turned into the global corporation Apple. Eighteen-year-old Mohammed Sadiq Mamdani founded something quite different: the Muslim Youth Helpline. It is a confidential telephone service to counsel young Muslims through personal difficulties. Fourteen years later it has 80 staff and has won numerous awards.

Despite facing scepticism about the initiative when it first launched, he says: 'I was determined to make my vision a reality and push-start the momentum towards greater recognition of the identity conflict which Muslim youth growing up endure.' He realised from his own personal experience that the 'lack of support systems both within their own communities and mainstream service providers fuels the sense of isolation and need.' So he set up the helpline as a response.

The social engagement that drives Mohammed and so many others like him is rooted in their faith and requires them to act – an itch to be constantly doing more, to help everyone, no matter what their background. He also set up Al-Mizan Charitable Trust, a Muslim grant-funder which supports disadvantaged people and deprived communities across the UK, regardless of their faith or cultural background. The trust provides small grants and interest-free loans of up to £500 to groups such as the elderly, infirm and disabled, single parents and those who have suffered bereavement, domestic violence or abuse.

He's a trustee of the Foundation for Social Entrepreneurs, a charity that promotes social entrepreneurship by offering financial awards and support packages to individuals with creative ideas for achieving social objectives. He has won numerous awards, including the Whitbread Young Achievers Award, which noted, 'Mohammed is an inspirational example of what young volunteers can do in their communities, through determination and commitment.'

Believing in Islamic values is the motor behind the actions of those like Mohammed, actions which must continue as long as they see that change is required. Mohammed says: 'The work never stops although we're also working in the sector where we strive to work ourselves out of a job!' There are four key ways in which this group reaches out not just to the ummah but to the wider global community, putting their faith values and their grounding in modernity to the uses for which they believe they were intended: arts and cultural exchange, charitable and community work, business and commerce, and politics. All of these ideals resonate with our Generation M individuals, each of whom will grasp one or more as their personal preference. Their Islamic values offer them a blueprint for their actions, and modernity offers new ways and new approaches to achieve outreach, engagement and success. It is all about the practical application of knowledge and belief.

Arts and Cultural Exchange: Standing in Each Other's Shoes

'Sometimes clothes have a larger impact than politics,' says Iman Aldebe. She is working on an Islamic clothing line for both men and women in the Arabian Peninsula, particularly Riyadh and Dubai. Now based in Stockholm, she grew up in Jordan, where she studied design at school and started creating dresses for friends. Her collections are sold in Sweden, Paris and Dubai. 'I'm always at the forefront because I've worked with Muslim fashion during a large part of my upbringing,' she says.

Making art out of fashion has always been a tool for her to try to eliminate prejudices. 'I want to show the emergence of strong, individualistic, intelligent, independent and driven women with a different background from the Swedish one, and that are Muslim,' she explains. 'I've wanted to eradicate the image of the oppressed Muslim woman that voluntarily isolates herself from society to live on welfare and produce babies.'

In the twenty-first century showcasing Islamic art has become an increasingly popular method for Muslims to reach out, and it has also been promoted by major institutions, particularly in the aftermath of the events of 11 September 2001. There is a palpable desire to open channels of dialogue and reclaim Islam's artistic heritage in the modern world through arts and culture. After all, art is traditionally a vehicle through which to make sense of our shared place in the world, and which acts as a safe space to discuss thorny cultural and political issues.

The Metropolitan Museum of Art in New York reopened its Islamic art galleries at the end of 2012 after an eight-year closure. Its curator, Navina Najat Haidar, described how Islamic arts can illuminate the meaning that Islam brings to a vast global population: 'Islam is not a single lens through which we view and interpret the art [...] Rather, it's an inverted lens that reveals great diversity.'

In the Louvre in Paris, an Arts of Islam gallery, with a specially designed roof inspired by an Islamic veil, has been recently opened. In Canberra, Australia, a Muslim group is seeking to build an Islamic art and history museum to 'educate people on their magnificent contribution' and on the nation's long history of trading with Muslims from what is now Indonesia, long before the arrival of the first white settlers. This development would also strengthen ties with two of Australia's biggest trading partners, Indonesia and Malaysia. There is a lovely symmetry to highlighting historical trade and cultural relationships in order to foster future trade and culture.

In 2012, the world's first known hajj exhibition was held at the British Museum in London, and gathered praise from around the world. It moved audiences away from the political discourse about Islam and into the human experience of being Muslim. One of the curators of the exhibition, British Muslim Qaisra Khan, captured this by expressing her aspiration that the show would allow people 'to stand in Muslim shoes'. In the Gulf too there has been a mushrooming of museums and galleries being commissioned and opened over recent years, attempting to tell the story of the region's heritage.

The idea of connecting via the human experience expressed through arts is captured by pop star Maher Zain, who says, 'Who can argue with a song?', which could apply to any form of artistic expression. In the UK, Khayaal Theatre Company brings together 'artists and audiences of different faiths and secular traditions to harness and mobilise the inclusive energy of shared story'. The aim is 'to connect hearts and foster greater intercultural and interfaith dialogue, understanding and engagement between Muslim communities and the wider world'. The company performs stories from around the Muslim world. Having toured globally, the founder and creative directors, Luqman Ali and Eleanor Martin, explain how shared spaces for Muslims and non-Muslims can create practical exchange. 'We believe that through working with these stories, making them more accessible to a wider contemporary audience, we can help to disprove the much bandied-around concept or thesis of a "clash of civilizations",' says Luqman.

Of course, cultural exchange doesn't need to be in the 'high arts'. Generation M are keen to pioneer street-level exchanges of culture too. In one cultural initiative in Norway, an invitation was sent out from Muslims 'to invite you to their house for a cup of tea'. A national TV campaign was run, with the advert introducing Muslims as individuals by their name, offering respect and personalisation. It also introduced something they enjoy personally, such as 'dancing' or 'being a princess', as one child explained. Invitations were sent to local leaders and communities. As this was a social campaign, Facebook was heavily utilised to share the invitation too. Even the queen received an invitation and went to tea at a Muslim home.

A concept deeply rooted in the Muslim psyche – hospitality – was thus translated into a concept deeply rooted in Norwegian culture – the welcome into the home. This was a mutual engagement. The invitation was personal: 'Will you come to my home for a cup of tea?', underscoring how Muslims believe the individual is part of a community, and that individual action is paramount. Further, the campaign humanised Muslims in their day-to-day lives, as ordinary people. The shared cultural symbolism of the cup of tea evoked similar values in both parties participating: peace, hospitality and neighbourliness.

Nahla from Cairo explains why she thinks art is the most powerful way to connect with Muslims, and why as a language of mutual exchange it resonates so deeply with her as a Muslim: 'I feel art elevates the soul to a different level, even more with Islamic art, it puts me in a state of meditation. There's always less of the self and more of the universe around. I believe it's contagious.'

Charitable Projects and Community Work

'Charitable and community work is where you can have a different perspective to the people you are working with but still collaborate on achieving the same goal,' says Anna in London.

The giving of financial resources is a core obligation as well as a recommended act for Muslims, but so is giving of your time and skills, hence there is also an emphasis on community work. Anna explains:

It creates a respect that bridges divides because it makes you realise that you can achieve great things together, even if you differ on your worldview. It is community work that taught me that mutual respect is an appreciation of the good in other people, in spite of their difference to you.

Her method is action-oriented. She talks about her own volunteering efforts working across communities:

It gave me humility towards difference, respect for other people's views and an unshakable knowledge that goodness lies in intentions and actions, not in the pathway you choose to reach God [...] There is something about working towards the better good that makes you realise that for all the intellectualising we do of faith, for all the politicking, actually the most important aspect of a person is their action, their morals and their desire to achieve good.

Generation M's eyes are always on the ultimate prize of spirituality and faith; action is the means. 'Community work I think not only opens your mind and ability to respect, it enhances your ability to understand the world and people in it at a higher spiritual level that goes beyond doctrine.'

In 2011, in the wake of the protests in Tahrir Square in Egypt, many public arenas were left in disarray. Individuals in civic society spontaneously got together to care for their shared spaces and return them to their previous state. This surge of civic pride was impulsive and showed that the community cared about its environment and felt that everyone shared responsibility for the improvements.

Household cleaning products Persil detergent and Pril dish-washing liquid were involved in volunteer drives to clean up districts affected during the uprisings. Volunteers cleaned, scrubbed and repainted sidewalks and walls either damaged or covered in grafitti. The objective of the activity was to help people make Egypt a cleaner and better place. The companies provided rubbish trucks and bags to dispose of trash, tools such as brooms, paint and brushes and general cleaning products made by Persil and Pril's parent company Henkel. Adverts to explain the project were aired for free on TV channels, and these were supported by social media campaigns. The concept of the project was 'El balad, baladna', 'This place is our country'.

This was about genuinely engaging with the community. There was a rising sense of community spirit, and the brands aimed to make their contribution to it by reaching across the commercial space into the shared area of the community. Generation M is constantly on the look out to see if brands are investing in the community and this was a great example of where they have played their part as good community members. However, the brands were rightly careful not to 'take over' the initiative, respecting that it was being led by the community itself, and being sensitive, participative and supportive. Muslim consumers are very quick to frown on those who appear to be doing good works just for show, and just to boast about their work. The brands let their good works speak for themselves and played a team member role, pulling together with the rest of the community.

In Singapore, Project ME encourages Muslims to enhance their level of environmental awareness and action. The Young Association of Muslim Professionals (Young AMP) in Singapore says the initiative aims to: 'build bridges with various sectors and other communities in finding solutions to environmental problems while meeting other concerns such as socio-economic issues'. The project says, while its focus is on Muslims, it is open to all: 'the more the merrier!'

Interfaith work is one of the planks of charitable and community work; faith-based activism is a way to build bridges between faith communities as well as improve wider social spaces. With their perception that the importance and role of faith communities is undervalued, and with politics too often exacerbating religious tensions, Generation M is part of a wider movement to build interfaith links to open not just dialogue but also action.

Giving to Charity

Zakat is the contribution to charity which should be given every year by Muslims if they have made a surplus on their wealth in the previous year. Sometimes it is given to those nearest and in need like family or local community members. Sometimes it is sent abroad to poorer regions or those hit by calamities. And sometimes it is invested into local community amenities such as mosques and schools which can be used for the benefit of all. In addition to zakat, some Muslims will also pay a further mandatory charity known as 'khums', which literally means one-fifth, and as the name suggests, is 20 per cent of surplus income in addition to the 2.5 per cent of zakat on wealth (which includes items such as gold, cattle and land). Again, this money is used for a mixture of help with poverty and welfare as well as community investment.

Mandatory charitable dues like zakat and khums are central to Muslim belief; Generation M are looking at modern approaches to charity, such as social entrepreneurship, as well as reviving historical Muslim ideas such as waqf to ensure a lasting and effective contribution. Waqf straddles the spheres between charity and commerce, referring to assets that are donated, bequeathed, or purchased for the purpose of being held in perpetual trust as ongoing charity or for a general or specific cause regarded as socially beneficial. This condition of perpetuity allows for an accumulation of societal wealth over the years, such that awqaf (plural of waqf) in many regions have become an important sector dedicated to the social and economic improvement of society. This philosophy fits neatly with Generation M's own view of using commerce to create the best for their communities.

Marwa El-Daly is the founder of the Waqfeyat al Maadi Community Foundation, a waqf foundation set up in 2007 in Egypt. She explains:

I am a believer in social justice philanthropy where giving in any form is directed to solve root causes of poverty, deprivation or any kind of injustice. My interest is to invest in change-driven philanthropy that brings people out of the vicious circle of poverty and dependence and helps them have equal access to opportunities and resources.

Marwa says that when she studied local charitable giving she found that 'people like to give in their own community, probably because of the religious belief that "al aqrabun awla bel ma'rouf" – those close to you by kin or geography are worthiest of your donation and help.' However, she found that much charitable giving was unstructured and ad hoc. She notes that charitable giving is huge in Egypt: 'normal people give over US$1.5 billion yearly donations to social causes that appeal to them.'

Once the organisation was established, it set out to persuade local philanthropists to contribute donations to set up a programme for income generation in the Waqfeya that would allow the Foundation to start small jobs for people while distributing their Ramadan bags, traditionally given to poor people in the fasting month. The Foundation became a hub for NGOs in the area and its work included establishing an arts centre, which then diversified into income-generation projects, the profits of which were reinvested in activities for those from shanty towns and other deprived areas. The ethos was to move from dependency to sustainability, the core of the waqf model. Marwa says: 'it's like creating this sense of belonging and interest to make your place a better, more beautiful place.'

Islamic Relief is just one of many large-scale charities turning towards waqf to stabilise their income and to allow for advance planning. The charity is also setting up waqf facilities for other communities so they can be self-sustaining, rather than reliant on charity. Set up in the UK 30 years ago, Islamic Relief says, 'Inspired by our Islamic faith and guided by our values, we envisage a caring world where communities are empowered, social obligations are fulfilled and people respond as one to the suffering of others.'

Whilst it draws heavily on the Islam of the founders and many of the donors and volunteers, working with all groups for effective change is important:

> exemplifying our Islamic values, we will mobilise resources, build partnerships, and develop local capacity, as we work to enable communities to mitigate the effect of disasters, prepare for their occurrence and respond by providing relief, protection and recovery; promote integrated development and environmental custodianship with a focus on sustainable livelihoods, support the marginalised and vulnerable to voice their needs and address root causes of poverty.

Again, here is the emphasis on outreach into mutual spaces, whether it is in how funds are raised, resources are developed and provided, or to whom they are offered: 'we allocate these resources regardless of race, political affiliation, gender or belief, and without expecting anything in return.' At a local level, in 2013, online UK charity website JustGiving conducted a study to look at giving habits and found that Muslims give more to charity than other religious groups. At almost £371 each, Muslims topped the poll of any religious groups that give to charity, including those who profess atheism.

There is rarely a sense of burden in undertaking these duties because to give away money is to consider the money to be 'purified' and therefore halal. Charitable giving falls into two types. The first is charity that brings with it a one-off reward – for example, feeding a poor person. The second type is 'sadaqah jaariyah', charity that keeps perpetuating – such as building a school in which children are educated, who will then go on to earn money, feed their families, and educate more children and thus continue the cycle. This form of charity is highly prized and holds special esteem among Muslims. That's why for any charity, projects that bring perpetual benefit are a very effective strategy. Schools, hospitals, mosques, water wells, even orchards and farms, are popular investments.

Business and Commerce

'Faith was a fundamental part of the very reason I started my business – something which would allow me to undertake a process of lifelong learning, as well as allow others to benefit,' says Hajera Memon, who founded Shade 7 Publishing. Her start-up company was the first global publishing house to offer pop-up and novelty books inspired by Islam to teach children in a fun way. Innovation and high standards are key to her ethos. 'We make the world a better place through publishing good quality books.'

Her company is very much a commercial enterprise, but engaging in the civic domain is just as important. 'In a time where cultural and faith-based misunderstandings are rife, the work we do is important. We have a strong social purpose.' It's not just what her business does that goes back to her Muslim values, it's the way the business operates that is crucial. 'For me, running a business as a Muslim goes right back to striving to follow the example of the man who was sent with the mission to perfect our character, our beloved Prophet Muhammad (PBUH).' She sees managing her company as completing the virtuous circle of making her a better Muslim. Running a business is 'important because it brings about practical qualities we must develop to better our character, like honesty, trust, generosity, leadership, accountability, humility, as well as having a bigger humanitarian vision, to the forefront of your daily actions.'

Engagement through brands, as we discovered earlier, is something that gives Generation M an opportunity to express who they are as individuals within the framework of being part of a wider community.

Ogilvy Noor's Brand Index was an attempt to understand what it means to be a Muslim brand in more detail. 'How friendly are global brands to Muslim needs?' was the question we posed about 35 global brands from five categories – beverages, food and dairy, personal care, financial services and aviation industries – to 2,500 Muslim consumers in Saudi Arabia, Egypt, Pakistan and Malaysia, countries considered majority Muslim markets, to help rank brands on a 100-point index that is based on agreement with the statement 'This brand is halal or shariah-compliant.' Lipton, Nestlé and Nescafé received top scores, with Lipton reporting the highest. Global brands like Kraft, Pringles, and 7-Up were also ranked in the top ten. The majority of the financial services and airlines that were surveyed, including Citibank, Singapore Airlines, Emirates and HSBC, received some of the lowest scores on the index.

In the commercial space, origin matters less than sincerity: a Muslim-friendly brand does not have to originate in a Muslim country, as the highest-scoring brands demonstrate. Genuine empathy and understanding, shown through all aspects of the brand's behaviour, are much more important. Having said that, the study clearly demonstrated that Islamic branding efforts must be holistic, not tokenistic or a marketing ploy. Generation M want to feel that the brand genuinely comprehends Islamic values in all aspects of its operations all over the world.

The commercial arena therefore offers Generation M the opportunity to engage with existing brands and ensure that they are treated with the same respect and care as any other consumer. Equally, young entrepreneurs and visionaries like the ones we've been meeting are creating new kinds of brands and businesses with the values that are important to them, but which also reach out on a universal platform to a broader global consumer audience.

In this commercial space where mutual exchange is important, and where the language of universal values is most powerful, we can think of Islamic branding as branding that is empathetic to shariah values in order to appeal to the Muslim consumer, ranging from basic shariah friendliness to full shariah-compliance in all aspects of the brand's identity, behaviour and communications. There is overlap with values that all organisations need to communicate today, such as honesty, respect, accountability and understanding.

Tagging on the 'Islamic' label is not enough. We can learn from a company in South Africa that allegedly labelled pork as 'halal'. When Muslim consumers found out, they were outraged, and Muslim companies took out a court order to prevent the company from using the halal logo. The company claims it has been the victim of a smear campaign, but admits that even if this is the case it will take years to rebuild its reputation.

Establishing the 'crossover' with the mainstream is particularly appealing to Generation M audiences, highlighting the values which they state over and over are important to them – values such as purity, cleanliness, wholesomeness, ethics, honesty and transparency. Of course, many consumers, not just Muslims, are looking for these qualities in their purchases.

Brands have the ability to bring clarity and guidance in an area of confusion, conflict and lack of trust, exactly the values that Generation M expect. It's up to the brand how halal-friendly or halal-compliant it wants to be, but understanding the impact of the decision is crucial. The challenge for brands – wherever on this spectrum they choose to position themselves – is how to convey their Muslim friendliness. For products other than food and beverages, an understanding of what it means to be halal is even more important.

Alongside integrating 'halal' status into products, clear communication, consistent processes through the sourcing, manufacturing, go-to-market business practices and transparency all build consumer confidence and loyalty. This is what leads to credibility and 'trusted friend' status, the ultimate prize for brands. In return, the brands are welcomed as allies in building a Muslim lifestyle.

Khadis, from Moscow, encapsulates the centrality of business and commerce to Generation M when engaging with the wider world. 'Personally, for me, the most important method is business and a strong economy,' because these equate to 'the ability to help the community and wider society. I even heard that the Prophet peace on him after the hijrah first constructed the mosque and then the second thing was the market. That shows us the importance of business and strong economy from an Islamic perspective.'

Politics

'We are Allah's khalifahs on Earth – His stewards,' says Naheda. 'Islam isn't just the five pillars like people think, like pray and that's it. Islam is a complete way of life and therefore social, political, economic frameworks are provided.' Getting involved is important to Generation M, whether it's arts and culture, charity and community, business and commerce or, yes, politics. They'll be the first to tell you that involvement in politics doesn't make them Islamists, or oppose secular states, or seek the establishment of a khilafah or believe shariah law should be imposed. Instead, it's about using this as one legitimate channel to make the world a better place.

Given the scrutiny afforded to Muslim organisations like Daesh, Generation M individuals feel understandably nervous about talking politics. But it can be a matter of pride as well as motivation. Naheda says,

> Under the political system of Muhammad (SAW) we had an amazing political and welfare system. The whole concept of the welfare system – the baitul maal – wasn't invented by the West! If we all gave a certain percentage of our wealth to the poor and needy, you think there would still be poverty?

Of the various methods of engagement, Naheda's preference is for the political.

> This connects with my values and faith as a Muslim because I need to act on the Qur'an and Sunnah: none of you is a believer until he loves for his brother what he loves for himself. If we don't get politically involved, we can't influence society and change things.

Despite the initial euphoria during the Arab Spring being dissipated by subsequent problems, it's clear that young people are electrified by the need to assert themselves politically.

Asmaa Mahfouz, whose video urging people to protest in Tahrir Square is credited with being one of the sparks that ignited the revolution, said in her appeal to her fellow Egyptians:

Fear none but God. God says, He will not change the condition of a people until they change what is in themselves. Do you think you can be safe anymore? None of us are. Come down with us and demand your rights, my rights, your family's rights. I am going down on January 25th, and I will say no to corruption, no to this regime.

The drive to make things around them better is all-encompassing. The languages through which Generation M interact with the world are rooted in their faith as Muslims but use the best tools of modernity. Generation M's passion for being in constant dialogue with the world is not to be underestimated. It is all encompassing, embracing the ummah and beyond.

Henrietta says: 'As a coach it inspires me to work with people and change what holds them back – negativity, anger, lack of confidence or whatever else it might be.' According to Sufian:

My faith inspires me to resist wasting natural resources. Whenever I am about to waste food, water, gas and so on, I feel that my faith comes along the way and stops me. So, it helps me to waste less and make the world a better place.

Rania sums it up: 'As a Muslim I know I've been entrusted with the welfare of everyone around me and beyond me in a way commensurate with my abilities and their proximity.' She smiles: 'It's simple.'

15   (DEEP) GREEN
CONSUMERISM

The Impact of Muslim Consumers
on the Global Economy

Zaufishan Iqbal is a British Muslim woman who runs the website
The Eco Muslim, which she describes as her '"eco-jihad", a
greener effort to make our community on earth that tiny bit purer
to live in'. Her playful and creative Islamic turn of phrase points to
the fact that being a faithful future-facing Muslim is more than just
about eating halal or living a Muslim lifestyle. This is about making
the world a better place. She says that everyone should live on less
and follow the '4R's: Reuse! (e.g. leftover water) Reduce! (how
much food you waste) Recycle! (your unwanted clothes) Reject!
(poverty, homelessness and exploitation).'

An 'eco-jihad' encompasses all of these as an 'effort to preserve
what's natural around us, to value resources from wherever they
are sourced and to improve the quality of life for others – people,
animals and plants,' explains Zaufishan. 'It could mean organising
a street clean-up, planting a tree or eating organic.'

Halal, shariah, jihad, ummah, zakat, prayer … every religious
concept we've considered is seen by individuals like Zaufishan to
be an aspect of the same goal of being a faithful Muslim whose
purpose is to be devoted to God and creation. The 'green faith' of
Islam is the blueprint for Generation M's eco-consciousness. There
is a connection between 'green faith', says Zaufishan, and 'social
action'. This kind of eco-consciousness is holistic, and the notion

of stewardship of the earth and respect for physical resources goes hand in hand with the spiritual. She notes that she will make 'dua' (supplication) that her generation of Muslims will be fearless in healing their malnourished communities.

Her faith is what informs her 'green' values and drives her to work in this field. Her website acts as a digital resource for ideas that can be shared, aiming to improve the ummah. Her avatar is a friendly woman in hijab with an earthy feel: a marker that her faith is the foundation for her ethos, and she's proud of that fact.

Which brings us back to where we started our story with Generation M. We can draw together the threads of their pioneering attitudes towards faith and modernity, their new Muslim culture, their belief in both individualism and community and their relentless faith-based march towards making the world a better place. This is faith-inspired futurism, individuals harnessing collective ideas and power to make a better world for all.

The fusing of faith and modernity has created a generation of Muslims who believe they are the living proof that these two can and must go hand in hand. But this identity is still developing; there are tensions that they are exploring which may never be fully resolved. One of the most fascinating of these is how their consumerism is mediated by their faith, which cautions against extravagance and which advises ethics in both consumption and production.

At the heart of this tension is the fact that halal consumption is a badge of identity for Generation M. This consumption is increasingly scrutinised not only to ensure it complies with halal criteria but also to ensure it upholds wider ideas of tayyab. This holistic 'spirit' of halal insists that every part of the supply chain must conform to ethical principles, from sustainability in production, through fair wages for workers, to the concept of the product, to the financing of the whole project, to the disposal of used goods. Even the language of communications must be ethical and contribute to the wider social good. It doesn't need to be expressed in Islamic terms, just in values that can unite communities.

It's here that Generation M find themselves aligned with – even leading – wider consumer trends. These are the influencers shaping all of our global futures, inspired by their faith. Generation

M are not shy of being in such a leadership position. They want to propel themselves and their Muslim communities as well as global trends in a more ethical direction. Their vision is that things should be better for everyone, not just Muslims. Whether it is eco-consciousness, ethical consumption, sustainable supply chains or diversity in beauty ideals, the goals and parameters laid out in their religion must be struggled for in order to benefit everyone. Their faith should not be self-serving, even while it's right to enjoy the good things of life. Faith must be employed for the greater good.

We've noted how groups that are originally seen as outliers can have huge impacts on wider society, predicated on ideas that are unbelievable at the time but which rapidly become a major cultural influence. Just think of how the Hispanic influence has shaped the USA, or the LGBTQ impact around the world. The mainstream can – and as far as Generation M are concerned, must – absorb influences from outside the mainstream in order to stay fresh and relevant. More importantly, consumers now expect dialogue in their relationship with authorities, institutions and brands and as a result expect to see themselves reflected in the fundamentals of those organisations.

Keeping our focus on consumption, we see that the State of the Global Islamic Economy Report 2015/2016 estimates that Muslim consumer expenditure on food and lifestyle will reach $2.6 trillion by 2020, and Islamic finance will reach $2.6 trillion. Among these are sectors such as Muslim travel, estimated to reach $233 billion by 2020. Muslim cosmetics spend was estimated at $54 billion in 2014. We've investigated these sectors and the Generation M attitudes that are driving their development in quite some detail throughout the book, but here we take a moment to zoom out and see where deep green consumerism is taking us, and how authorities, institutions and brands must respond.

So now we step across the blurry line of the cutting-edge present into the near future, looking at the faith-inspired trends that Generation M are pioneering. With a better global future envisioned through the lens of their faith, many of the trends they are pioneering are in sync with wider consumer movements, and in many cases may even be the trigger for development. Through their sheer numbers, their growing middle-class stature, the shift of economic and political power towards the Middle East and Asia, home to most of the world's Muslims, through the Muslim minorities that act as influential and well-connected leaders, by the inspirational force of their faith and their refusal to accept the status quo, Generation M are determined to make change. And what a change it's going to be.

Tayyab, the Environment and the Ethical Supply Chain

> I'm British and I'm Muslim – the two aren't mutually exclusive, yet when I was growing up supermarket shelves told me otherwise. I've always wanted to enjoy a good shepherd's pie or a lasagne; funnily enough Muslims don't eat curry three times a day!

Shazia Saleem, whom we met briefly right at the beginning of our story, is talking about her passion as a foodie. In 2014, she launched ieat foods in the UK, a range of halal ready-meals.

Her insight into the changing identity and tastes of Generation M consumers landed her a deal with one of the UK's leading supermarket chains and in less than nine months her company's products were available in 150 British stores. There is more to her tale than identifying the Muslim consumer audience and developing a new product and marketing line. The backstory to her company involved developing her supply chain in line with eco-principles, and places her as part of wider industry trends towards wholesome and ethical consumption. For Shazia, she had to be true to her Islamic principles to run a business in the most ethical way possible.

This meant that setting up her supply chain wasn't as simple as commissioning a manufacturer and sourcing the cheapest halal meat. 'A lot of time is spent focusing on halal, and 50 per cent of the instructions – the tayyab part – often get ignored.' To ensure the tayyab aspects of her products, she went back down the supply chain to the farm and animal conditions, as well as forward into packaging and communications. The products are made only from 'store cupboard ingredients', so additives don't feature on her ingredient list. She also wants to invest a percentage of her profits into a charitable foundation. Keeping her supply chain tayyab costs 'a huge amount of money', she says. She hopes that by pioneering a tayyab supply chain she can be part of a movement to improve the halal industry.

In the UK the Radwan family gave up traditional nine-to-five life to open a halal organic farm outside Oxford. Lutfi and Ruby Radwan and their five children set up Willowbrook farm, aiming to raise animals as they feel the Qur'an intended. The sheep, goats and chickens strut around the farm freely, munching on chemical-free grass. They look plucky and wild, living a good, free life. When it's time for slaughter, the Islamic rituals are followed. This is about 'acknowledging a spirituality behind all material existence,' says Ruby. 'It takes you back to humans being stewards of God's earth.'

Lutfi is frustrated at how much emphasis is placed on how animals die rather than how they live – a problem that faces both the halal and the wider mass-food industry. But for Lutfi this can be addressed by upholding Islam's emphasis on sustainable living and kindness to animals. The Qur'an commands Muslims to 'eat of what is in the earth lawful and wholesome,' says Lutfi. 'We can't allow ourselves to be subsumed in what's wrong with the British food industry already. If halal means anything, it's got to be a bit more holistic. It's got to distinguish itself.'

The *Chicago Tribune* looked at the trend of rising farm-to-fork consciousness among Muslims, reporting that 'some Muslims are making sure their food is not just halal, but organic, free-range and *tayyab* – Arabic for wholesome. They care as much about how the animal was killed as they do about how it was raised.'

Halal observance and tayyab preferences are among the many growing global dietary trends such as organic, vegetarian, vegan, kosher, gluten-free, farm-assured and so on. Like halal, these are purchasing compasses which allow consumers to blank out non-compliant options and look for products that meet their personal consumption principles.

In 2012, Dutch research company Innova published '10 Key Food Trends', which included the values of purity, authenticity, sustainability and corporate social responsibility. These values show a remarkable crossover with halal and tayyab values. Consumers who are not Muslim also state that halal (and kosher) foods are preferable due to the care and cleanliness that go into preparing them.

In the Ningxia region of China, which has a high Muslim population, Malaysian firm Fahim is implementing a 'halal integrity management solution'. This will deliver exactly what we've been discussing here – an end-to-end solution for monitoring halal status from farm to fork. The chairman of Fahim's parent company explains the potential for crossover in his region: 'Our target is not only the Muslims but also the non-Muslims. I was told by some Chinese people that they preferred halal food products to allay food safety concerns as halal in Chinese literally means pure and good.'

Highlighting the idea of tayyab is just one aspect among many of the growing momentum for an Islam-inspired ethical supply chain of production and consumption. Resources must be properly respected, workers in primary industries must not be exploited. Sustainability and renewability are part of the Islamic idea of 'stewardship of the earth' which Generation M eco-Muslims like Zaufishan Iqbal are championing. Improving nutrition, reducing waste and diminishing the use of harmful chemicals and additives in food are rising in the Generation M conscience. Civic duty, community investment and charitable giving are all part of this broader connected view of consumption that ensures the spirit of Islamic values are upheld as much as the rules.

Zaufishan challenges global corporations as well as existing Muslim providers to think about what tayyab means, even while not using the word itself.

One can blame the corporations; however, the food chains of many of the Muslim community's own companies are flawed. We are churning out our own varieties of nuggets, sausages, and cold meats, which follow similar production processes to the global chains.

In Zaufishan's eyes, those supply chains are problematic because of the low-quality products they produce. And she raises questions about whether fast food can ever be totally tayyab if its inherent healthiness is in question. Her wider discontent with a failure to offer a wholesome, eco-conscious vision for society is what prompts her to set course on an eco-jihad.

With global newspaper headlines regularly featuring discussions about whether halal is 'humane' and 'modern', Generation M are aware that the implementation of tayyab rules has to be a prominent feature if the industry is to meet the aspirations of their Generation M peers, as well as the wider global population. The social activism and grassroots movement to push halal towards its tayyab roots reflects Generation M's push for their own identity to have a place in the wider world, and halal and tayyab are strong ways in which they can contribute holistically to improving consumer and corporate behaviour towards the environment. Watch this space, as Generation M becomes ever louder in championing tayyab as a must-have for both Muslims and wider society.

Dressing Green

Similar concerns are slowly extending into other sectors like fashion. The exploitation of factory workers who produce garments for the world's biggest brands raised an international outcry in 2014 after fatal fires in factories in Bangladesh. At the other end of the chain, a growing number of consumers are concerned about sustainability and are looking at how the fashion industry can be more resource conscious. Muslim consumers are no exception.

The 2015 Corporate Social Responsibility campaign by global fashion retailer H&M caused a stir by featuring a Muslim woman who wears a headscarf, as we noted earlier in the book. The campaign was for 'Close the Loop', advocating recycling and sustainability in fashion, a fascinating and pertinent choice of subject to intersect with the growing consciousness by Muslim women about sustainability in fashion. The brand was challenged on what were seen to be inconsistencies. As @kathrynmedien noted on Twitter: 'We are quick to celebrate H&M hijabi campaign. Don't forget: Muslim women make those clothes in sweatshops. Hijabis die making those clothes.'

Mariam Sobh is the founder of Hijabtrendz, one of the earliest hijabista websites. She advocates eco-fashion for Muslims and is concerned about recycling and sustainability. In one example she criticises the Middle East because of the influence the region wields over Muslim fashion.

> In places like the United Arab Emirates I think it's imperative they try their best to find more sustainable materials for their designs. They have become quite the hub for abayas [long dresses] and shaylas [scarves] and many people look to them for the next 'big' thing in the area of hijab fashion. But items from the UAE also tend to symbolize 'excess' and wastefulness. So it's important to showcase that Muslims can be rich and have luxury, but at the same time be conscientious enough to do so in a responsible way.

She suggests, by way of example, 'incorporating some recycled pieces of fabric/trim into their designs'.

The 'hijab swap' is a growing cultural phenomenon. Mariam says, 'If you are sick of your old hijabs, have a hijab-swap party with your friends. Trading scarves will make you feel like you just bought some new stuff. And it's a form of recycling.' Many Generation M women are doing exactly that.

Melbourne Madinah in Australia advertised a 'Hijab Swap Party' by announcing: 'Bring along all your neglected scarves (as long as they're in good condition) and swap them with other sisters' hijabs that you like better!' as part of World Hijab Day events. Masjid Omar in Columbus, Ohio, invited 'sisters of all ages' to bring 'gently used scarves and trade with other scarves'. The suggested list of items to bring included hijabs, modest clothes and 'a smile'.

Ibrahim Abdul-Matin is the author of *Green Deen: What Islam Teaches About Protecting the Planet*. He believes that looking after the environment is 'our God-given duty'. He says about the earth that 'Allah has generously given us these things and that we cannot forget to be grateful. We also must serve with justice and not destroy, pillage, or hurt any of the things He has provided.'

Ibrahim grew up in Brooklyn, New York, the son of two African-American converts to Islam. He says he remembers seeing nothing but concrete buildings until he was five years old, when his father took him hiking in the mountains.

The beauty of nature completely stunned me. I remember seeing my father pray on the mountain. He told me, 'The Earth is a mosque. You can pray everywhere, everywhere is sacred.' From that moment on, I felt a deep sense of responsibility to protect the planet. Allah created this space for us to worship Him – destroying it not only prevents us from properly worshipping, but it is disrespectful to His creation.

He says that his book is an illustration of 'how the power of religion can be used to involve people of faith in the environmental movement.'

Conscientious Consumerism

'I view Islam as a way of life. My faith encourages me to be aware of what I drink, eat and what I put in/on to my body,' says Faiza Hussain, the founder of H&O Skincare. She describes her company as offering an 'ethical skincare range'. H&O stands for halal and organic.

Available online, her products are most popular in the Middle East, Africa, Australia and the UK. Like many Generation M entrepreneurs, she founded her company because she felt her own needs were unmet by the marketplace. She wanted a skincare range which reassured her that 'all the ingredients are completely natural and without alcohol and animal content.'

The goal of being both halal and tayyab means that Faiza faces challenges that less socially and religiously rooted businesses might choose to ignore. There are fundamental challenges in:

making decisions of recycling and reprocessing of items when they reach end of life as all of the products are completely chemical free using natural preservatives to hold the shelf life. We reviewed these challenges from the very beginning, so all of our products are handmade in small batches so they can last longer and to prevent wastage.

The concern for both the social and natural environment is evident in every aspect of Faiza's vision. Ingredients should 'nourish the skin and respect the environment'. And, 'as an independent business our aim is to demonstrate the importance of making a living whilst maintaining focus on the effects businesses of any size can have on the environment.' In the medium term she hopes that she will be able to introduce her products to independent stores which support economically ethical initiatives.

Selecting the right investors is important too, says Faiza, who believes they should also 'support similar economically ethical and fair trade initiatives'. Even ensuring the communications and branding aspects are aligned with holistic Islamic values is on her radar. 'What method of advertising would be appropriate?' she wonders; she notes the importance of being honest with customers.

It is important to inject ethics back into the consumer culture, which Generation M are so comfortable with, as those ethics go to the core of these young Muslims' identity. Every aspect must aspire to the highest ethical standard, as inspired by their Islamic faith. Much of tayyab concentrates on the supply chain, but, as Faiza explains, this extends forward into disposal and laterally into advertising, branding and finance too. This latter point about financing is important, and one that small businesses often struggle with as investment vehicles that avoid interest are limited.

More generally, consumers – both Muslim and non-Muslim – are seeking Islamic finance alternatives to conventional banking which they believe are more ethically sound and fairer to consumers. In South Africa, Islamic finance products are growing in popularity among those who are not Muslim. According to Arrie Rautenbach, head of retail markets at Absa Bank in South Africa, 'Many non-Muslims choose Islamic banking products because they like knowing that their funds will never be invested in industries that are potentially negative for society, such as alcohol, tobacco, gambling and pornography.'

In a study by the Islamic Bank of Britain (IBB), speaking to Muslim and non-Muslim consumers, they found that 60 per cent agreed that shariah finance is relevant to all faiths, and there was no significant difference across faiths in this belief. Of those questioned, 58 per cent considered Islamic finance to be an ethical system of finance which considers the impact of its activities on society. In addition, the IBB also found that in the year 2012/13

87 per cent of applications for its fixed-term deposit accounts were from non-Muslim customers.

Crowdfunding options are increasingly popular with this entrepreneurial segment as they avoid interest and as a result are more shariah-compliant, as well as retaining control of the business for the founders, who thus have a greater ability to remain true to their principles. LaunchGood is a crowdfunding platform focused on the Muslim community worldwide. In its first two years it raised more than $3 million for more than 370 projects across 30 countries. LaunchGood has been used to fundraise for several nationally recognised projects, including a campaign to help rebuild African-American churches destroyed by arson in the summer of 2015. It says it aspires to bring goodness to society. 'The Prophet said, "The believer is like a life-bringing rain, wherever they are they bring benefit." We believe in Muslims doing great work that benefits everyone, not just Muslims.'

According to one of the founders, Chris Blauvelt, the aim of the site is to be the best crowdfunding site. 'Sometimes we get used to Muslims doing a business and it's kind of a cheap version of the mainstream business.' The work the platform does is designed to make the world a better place, but its very existence can diffuse negativity.

> NeoCons and pundits like to say that Muslims don't contribute anything to society and we don't even need to say anything, we can just point them to LaunchGood and they have to say, 'You know what, Muslims actually do a lot of really great stuff.'

Tausif Malik, founder of Muslim Spelling Bee, says, 'The role of the business to be fair and just in their business creates more business opportunities so people get jobs and suppliers get additional business and in the long run there is limited poverty in society.' According to Tausif, businesses are not detached from wider society but instead play a role through the values they embody, how they are structured and the way they interact. Seeing business and finance as a way of improving society rather than as money-making machines is crucial to overall prosperity and growth.

In Islam the Prophet always encouraged people to conduct business as it helps not only the individual but the family and community. This results in overall economic development, hence if we revisit Islamic history there was prosperity and growth. Islam encourages free enterprise, but unlike capitalism where the survival of the fittest theory is implemented, compassion and care is given to the weaker section, so it is an holistic growth approach.

Tausif adds, 'In our business model, we work with non-profits and we share revenue with them.'

Our Generation M entrepreneurs are consistent in ensuring that a share of profits goes towards charity. Entrepreneurs believe their businesses do better when connected to the community, and consumers look favourably on businesses who take on social responsibilities. Honesty is also important, says Tausif. 'If you keep your prices fair and announce the weakness of the product or service to the customer, then if the customer buys, he becomes loyal to the business.'

Bringing in New Images of Fashion

Imagery and advertising, as Faiza Hussain mentioned earlier, are also part of the ethics of how a business operates. The power of the beauty and fashion industries when it comes to imagery is one which is being increasingly challenged in the face of an industry struggling to deal with harmful practices such as size zero models and sexualised images.

Generation M women we interviewed told us that the women displayed in Western beauty brands 'are not the kind of thing I aspire to'. As already described, Muslim beauty attempts to challenge the idea of beauty for external judgement with a more spiritually determined kind of beauty, one that is part of dignity, self-respect and grooming. The Muslim women in this type of imagery display a kind of inner strength, a self-possession that is concerned with making their presence felt on their own terms rather than being presented for visual consumption, which is how

Generation M see the modern beauty industry. There is instead an attempt to inject boldness and personality, a powerful portrayal of woman as an individual.

We have seen how existing global campaigns already adjust their imagery when rolled out in majority Muslim countries. What Generation M are exploring is a new approach to beauty – one that acknowledges the importance of the external, but sees it simply as one component of a successful life. Being well-groomed for both men and women in this new paradigm of beauty is a responsibility to self and God, and a duty. Further, what goes on the body affects what is absorbed into the body, meaning that it must live up to the same halal principles as food, and increasingly the same tayyab principles.

Jana Kossaibati, a blogger and medical student, runs the website Hijab Style and says that there is a danger of Muslim fashion running into the same image challenges as mainstream fashion, rather than finding a way to project Muslim ideals through their visual identity.

> It would be quite refreshing though, to see companies try to come up with effective, creative advertising, without just imitating mainstream glossy magazines, albeit with the model wearing a scarf on her head. In terms of what image they project, at the end of the day, the companies are selling clothing that although may primarily be aimed at women wearing hijab, can be worn by anyone, and in any setting. It's up to the consumer to decide how they want to wear the clothes.

She sees this as part of the wider changes that need to be made to beauty and fashion with regard to conscientious consumerism.

> Hijab fashion companies have a great opportunity here to showcase women of different shapes, sizes, ethnicities and ages, if they do choose to use models. I know lots of company owners ask friends and family to model for them, or even recruit their own customers! In this way I think they make their clothing feel a lot more accessible and wearable for all women, and this helps to counteract the negative messages that mainstream advertising may be sending out.

Even beyond imagery, the messages underpinning a sales promotion, the concepts of beauty, consumption, travel and so on, must all also be ethical. This is more specifically called 'Islamic branding', something yet to be fully embraced by industry. Some soul-searching is required to determine whether certain messages and positioning are ethical, even while they may be effective. Generation M have so far expressed their aspiration for better communications values, but are focusing so heavily on product and business development that they have not yet fully turned their attention to this aspect of consumption as an area where a new model and principles need to be developed.

That's why the language of 'values' rather than technical Islamic terminology appeals to Generation M: they want everyone to benefit and understand this is a consumer good that is being pursued rather than something for Muslims only. In the USA, Whole Earth Meats is halal and organic, but the halal accreditation is not explicit and is found only on its website. It markets its burgers based on tradition and wholesomeness, using these values to appeal implicitly to Muslim consumers but to be accessible to wider consumer trends related to ethics.

Ensuring corporations are behaving in trustworthy ways is being championed. There's a process via the halal certification bodies that is already being instituted by Muslims and through which corporations can be held accountable. The horsemeat scandal in the UK and Europe in 2013 raised significant questions for all consumers: what is in the food we eat, how can we be sure it's properly labelled, and most importantly, who can we trust? For Muslim consumers who observe halal in their food and beverage consumption, these are of course questions that they ask daily. For them, halal certification from a trusted authority is vital, otherwise they simply won't buy. No trusted halal logo, no sale.

Consumer confidence underpins this market. Consumers want reassurance from a trusted authority. The infrastructure established by Muslim consumers to require inspections and certifications has something to offer the wider global movements. Equally, halal certification bodies are slowly beginning to incorporate 'tayyab' criteria into their certification requirements. In South Africa a Muslim consumer council is being set up to hold service providers, suppliers, and producers accountable. In Europe, the European Halal Development Agency is setting up rigorous criteria that look at not just slaughter processes but the provenance of ingredients when it comes to halal. It will be exciting when such agencies expand their remit beyond halal into the language of ethical consumerism. Equally, partnerships with organisations such as Fairtrade will be a natural coming-together of consumer interests.

Collective Power

News stories about the power of the Muslim consumer often focus on the mistakes brands make (usually inadvertently) which anger this target group. Perhaps the most enduring tale is that of Nike, which stylised one of its logos for placement on its trainers, only to be greeted by angry Muslim consumers saying that the new design looked like the Arabic text for 'Allah' (God) and that placing it on shoes was an insult.

More recently in 2014, the Malaysian Consumer Group was angered when bottler Chuan Sin Sdn Bhd placed the image of a Hindu deity, Lord Murugan, next to the halal logo. They felt that this was making a mockery of the halal logo. In both cases, Muslim consumers felt that their concerns were being addressed only as an afterthought. What Muslim consumers want to feel, just like other consumers, is that companies take their concerns seriously, rather than seeing them as opportunities for commercial exploitation.

These are the kinds of stories that attract interest, worry and even fear when it comes to engaging with Muslim consumers. However, businesses need to take note of growing Generation M demands for better corporate ethics and governance when it comes to the overall management of the business. When Generation M demand that companies behave better, their demands are set in the context of wider consumer movements demanding better corporate behaviour.

For Muslim consumers, businesses should not be making donations for the sake of show. Corporate social responsibility programmes must never be about paying a 'tax' to operate as a business in order to provide the business with absolution for other misdemeanours. Instead, a business must act like a good social citizen, just like an individual. Business must make the world a better place.

A Colgate-Palmolive Ramadan campaign has been running since 2008 tying product purchase to charitable giving, focusing its activities in the run-up to and during the month of Ramadan. This particular campaign donated a proportion of the sale of each tube of toothpaste during August and September towards 15 orphanages across Malaysia.

If companies do want to do good works, the key is to avoid doing it for publicity – Muslim consumers can sense this cynicism. But if it is part of the community's overall charitable aspirations and the brand becomes a trusted community member by showing its genuine intentions, then the charitable-giving campaign will take root in the community's heart.

Protest is important too, as a powerful means of direct action to hold organisations to account. The assertion of collective consumer power has become globally more prominent, and many Muslim consumers often play a part. In 2014, as an attack from Israeli forces against Gaza escalated, Muslim consumers reignited a boycott against companies of Israeli origin, but notably also against global companies they perceived to be violating international conventions of not trading from occupied territories. The Israeli finance minister Yair Lapid noted the negative effect of the boycott on the Israeli economy. The *Washington Post* reported that the export of Israeli goods dropped by 14 per cent after supermarket chains in Europe had these products boycotted. A broad coalition of interest groups beyond Muslim activists were campaigning for the same boycott goals. YouTube videos went viral of activists – most of whom were not Muslims – at supermarkets, filling trolleys with goods produced in occupied territories and then abandoning them at the checkout. The assertion of collective Muslim power is in confluence with wider consumer movements.

During the 2014 Gaza conflict, Muslims turned to the Buycott app to identify the brands that they wanted to boycott. The app is used by consumers around the world to identify the source of products instantly so that their purchases do not conflict with their beliefs. People can set up banned product lists to support their own particular interests or causes. The creator of the app, Ivan Pardo, noticed a spike in traffic during the Gaza conflict. 'Next thing I knew Buycott was a top 10 app in the UK and Netherlands, and number one in a number of Middle Eastern countries. Word was spreading through social media.' Ivan pointed out that the app was not written for the Gaza conflict: 'It bothers me that a lot of people are downloading Buycott and thinking that it was written specifically to boycott Israel. It was not,' – and here is the crux of the argument – 'because all brands and businesses whatever their misdemeanour, should be held to account.'

The global drinks business SodaStream launched a new advertising campaign in 2014 featuring the Hollywood actor Scarlett Johansson. At the time she was also an ambassador for the global development charity Oxfam. SodaStream's factory is located in occupied territories, which is in contravention of the Geneva Convention. Oxfam declared that Johansson's position for Oxfam was irreparably compromised and she stepped down from her role. The media furore, which was a perfect storm of social anger, Muslim consumer fury and general consumer protest, highlighted SodaStream's ethics and had a negative commercial impact in a number of countries.

As already mentioned, in the fashion world, the growing sector for modest clothing being instigated by Muslim women is being embraced by women of other faiths such as Judaism and Christianity. Not only have Muslim women made modest wear more acceptable generally for women, but the commercialisation of this idea has made it more accessible for women in general to purchase such goods.

Bringing alternative viewpoints into the global discussion and presenting alternative lifestyles is also something that Generation M are keen to promote. Whilst the news channel Al Jazeera was set up at a government level, its 'alternative view' resonates strongly with global consumers in general, as they turn to alternative media for a broader perspective on local and global events. During the Iraq War and the Israeli attack on Gaza, citizen journalism, YouTube and local TV channels, rather than the dominant global players, became the go-to sources for news. Local on-the-ground Generation M activists are pushing hard for their perspective to be heard globally. Other examples that we've already seen are

Emel magazine and the Alchemiya TV channel. If we've learned anything from the development of social media journalism in the last decade it's that consumers all around the world want broader representation of news and culture.

Creation and curation of world-class ideas and content not only contribute to grassroots activism, but also bring Generation M back full circle to one of their driving forces, which we started with at the beginning of the book: to assert their right to be in the modern space, inspired by Islamic values, to represent themselves on their own terms and to shape the future in a way that is positively influenced by those Islamic values.

Middle-Class Tastes and Aspirations

'They are the Lexus and Mercedes of the cattle world,' says Indonesian saleswoman Desnia Yoshie. She's standing in a showroom in Jakarta, behind her a range of cows. They are waiting to be purchased by upwardly mobile Muslims, ready to be slaughtered for the upcoming Eid ul Adha festival. The economically affluent middle classes are on the rise, and purchasing the top of the range animals is a matter of taste as well as an assertion that they've arrived as the middle classes.

The showroom is usually for cars, but a month before Eid it is converted to sell cattle. It's good business. In 2014, the owner sold more than 5,000 cows. Most cost around $1,000 to $1,600 but some fetched nearly $25,000. The showroom is a clean, organised environment in which to make the sacrificial purchase, which appeals to this segment, used to shopping in malls. Animals for slaughter are usually bought from pop-up shops that appear on the roadside ahead of Eid. David, a manager at Samsung Electronics, who was shopping at the Depok showroom for a cow on behalf of his company, praised the set-up: 'They have health certificates from the government, we can pay by credit card so we don't have to carry a lot of cash.'

Commenting on this new trend, Noorhaidi Hasan, a lecturer on Islam and politics at the Islamic University of Sunan Kalijaga in Yogyakarta, explains that it's a familiar story about the growing middle classes around the world, but with one difference: 'Their economic status improves' but 'at the same time they do not want to let go of their religious identity.' Or, in short, faith goes hand in hand with modernity, and halal consumption is a badge of identity and status.

The creation of such new products, services and marketing techniques is fuelling economic growth and socio-economic change. The growth of the premium and luxury markets is a wider global trend. According to Bain & Company's 2014 Annual Luxury Study, the overall market for luxury goods has tripled over the past two decades to €223 billion in 2014. The lead author of the study highlights a shift away from local trends and tastes towards global brands. It's a short jump to our global Generation M sector and their increasingly luxurious taste. The Bain report suggests international tourism is a big chunk of this industry, and again is reflected in the growing Muslim travel sector which we explored earlier.

'When our parents and grandparents came to France they did mostly manual work and the priority was having enough to feed the family,' says Yanis, aged 33, who arrived in France from Algeria at the age of three.

> But second- or third-generation people like me have studied, have good jobs and money and want to go out and profit from French culture without compromising our religious beliefs. We don't just want cheap kebabs, we want Japanese, Thai, French food; we want to be like the rest of you.

So far, so familiar to the stories we've heard from Generation M Muslims we've met along our journey. But there are some interesting new twists which are proving contentious, given the equally pioneering trends of ethical consumption and conscientious consumerism. Halal foie gras is a new product, but one that is proving popular both as a sign of being involved in mainstream society, and as a sign of premium tastes and sophistication. According to Cyril Malinet, who manages a major Carrefour supermarket: 'It's one of our best sellers; we have around 30 foie gras bought a day.' Annick Fettani, head of Bienfaits de France, which specialises in halal duck, said: 'Until now we've had to fight to sell our foie gras but today everyone wants it.'

Premium and luxury segments are growing among Muslim consumers. Saudi Arabia has the world's highest per capita consumption of perfume, a product by its very nature premium. In neighbouring Oman, the brand Amouage launched itself as 'the world's most expensive perfume'. In the Middle East, the world's most expensive non-alcoholic drink Ruwa was sold at $5 million per bottle, encrusted with diamonds and with free refills indefinitely.

London's luxury hotel The Dorchester informs guests that its Chinese restaurant China Tang is halal. In nearby global luxury hub Mayfair, the halal Benares restaurant is Michelin starred. The gourmet date brand Bateel, based in the Middle East, is growing its chain of shops and coffee houses offering high-end date confections and even quality traditional drinks like pomegranate juice.

Earlier we met the owners of Willowbrook Farm, who espouse a holistic approach to production. They can only afford to do this because there are a growing number of middle-class Generation M Muslims who can afford to buy its £18.50 chickens. Other chickens are available for as little as £3.

The variety that Generation M can access in its consumption is crucial. Shazia Saleem's ieat foods highlighted that the pigeon-holing of Muslim tastes as traditional and homogenous is a huge frustration for Generation M. Her launch advertising campaign teased ironically: 'Muslims only eat curry, right?' offering a know-ing wink to Generation M, who know very well that they want to – and do – consume a wide variety of foods. As one Generation M woman in Jakarta said, 'I am a global citizen'; the desire for global cuisines and products reflects that. In the UK, Generation M want to eat a halal tayyab Sunday roast. In Jakarta Generation M are going out for spaghetti bolognaise. In the Middle East, housewives attempt to wow their families at weekends, family gatherings and Eid lunches with their expertise at producing international food dishes.

The sophistication and globalisation of taste go beyond food and beauty. Travel too is growing for the sophisticated middle-class Muslim traveller who wishes to explore the world in luxury while upholding her Islamic principles. Serendipity Travel in the UK, and

10. Food entrepreneur Shazia Saleem, founder of ieat foods

Andalucian Routes, which take travellers to the historical home of Islam in Europe, both cater to this premium traveller, offering a personalised one-to-one service and tailor-made tours. They are focused squarely on the middle-class trend that is being led by Generation M.

Dina Zaman, a writer at the *Malay Mail Online*, describes the growing Malay Muslim middle class:

> Once upon a time, you would be hard-pressed to find a tudung-ed Malay woman toting the latest It bag. Today, go to Bangsar Village or Bangsar Shopping Centre, and throw a coin – one in two hijabbed women will be sporting a handbag that probably costs someone else's two months' pay. I will admit that I find this progression refreshing. As a Muslim woman, I am tired of hearing about the poor downtrodden Muslim woman who wishes she could be as modern and wealthy as her Western counterpart.

She adds: 'The numbers are burgeoning, and this is not a silent group. They are critical, articulate and financially savvy.'

The Risk to the 'Real Meaning'

Our faith-conscious consumers are faced with a tension when consuming premium and luxury products. Whilst the more sophisticated tastes of the Muslim middle classes and their awareness and openness to international tastes mean that halal supplies of such products are increasing, there is a counter-argument about whether this meets with ethical principles.

Syed says:

> foie gras does not meet the two requirements of the Islamic law which clearly states that an animal before its slaughter must not be under stress or discomfort, and that it must not be diseased and no part of the animal's body be mutilated or deformed. The above departures from the Islamic halal law, make the foie gras unquestionably haram.

Not only does he believe that such a product violates tayyab teachings, he believes corporate ethics compel brands selling this product to be honest and transparent about its production values. 'It is the obligation of the foie gras producers to bring to the knowledge of their Muslim customers how this meat is produced and refrain from the deceptive labeling of halal foie gras.'

Commercialisation more generally, leading to a mourning for 'losing the real meaning of …', is something that Christian-heritage countries have been increasingly bewailing when it comes to occasions like Christmas and Easter. Increasing affluence and the taste for premium products and services are causing our faithful, futurist Muslims to wonder if they are facing the same dilemma when it comes to living a Muslim lifestyle, and what, if anything, they need to do about it.

Journalist Arwa Aburawa asks if the explosion of luxury architecture in Makkah is causing hajj to lose its egalitarian spirit. She describes the image of the Ka'ba in Makkah as one of 'striking simplicity. Covered in black material it's a bold yet uncomplicated structure, with bare walls and a simple interior consisting of lamps and three supporting arches.' The global Muslim luxury consumers and the wealth and corporations which the Muslim audience attracts mean that 'This simplicity has been undermined by the proliferation of luxury hotels, malls and towering skyscrapers which surround the holy site. You can even start your day with the usual Starbucks coffee if you like or pick up a MacDonalds [*sic.*] after prayers.'

Saudi architect Sami Angawi expresses frustration at the zeal for luxury eclipsing true meaning. 'The hajj was always supposed to be a time when everyone is the same. There are no classes, no nationalities. It is the one place where we find balance. You are supposed to leave worldly things behind you.'

While Generation M believe they have struck the right balance with their faith and modern life, they are very anxious that their embrace of modernity should not veer into the worst excesses of commercialisation and extravagance. For example, on one fatwa website (for asking religious questions), Tarek poses the dilemma, 'Is VIP hajj permissible?'

In Makkah, at the geographic focus of Muslims wherever they are in the world, we see brought to life the tensions that sit at the core of a generation that wants to be fully devoted to their faith principles while enjoying the best that modernity has to offer. Every so often these tensions burst open and the flux in which their identities place them mean that they are still seeking solutions. That's what drives them to be pioneers, never settling for the status quo, believing things can and must be better. We can see the tension in all its glory here, precisely in the cradle of Islam's birth.

Generation M Production, Marketing and Consumption

'It is important for Muslims to be fully integrated into the global economic mainstream. And the best way to achieve that is through business,' explains Muhammad Ali Hashim, the CEO of Johor Corporation, one of the world's largest Muslim-run companies. He declared a surprising new concept: 'business jihad'. The Johor

Corporation is a Malaysian conglomerate composed of over 280 companies that cover everything from palm oil to healthcare, KFC franchises and shipping. It was established in 1968 as a corporation owned by the Johor state government.

Muhammad knows that he is playing with fire, juxtaposing the idea of business with the contentious concept of jihad. 'Jihad cannot be allowed to be hijacked by the extremists and those who pursue violence,' he says. Instead, he paints a compelling vision: 'Imagine if all the energy and motivational force of a jihadic war effort is harnessed, mobilised and channelled towards wealth creation to prosper the ummah (Islamic community) and the world.'

This sharing across boundaries of creativity is Generation M's hallmark. Business is a channel to fulfil their aspirations to engage, and it fits perfectly with their Islamic worldview of encouraging success. 'Not only must business pursue profits and add economic value. It must also result in enhancing the good through high ethical conduct and moral principles,' says Muhammad. He is inspired by the greatness of the Muslim civilisation and believes that Islamic values can be the inspiration to improve Muslim conditions today, but more importantly to make the world a better place for everyone. 'The world today is business-driven, and Islam is not anti-wealth creation,' he says. 'Islam teaches that to succeed, an enterprise must be led by the most able and competent, irrespective of whether he or she is a Muslim or not, and the fierce competition in the market demands exactly that.'

We've met many Generation M entrepreneurs during our journey, building products and brands that bring to life their aspirations as faithful, modern Muslim consumers, but which can also bring benefits to all. When Salma Chaudry was diagnosed with breast cancer, she started investigating what she was eating as well as the ingredients of the cosmetics she used on her face and body. What she found shocked her: they contained animal products and alcohol, and a range of harmful ingredients; as a Muslim she was concerned that she didn't know if this could comply with her Islamic principles. After her recovery, Salma set up the Halal Cosmetics Company, ensuring her products are both ethical and halal, supplying hand and body washes and lotions, face creams and moisturisers. Her products are free of parabens and all known harmful chemicals. She only uses natural ingredients. She's also added what she calls a 'miracle ingredient' called astaxanthin, which is derived from marine algae and acts as an antioxidant. She emphasises that the products are also suitable for vegetarians.

Whilst the company name may carry the term halal, the messages are clearly aimed at a universal audience, who share the aspiration to avoid putting things into their body that cause the kind of issues Salma experienced. The headline messaging on the website talks of 'an innovative formula for ethical skincare', 'the miracle of nature' and 'peace of mind from dawn to dusk'. This last is a lovely choice of words: 'dawn to dusk' is likely to resonate with Muslims as these are the words (rather than morning to night) that refer to the daily prayers. The business is already looking at expanding to the Middle East, the Indian subcontinent, Europe and North America.

We've met many small entrepreneurial brands set up by Generation M individuals and groups, and we've heard the passion and creativity of their founders. With the growing global Muslim population and the prominent role of Generation M within it, there are bigger prizes to be had at a global scale by reinventing what it means to be a brand from scratch, how values and promises are established and the kind of dialogue companies engage in with their consumers. We are likely to see the emergence of global brands from Muslim contexts, infused with a worldview from their faith as Muslims, that deliver to the cutting edge of modernity.

A Prediction: The Rise of Global Muslim-Inspired Brands

There is a perfect storm brewing for the emergence of Muslim-inspired brands: a vast, young, global Muslim demographic with consistent values, brand conscious and loyal; the will to create and promote brands; tech-savvy and globally connected consumers; pioneers of new consumer trends such as eco-friendliness and sustainability in line with wider consumer movements; the ability to harness collective power both within the ummah and across wider sectors and the sophisticated taste and affluence of a growing middle class. The reason that this is not the story of any other sector, and the reason why brand and commercial development will not replicate existing global brand formats is precisely because Generation M's faith demands consideration of the ethics of their work, a constant assessment of meaning, overconsumption, extravagance, giving back and stewardship. Of course, these values exist in other business and consumer groups but, as we've seen consistently throughout this book, the nature of the faith imperative makes these values non-negotiable in production, marketing and consumption as a means of achieving spiritual as well as worldly success.

We're not there yet. Muslim marketing consultancy Dinar-Standard looked at the brands of global stature emanating from the Muslim world and found that, apart from a handful, like Emirates Airline, most brands dominating the commercial space are of Western origin. In fact, in 2012, of all the Fortune 500 companies, only three had their origins in OIC countries. Whilst innovation and entrepreneurship are on the rise, and even while Generation M are keen to bring Islamic values to a global audience for the benefit of all, DinarStandard noted that in the OIC there is 'No Silicon Valley as yet, no Google, no values driven truly global "Islamic brand"'. As we've seen, there is a rich diversity of exciting brands emerging from the Muslim lifestyle, but these are relatively small in scale and have yet to achieve their global potential.

The momentum is building for Muslim-inspired brands. In his book *Made With: The Emerging Alternative to Western Brands from Istanbul to Indonesia*, strategic marketing expert John Grant explores a growing phenomenon among brands arising within the Western world. Grant argues that this new brand culture is 'both modern yet non-Western'. He believes that there is a shift in how brands are created and therefore in their ultimate resonance with consumers. He says that this is a reflection of the difference between the personality and identification of the 'Made By' brands which originate in the West, and the 'Made With' brands which are less about ego, and are more authentic and holistic. In short, these are the brands which demonstrate values which Generation M hold at their core.

Ogilvy & Mather's CEO Miles Young explains that the 'third one billion' of Muslim consumers 'is coloured green; not the familiar grass green of the environment, but the deeper green of Islam'. Young thinks that the reason that existing global brands have been slow to reach out is that global enterprises still operate within matrix structures in which the primary axis is geographic. Instead, the Islamic world is a powerful segment which unifies attitudes and behaviours, but not always by geography. He adds that his belief is that this problem will be solved by global product management.

This was borne out by the Noor Category Index. As we saw earlier, the number of categories that Generation M felt should be shariah-compliant expanded to include technology, travel and finance. Airlines and hotels were originally considered less important to be Muslim-friendly, with Muslims believing that there was not much that could be done. However, in recent years hotels, resorts and booking mechanisms are showing greater sensitivity to Muslim travellers' requirements. For example, the Retaj Hotel Chain based in Qatar announced a $500 million investment programme in 20 Muslim-friendly hotels. Halalbooking.com is valued at £30 million and estimates it serves consumers in 50 countries.

Tech brands too, initially categorised as of lower importance, are increasingly aware that they need to appeal to Muslim audiences and offer shariah-friendliness through their content, positioning and social initiatives. That's because the Muslim consumer, like the wider market, is increasingly conscious of brands engaging in a holistic and socially conscious approach to business. Part of a business's perceived compliance is derived from its engagement with its Muslim audiences and the sensitivity and depth of understanding with which it treats them.

In the area of healthcare we might see the development of 'holistic healthcare' that caters for physical and spiritual aspects, something that a wider consumer audience might also take up as part of a greater focus on alternative medicines and the importance of well-being and environment in health outcomes. Spiritual welfare is increasingly being investigated as a core component of physical recovery. We may see places of care offering space for family support and accessible prayer spaces for patients and visitors alike.

Young says that the second challenge for brands reaching out to Generation M consumers is:

the tendency of the marketing and advertising industry to see it as just another interesting segment. In this mindset, it becomes equated with 'greys', or the 'pink dollar', or Latinos in the US. Of course, all these are very valid targets for segmentation strategies, but the Islamic opportunity surely differs qualitatively. We are not looking here at a segment which is qualified by one primary difference, be it age, orientation, language or skin colour, and then whether attitudes and behaviour vary from a norm in accordance with that.

Here is the central point: the kind of brands that we are predicting will arise from Generation M, who bring together faith and modernity. Young says: 'we are looking at an alternative norm, one where the starting point is Islamic identity, and everything else fits into it.' And because the Islamic ideals Generation M aspire to are discussed in terms of 'universal values' that appeal to everyone irrespective of faith (or its absence) rather than specific religious prescriptions only for Muslims, these brands have the potential to appeal across the board and offer a refreshing and bold alternative to existing brands.

In the short to medium term, Young's advice is significant:

Brands must inform, educate, reassure the consumer about the highest levels of product quality through innovation; and also demonstrate a proactive anticipation of their informational needs – the surest way of garnering trust. In other words, techniques which may be regarded as marginal in the non-Muslim world need to be used or developed.

In a world where there is constant hostility towards Muslims but also increasing scepticism about corporations and their branding efforts, new Muslim brands must be able to navigate existing consumer concerns as well as bringing to life the Islamic ideals they aspire to. Thomson Reuters noted that: 'the global Islamic economy has a potential bigger than every country in the world except China and the United States.' The question is how the Islamic economy will draw in other consumers who find its core values and methods appealing. Throughout our stories we've seen how Generation M's products and brands right across the board can be attractive to non-Muslims, whether it is halal food, Muslim cuisine, modest fashion or Islamic finance.

'We are still in the pioneering days of Muslim-inspired brands, so it's very exciting to explore the potential individually and collectively,' says Peter Gould, an Australian Muslim who specialises in art, design and brand development for Muslim and mainstream audiences. 'I am convinced that Islam-inspired creativity and entrepreneurship can have a massively positive impact on our global community.' He believes that the spirituality within Islamic teachings has the ability to inspire creativity, and the core Muslim values can offer something more to consumers than the existing range of brands in the marketplace. He also sees such brands as part of a cultural tradition, alluding to how Muslims see commerce and culture as part of faith.

> Muslims globally have an incredibly beautiful artistic heritage and creative legacy that has shaped cultures in a profound way. Modern Muslim-inspired brands founded with the right intention and developed with ihsaan [spiritual excellence] have a role to play in continuing this tradition.

He believes that the authenticity which drives Muslim-inspired brands makes them potent and ensures that their appeal stretches beyond only Muslims.

> Most mainstream brands work hard to weave their stories and heritage to become embedded into culture. Muslim brands are inspired by something much deeper and more meaningful to the people creating them, the very essence of who they are. We aren't just about selling sneakers and soda, our brands are coming from a beautiful, powerful well of positive inspiration.

Or, as he puts it more succinctly, 'Purpose before profit.'

From his own experience travelling around the Muslim world to visit its heritage, take photographs and deliver workshops on Islamic art, design and branding, he believes unequivocally that Muslim-inspired brands can appeal to wider audiences.

The Alhambra Palace in Granada is one of the most popular tourist attractions in the world, drawing thousands of visitors weekly. To me it's a great example of how Islam-inspired art, design and creativity can create a powerful experience for anyone.

Just like our discussion of the culture of beauty that Generation M is pioneering, a well-designed visual identity for brands is important to offer up, but it is the inner beauty that's important. Peter extends his example of the Alhambra in a similar way:

The key is that it's not simply a beautiful visual effect, people actually *feel* something in their hearts as they walk around. I hope that some emerging Muslim brands will aspire to create rich, deep emotional experiences that can be universally appreciated and loved.

Peter's journey started ten years ago, when he became Muslim and found himself inspired by a series of spiritual and artistic journeys through classical cities such as Fes, Damascus, Istanbul and Makkah. He is the creator of a whole host of pioneering projects, including children's apps such as Kids of the Ummah, which showcases different Muslim nationalities. He's one of the founders of the online platform Creative Ummah with the strapline 'Inspire. Empower. Change.' The aim is to connect with 'incredible change makers and creatives from right around the Ummah'.

His most recent project, 'Islam Imagined: A Journey to the Future', aims to create an inspiring and uplifting space where people can share their visions of how the future might look.

Creativity, design, innovation and entrepreneurship are the tools our global community desperately needs to embrace. Islam Imagined is my personal effort to inspire and motivate young people around the world to think positively and optimistically about the future, and encourage them to proactively create the future they want.

Peter, like his Generation M peers, takes us right onto the doorstep of the future. They paint us a grand vision of how their faith is inspiring a better modernity for everyone. They believe they are not just imagining a better future, they are going to create it. 'We need to dream big, be bold, and spark the imagination of people around the world,' says Peter passionately. 'We must raise a generation of creative thinkers and innovators to face the challenges we all share as human beings, thinking about being sustainable and civic-minded so we can build together the kind of future we all aspire to.'

If we've learned anything from the stories of our heroes, it's that no challenge is too great. Peter outlines the path ahead: 'It's ambitious, but I believe we have the technology, energy and drive to make it happen. Inshallah.'

POSTSCRIPT

I set out on this journey with two huge aims in mind. The first was to get to know today's young Muslims by listening to their voices, expressing their own stories, told in their own words. The key was to explore how they live a life that they see as both faithful and modern. If I have learned anything it is that respecting their agency is absolutely crucial to hearing what they have to say.

What I discovered was an open, engaging group of people around the globe who warmly welcomed my explorations. They found questions about their lives, inspirations, habits and motivations fascinating and enjoyable to answer. Whether it was mundane questioning about what they ate for suhoor, or grand questions of meaning, like how their faith inspired them to make the world better, they responded with enthusiasm, self-reflection and a sense of duty to help others understand their views, a duty that they took very seriously. Yet it never felt worthy on their part; rather, there was a sweetness and honesty in all their engagements. My research notes overflowed with far too many fantastic examples and insights, which I am sad that I can't include.

I find myself at the end of this journey with a powerful sense of optimism. It is exciting that we are being beckoned into the future through the actions and attitudes of a segment like Generation M who believe we have the right to enjoy the best of life, but we must do this with respect for our humanity, our bodies, our environment and, most of all, with respect for each other, no matter how different we are. They inspire confidence through their pride in being pioneering, and being a positive and creative force for change in spite of the social, political and economic challenges they are facing. Their zeal to leave their mark is breathtaking.

I also rather enjoyed their acknowledgement of the limits placed on how they ought to behave and their joyful disregard of those limits. Instead of rejecting modernity as some extremists might want them to do, they embrace it and integrate it into their lives. Instead of apologising for or even rejecting their faith as a means of demonstrating their loyalty to nation or modernity, they take pride in their faith and believe it can make things better for everyone.

Young Muslim architect Maryam Eskandari, based in Cambridge, USA, encapsulates this perfectly. She says, 'I have a passion to expand the boundaries and create a new vocabulary for the next generation.' She says about her profession: 'I am an architect. We create things and leave our impressions on earth.'

On her identity and the future:

> I am you. I am not defined solely by where I am from, my traditions, heritage, rules, and culture. I believe in the best from everybody, everywhere, and everything; morphing it into a modern culture. We all should be global citizens where we learn from each other and import the best things from others into our own lives. We should be open and yearning to change; push for new things and be unique.

Given the influence of Generation M socially, economically and politically on our global future, the second aim I had set myself was to consider how we could do things differently when engaging with young Muslims. The most obvious – and reading this book is a great start – is to go beyond the repetitive and frankly tedious public tropes of 'Muslims are terrorists', 'Islam is medieval' and 'Muslim women are oppressed' that form the backbone of discussions about Muslims. Hearing Muslims on their own terms, as a dialogue of equals, is a crucial beginning.

It feels only right that as a final personal word I share some brief thoughts on how we can move forward towards opening a conversation. A detailed explanation of how to establish and engage this audience would be its own full-length book. But here are some preliminary suggestions.

Engagement is required, in the languages most dear to Generation M. These key languages through which communication can be established include arts and culture, charitable work, business and commerce, and politics. If these languages are deployed in a way that is forced and inauthentic, they will sound pious and righteous in all the wrong ways. Generation M should be spoken to not with the wrinkled brows and earnestness of someone who has studied a language in a textbook. In fact, they shouldn't be spoken 'to' at all. They want dialogue.

Getting advisers on board is worthwhile, especially those who have professional expertise. A formulation often repeated is to know the difference between a Muslim who is a professional, and a professional Muslim, who takes it as their career to 'be Muslim'. It's okay to make some gentle mistakes, to test out some outreach and to look to native speakers for help. It's okay to speak to them in your own accent and style, as long as your thoughts are spoken authentically, with trust, honesty and transparency but most of all with respect.

Connecting with faith values, not labels, is crucial. And ensuring that the techniques of modern life are applied in the same manner as to any other sector is equally important. There must be no short-changing in either domain.

It's important to ensure a healthy dollop of humour. Generation M are happy to laugh at their predicament, as long as they are being laughed with, not mocked. They are willing to laugh at their foibles as Muslims. People, cultures and traditions can be treated with humour, but it takes skill and insight and a true dedication to see the struggles of Muslims as they really are, not their stereotype.

Arab comedian Mo Amer, who does stand-up comedy and has been part of a Muslim-Jewish interfaith stand-up tour, explains that 'Historically, in Islam, the Prophet Mohammed – peace be upon him – used to commission jesters and poets to entertain the people. That for me is a prime example of how humour was used to lift spirits.' Humour is core to Mo's view of the human psyche. His ideas resonate with the Islamic idea of 'fitrah', the instinctive human nature.

Laughter comes from the heart, just as weeping and crying do. It all comes from the same place. Sometimes you laugh too much and you start crying, and sometimes you cry so much [that] at the end you start laughing. So they're all connected, and this is all an emotion that we all experience. That in itself is very, very spiritual.

When talking with Generation M, in whichever language you mutually select, remember this is not an audience of one. Everything is being shared with the ummah. It's their duty to connect with, support and guide other members, whether they live next door or on the other side of the world. The online world plays a pivotal role in shaping identity, relationships and connectivity, but Islam is a religion of real places, spoken words and real actions: the mosque, the family, the community, rituals and sermons are all testament to this. The digital world only complements, and does not replace them.

Whether online or offline, communications must be consistent. Whether spoken by an organisation, brand, an ambassador or a consumer, honesty, transparency, clarity and integrity must resonate from every word, image or video.

Engagement is important, but Generation M will only engage with those who speak with them on equal terms, those who aren't blinded by stereotyping and those who are respectful. Generation M have human stories that are hugely important and effective at conveying their humanity, especially if they are given space and autonomy to direct this storytelling on their own terms.

It's vital to check and check again that this is not exploitation for commercial or political gain – or beware their wrath. As @muniwah from Kuala Lumpur tweets, 'When being Islamic is a trend, people would make money out of it,' and then cautions Muslims, 'Seek knowledge. Don't follow blindly.' Honesty and transparency, even in the face of mistakes, are essential. The format of the anger is likely to be boycotting, protesting and civil resistance.

So, you'll need to be a bit brave sometimes. Being funny takes courage. Reaching out across any political or religious divide can cause anxiety. But consistency is key; no sneaking around behind their backs, because of course you can't manufacture integrity. As one Muslim consumer said: 'You cannot fake it. We will know.' The loyalty you'll gain will pay you back in spades.

Exploitation is reviled precisely because it violates the trusted relationship, so openness and honesty are important, and Generation M expect them from individuals, organisations and brands. It's best to avoid overclaiming, fluff or hype.

In Indonesia, @ekashanty1 explains,

> The approach of Islamic Marketing is taken from the Prophet's wisdom in his business life. It's an art of sustaining brand with a value mission statement. For Muslims, using this approach in Brand and Company's value will gain two benefits, TRUST and WEALTH in life and here after Inshallah.

Perhaps the most challenging topic is how to engage with Generation M while we live in a world where violent extremists such as Daesh dominate so much of the discussion about Muslims, and into whose arms a small but worrying number of vulnerable young Muslims are found fleeing. As I've been writing this book the exploits of Daesh have intensified, and the horrors they have been perpetrating have escalated. The difference between such groups and Generation M is like night and day. These violent groups do not believe in faith and modernity going together hand in hand. Unlike Generation M's belief in people working together across differences of faith and culture, such extremists believe in oppositions and binaries.

Daesh promises an Islamic utopia, predicated on a black-and-white view of the world. It connects to the growing push towards literalism and losing the spirit of Islam. It's not a surprise to read that two young men who set off to join Daesh bought a copy of *Islam for Dummies* before they went. It is their very lack of faith that makes them vulnerable. Most dangerous of all is that these groups are defining being Muslim in opposition to anti-Muslim hatred, and the two feed off each other in a vicious cycle. This cycle can be broken by Generation M.

Generation M is the platform from which conversation, dialogue and healing can come. If I had to choose a handful of words to describe why this is, I'd talk about togetherness, better futures, communities, diversity and stewardship. Generation M believe in these things for everyone and see their fundamental duty as improving the lives of all, not just their own group, or country, nor just Muslims.

Many young Muslims are finding a strength and pride in such a shared identity, and discovering inspiration from their faith values to build better communities and societies. This requires resilience and wisdom. The ability to discern the difference between good voices and loud voices – withstanding the latter in favour of the former – comes with experience as well as the right resources and support. Without them, it's easy to run into the arms of those who appear to be offering solutions, but who instead are perpetrators of the cycle of hate. Generation M is the perfect place to seek out these resources, and gaining their support is vital.

The challenge for young Muslims is to avoid the lure of political extremists at either end of the spectrum – whether anti-West or Islamophobic – and instead find an expression of their Muslim consciousness and identity that rejects both. The obvious conclusion is that we should and must support the young Muslims of Generation M in celebrating their identity built on faith and modernity. Their faith as Muslims must be bolstered.

This is a generation in flux. They are still exploring and refining their identity, and that is what makes them such an exciting group. They are constantly questioning and evolving. There are some exciting tensions at the heart of their identity which are yet to be resolved; in fact they may never be put to rest, but it is the momentum in those tensions that will give continued life to this group. How do they balance their growing sense of individuality versus their responsibility to family and the wider ummah? How do they square producing and consuming more products with the edict to avoid extravagance? How should you enjoy the good things in life while avoiding indulgence? Does being fashionable run the risk of stepping into the domain of immodesty?

It will be exciting to watch how these questions will be posed and discussed, and the ebb and flow of different solutions. It is these paradoxes which make Generation M so fascinating; I am intrigued to see how they will impact our future. They will undoubtedly affect global politics as we've discussed above. But I wonder when we will see our first truly global Muslim brand. Will the processes of halal food be so rigorous and ethical that wider consumer groups are attracted? Will the imagery and ethics of Muslim fashion reshape the fashion and beauty industries as we know them? I anticipate the answers with relish.

As is only right in a book bringing you voices, I leave you with the words of Basem Hassan, a photographer and new media artist in the USA. Basem's words take our story full circle.

'I'm part of the birth of a new Muslim cultural identity that's truly a historical event to witness,' he says, reminding us that this is truly a new and unique group of Muslims. 'I do not see colour or ethnicity as a hierarchy, but as an opportunity, the same opportunity that exists in teaching and learning about each other's religions. This is the true essence of Islam.'

Of course, being committed to faith has demands, but it brings rewards, constraints that lead to the flourishing of creativity:

Yes, we have limitations on what we can and can't do – how much or how little we are permitted to engage with certain aspects of any society. But those parameters are hardly limiting, actually liberating in knowing you are safe to indulge in the permissible.

As always, there is an open invitation from Generation M to get to know them as human beings.

We skate, we snowboard, we make art, we make music, we fall in love, we slam poetry, we go baggy, we go skinny, we get emo, we get big. But we also pray, we memorise Qur'an, we fast, we give in charity, we educate, and we represent … I hope one day we'll break fast together.

GLOSSARY

abaya: full-length, long-sleeved, loose over-garment, like a cloak, often worn by women in the Gulf, typically black. Now being re-invented in colours and prints.

adhaan: call to prayer, recited in Arabic, usually in a melodious voice.

alhamdulillah: 'thanks to Allah', a commonly used phrase to denote gratitude, and that all good things come from God, often used as a response to the question 'how are you?'

aqiqah: the sacrifice of an animal on the occasion of a child's birth. The meat is shared between friends, family and the poor, and as a result 'aqiqah' often is used to refer to the entire occasion of the birth celebration.

arba'een: day of mourning, 40 days after ashura. Arba'een means 40 in Arabic.

ashura: the tenth day of Muharram, the first month of the Islamic calendar, the day that Hussain, the grandson of Prophet Muhammad, was killed along with family and supporters for opposing the Caliph Yazid's regime. It is marked as a day of mourning, in particular by Shi'a Muslims, to remember the fight against injustice. Sunni Muslims may fast. It is also believed that ashura was the day Moses was freed from the Pharaoh.

astaghfirullah: 'I seek forgiveness from Allah', said when a person has committed a sin, or when they see or hear of wrongdoing being committed.

awrah: parts of the body that should be covered for reasons of modesty.

da'wah: Arabic for 'invitation', denotes the action of inviting someone to become Muslim or to improve their Islamic actions.

dawlah: Arabic for 'state', although now used by supporters of Daesh to refer casually to the 'Islamic state'.

dua: also spelled du'aa – meaning prayer or supplication to Allah.

eid: festival or celebration. Usually referring to Eid ul Fitr, the festival of breaking of the fast, which follows Ramadan, or Eid ul Adha, the festival of sacrifice, which falls during hajj.

fajr: the obligatory morning prayer performed before dawn.

fatwa: Islamic legal pronouncement, issued by an expert in religious law with regard to a specific issue, usually at the request of an individual to resolve a matter that is not clear.

fiqh: the body of Islamic law that is extracted from Islamic sources. These deal with the rules and regulations applied to religious acts and everyday activities.

fitrah: the instinctive human nature to be and do good, and also to believe in a Creator.

ghutra: the cloth used by Arab men to cover their heads, usually kept in place by a black rope called an igal.

hadith: report of the statement or action of Prophet Muhammad.

hajj: pilgrimage to Makkah undertaken during the month of Dhulhijjah. It is a religious obligation on all Muslims to undertake hajj at least once, providing they can afford it and are of good health. Religious visits to Makkah outside of this period are known as umrah.

halal: permitted.

halaqa: study group, study circle or religious gathering for learning.

haram: forbidden.

hijab: colloquially used to mean the act of covering up generally, but is often used to describe the headscarves worn by Muslim women.

hijrah: literally 'migration', but may be used to refer specifically to the journey made by Prophet Muhammad in 622 CE to leave Makkah and migrate to Yathrib, which was subsequently named Madinah. The Islamic calendar is dated from this event and is known as the hijrah calendar.

iftar: the meal taken to break the fast.

jihadi/jihadist: someone who undertakes jihad, but the term is generally used to refer to violent extremists who justify their acts as a form of jihad.

kebaya: a traditional blouse-dress combination that originates from Indonesia and is worn by women in South East Asia.

khums: religious obligation to give one-fifth of one's annual surplus income to charity.

madrassah: school; often used colloquially to refer to religious school, similar to Sunday school.

mahr: gift given by the groom to the bride as part of the nikah ceremony in order to complete the Islamic marriage contract, usually takes the form of money.

makrooh: religiously disliked or discouraged.

masjid: (pl. masajid) mosque or place of prayer.

mawlid: the celebration of the birthday of Prophet Muhammad.

mubah: an action that is religiously neutral – neither recommended, forbidden nor obligatory.

mufti: expert in religious law; in some countries the mufti may be a specially appointed position and refers to the most senior scholar or religious leader.

mushaf: (pronounced mus-haf) physical bound volume of the Qur'an.

muslimah: Muslim woman.

mustahab: religiously recommended act.

namaz: colloquial term for the obligatory prayer (salaat) used across subcontinental languages as well as Persian.

nasheed: Islamic devotional song.

nikah: the Islamic marriage ceremony; also refers to the marriage contract between husband and wife.

niqab: cloth that covers the face, but generally leaves the eyes clear. Accompanied by a hair covering and sometimes a veil to cover the eyes.

PBUH: 'peace be upon him' – blessing recited when the name of Prophet Muhammad is mentioned.

qawwali: devotional music popular in South Asia.

qibla: the direction to face when praying – facing towards Makkah.

revert: someone who has become Muslim, suggesting they have reverted to their original God-given nature of being Muslim. Also called convert.

salaat: the five obligatory ritual prayers each day.

SAW/sallallahu alaihi wa-salam: blessing added following the mention of the name of Prophet Muhammad, Arabic for 'peace be upon him' (PBUH).

shariah: literally 'the way', encompassing personal and familial, religious and social, moral and political, economic and business aspects of life. It may also refer to the body of moral and religious guidance derived from the Qur'an and hadith.

shayla: long rectangular scarf traditionally worn in the Gulf.

shisha: hookah or waterpipe, used to smoke molasses-based tobacco fragranced with a variety of flavours.

suhoor: the meal consumed just before beginning the fast.

sukuk: Islamic bonds, structured in such a way as to generate returns to investors without infringing Islamic law (which prohibits riba, usury).

sunnah: religiously recommended; also refers to the statements and actions of Prophet Muhammad which Muslims are encouraged to emulate.

suratul kahf: chapter of the Qur'an that Muslims are encouraged to read on Fridays in particular.

tayyab: literally 'good', but refers more broadly to good ethics, wholesomeness and integrity.

thobe: a loose ankle-length garment, usually with long sleeves, worn by men, originating from the Arabian Peninsula.

ummah: global Muslim nation.

waqf: (pl. awqaf) an Islamic religious endowment.

wudhu: the ritual washing performed by Muslims before prayer.

zakat: religious obligation to give 2.5 per cent of surplus wealth in charity every year.

zikir: (also spelled zikr or dhikr) the repetition of the names of God as an act of worship.

MORE ABOUT THE
PEOPLE WE MET

and the Stories They Tell

This book is all about meeting real-life characters from Generation M, and we've met plenty along the way. Here is a selection of some of those featured in the book so you can read more about them and their work and even see some of their creations. I've also picked out some of the events and stories that I thought were more interesting to explore in depth. There are many, *many* more stories out there, which I hope this book will encourage you to explore.

Abdel-Fattah, Randa, author: 'Veils and Vegemite', first published in the *Sydney Morning Herald*; reprinted in Tony Jones (ed.), *The Best Australian Political Writing* (Melbourne, 2008).

Abdul-Matin, Ibrahim, green activist: Willi Paul, 'Watering the Well of Zamzam: Interview with Ibrahim Abdul-Matin, Muslim Green Activist', PlanetShifter, 11 January 2011. Available at www.planetshifter.com/node/1774 (accessed 1 May 2016).

Aboulela, Leila, author: Claire Chambers, 'An Interview with Leila Aboulela', *Contemporary Women's Writing*, iii/1 (2009), pp. 89–102. Available at cww.oxfordjournals.org/content/3/1/86.full?sid=e9f9c 39a-5670-4d88-b288-60e45221ef16 (accessed 1 May 2016).

Aburawa, Arwa, journalist: 'Luxury Architecture in Mecca: Has Hajj Lost Its Egalitarian Spirit?', Green Prophet, 6 January 2011. Available at www.greenprophet.com/2011/01/mecca-hajj-equality-luxury/ (accessed 1 May 2016).

AbuSulayman, Muna, entrepreneur, social activist, TV presenter: speaker profile, Global Speakers Bureau, n.d. Available at www.gspeakers.com/speaker/?speaker=AbuSulayman_Muna (accessed 1 May 2016).

Adam, Haneefah, creator of Hijarbie Instagram account: Sarah Harvard, 'Hijarbie Might Be the Best Doll that Barbie Forgot to

Create', *Teen Vogue*, 3 February 2016. Available at www.teenvogue. com/story/instagram-user-creates-hijarbie-muslim-barbie-doll (accessed 1 May 2016).

Adritia, Tia, committee member of Hijabers Community: 'Hijabistas of the Region', *Aquila Style*, 5 June 2012. Available at www.aquila-style. com/lifestyle/cosmopolitan-living/hijabistas-of-the-region/7943/ (accessed 1 May 2016).

Akbar, Javaria, feminist: 'I Had an Arranged Marriage – But I'm Still a Feminist', Vice, 26 November 2014. Available at https://www.vice. com/en_uk/read/you-can-have-an-arranged-marriage-and-still-be-a-feminist (accessed 1 May 2016).

Akhtar, Navid, journalist, TV producer, founder of Alchemiya: Aisha Gani, 'Afghan Skateboarding? A Call-to-Prayer Contest? New Muslim Channel Has it All', *Guardian*, 21 March 2015. Available at www. theguardian.com/world/2015/mar/21/afghan-skateboarding-muslim-tv-channel-alchemiya-islamic-culture (accessed 1 May 2016).

Ali, Luqman and Eleanor Martin, founders and creative directors of Khayaal Theatre Company: Marian Smith, 'Demystifying Islam in a Strained Britain', NBC News, 23 February 2011. Available at www. nbcnews.com/id/41642329/ns/world_news-europe/t/demystifying -islam-strained-britain/#.Vx-50fkrLIU (accessed 1 May 2016).

Ali, Samina, curator, Muslima: Muslim Women's Art and Voices exhibition: 'What You'll Never Hear From the Media About Muslim Women', *Huffington Post*, 3 July 2013. Available at www. huffingtonpost.com/samina-ali/not-without-my-daughter-t_b_3536599.html (accessed 1 May 2016).

Allam, Norédine, creator of *The Muslim Show*: Warda Mohammed, 'Muslim Show: A French Comic Book Series Takes on the World', OrientXXI, 29 May 2014. Available at http://orientxxi.info/ magazine/muslim-show-a-french-comic-book-series-takes-on-the-world,0582 (accessed 1 May 2016).

Amanat, Sana, series editor Marvel Comics featuring Kamala Khan: Lisa De Bode, 'Ms. Marvel Returns as Muslim Teen', Al Jazeera America, 5 November 2013. Available at america.aljazeera. com/articles/2013/11/5/ms-marvel-returnsasmuslimteen.html (accessed 1 May 2016).

Amry, Hend, creator of LibyaLiberty: libyaliberty.tumblr.com.

Angawi, Sami, architect: Nicolai Ouroussoff, 'New Look for Mecca: Gargantuan and Gaudy', *New York Times*, 29 December 2010. Available at www.nytimes.com/2010/12/30/arts/design/30mecca. html?_r=0 (accessed 1 May 2016).

Anuar, Muzdalifah, founder of Pearls of Paradise, Women of Wellness (POPWOW), Singapore: 'Working Out Your Beauty Inside and Out', goodvirtuesco, n.d. Available at www.goodvirtuesco.com/ working-out-your-beauty-inside-and-out (accessed 1 May 2016).

Aouragh, Abdelaziz, founder of El Asira: www.elasira.com.

Ataya, Rabea, founder and CEO of Bayt.com: 'Should Men in the UAE Be Entitled to Paternity Leave?', 7Days, 13 January 2015. Available at 7days.ae/men-uae-entitled-paternity-leave (accessed 1 May 2016).

Backer, Kristiane, former TV presenter and convert: Arwa Aburawa, 'Presenting Islam: Kristiane Backer on Embracing the Faith', *Aquila Style*, May 2013. Available at www.aquila-style.com/converts-corner/ presenting-islam-kristiane-backer/86999 (accessed 1 May 2016).

Bouarbi, Yanis, IT specialist, France: Kim Willsher, 'Middle-Class Muslims Fuel French Halal Boom', *Guardian*, 5 April 2010. Available at www.theguardian.com/world/2010/apr/05/france-muslims-halal-boom (accessed 1 May 2016).

Chaudhry, Salma, founder, Halal Cosmetics Company: www.halalcosco. com.

Chelby, Muslim convert, Canada: 'Ottawa Muslims Seek to Debunk Myths Around Converts', CBC News, 27 July 2015. Available at www.cbc.ca/news/canada/ottawa/ottawa-muslims-seek-to-debunk-myths-around-converts-1.3168288 (accessed 1 May 2016).

El-Daly, Marwa, founder of Waqfeyat al Maadi Community Foundation: 'Why I Give: Marwa El-Daly', News24, 27 October 2012. Available at www.news24.com/Archives/City-Press/Why-I-give-Marwa-El-Daly-20150429 (accessed 1 May 2016).

El-Katatney, Ethar, journalist: 'I'm Tired of Hijab', altmuslimah, 5 June 2015. Available at www.altmuslimah.com/2015/06/im-tired-of-hijab/ (accessed 1 May 2016).

Eskandari, Maryam, architect: 'I Am an Architect: We Create Things and Leave Our Impressions on Earth', On Being, n.d. Available at www. onbeing.org/project-feature/one-voice-maryam-eskandari/6525 (accessed 1 May 2016).

al Fahal, Tamadher, artist, creator of 'Diary of a Mad Arabian Woman' zine: muslima.globalfundforwomen.org/content/diary-mad-arabian-woman.

Gora, Bana, CEO, Muslim Women's Council: Aisha Gani, 'Meet Bana Gora, the Woman Planning Britain's First Female-Managed Mosque', *Guardian*, 31 July 2015. Available at www.theguardian. com/lifeandstyle/2015/jul/31/bana-gora-muslim-womens-council-bradford-mosque (accessed 1 May 2016).

Gould, Peter, designer, creative entrepreneur, artist: www.peter-gould. com.

Gümüşay, Kübra, journalist: Laura Scorun Palet, 'Kübra Gümüşay: The Power of Small Stories', Ozy, 17 June 2014. Available at www. ozy.com/rising-stars/kbra-gmsay-the-power-of-small-stories/32038 (accessed 1 May 2016).

Haidar, Navina Najat, curator and co-ordinator of Metropolitan Museum of New York Department of Islamic Art: Ellen Freilich, 'NY

Museum Galleries Refocus Gaze on Islamic Art', Global Good News, 17 November 2011. Available at www.globalgoodnews.com/cultural-news-a.html?art=132154662110215590 (accessed 1 May 2016).

Hasan, Mehdi, journalist, TV presenter: 'Mehdi Hasan: Islam Is a Peaceful Religion', Oxford Union speech, posted 3 July 2013. Available at www.youtube.com/watch?v=Jy9tNyp03M0 (accessed 1 May 2016).

Hashim, Muhammad Ali, CEO of Johor Corporation: James Melik, 'Business Jihad: How Muslim Firms Can Achieve a Bigger Global Presence', BBC News, 23 August 2010. Available at www.bbc.co.uk/news/business-10942331 (accessed 1 May 2016).

Hassan, Basem, photographer, new media artist: 'We Are the Fruit of the American Melting Pot, Where the Divisive Cultures of Our Parents' Homelands Are Foreign to Us', On Being, n.d. Available at www.onbeing.org/project-feature/one-voice-basem-hassan/6545 (accessed 1 May 2016).

Hassan, Yusuf, creator of Tutlub app: 'Young Nigerian Launches Tutlub, a Mobile Social Network App for Muslims', Olisa, 9 December 2015. Available at www.olisa.tv/2015/12/09/young-nigerian-launches-tutlub-a-mobile-social-network-app-for-muslims (accessed 1 May 2016).

Al-Hassani, Salim, creator of 1001 Muslim Inventions: 1001inventions. com.

Hijabman, 'feminist, activist, thinker': hijabman.com.

Hussain, Aliya, author: *Neither This Nor That* (Raleigh, NC, 2010).

Hussain, Faiza, founder of H&O Skincare: 'Interview With H&O Skincare Founder Faiza Hussain', MADE blog, 9 October 2013. Available at www.made.ngo/updates/2012-11-21-13-50-22/item/interview-with-h-o-skincare-founder-faiza-hussain (accessed 1 May 2016).

Hussain, Mina-Malik, writer: 'The Sheepification of Bakistan', *The Nation*, 7 July 2014. Available at nation.com.pk/columns/07-Jul-2014/the-sheepification-of-bakistan (accessed 1 May 2016).

Hussein, Faisal, activist, music-maker: 'Halal! Is it Meat You're Looking For?', posted 28 September 2010. Available at www.youtube.com/watch?v=9W9s6rzxZ7c (accessed 1 May 2016).

Iqbal, Zaufishan, ecomuslim: www.theecomuslim.com.

Isamael, Furqan, member of Thai Muslim group Halal Life: 'Fighting for Islam's Moderate Voice', *Bangkok Post*, 23 February 2015. Available at www.bangkokpost.com/news/special-reports/481146/fighting-for-islam-moderate-voice (accessed 1 May 2016).

Jabbar, Amina, doctor: 'Limits on the Professional Muslimah: A Different "Glass Ceiling"', *Aquila Style*, 9 September 2014. Available at www.aquila-style.com/lifestyle/cosmopolitan-living/limits-professional-muslimah/78598 (accessed 1 May 2016).

Jackson-Best, Fatimah, healthcare researcher: 'The Sunnah of Smelling Good: It's for Men as Much as Women', *Aquila Style*, 20 June 2014. Available at www.aquila-style.com/fashionbeauty/vanity/spruce-smell -good/68906 (accessed 1 May 2016).

Jarrah, Samar, USA: 'Being a Muslim in America Makes Me a Better Muslim. A More Hopeful One', On Being, n.d. Available at www. onbeing.org/project-feature/one-voice-samar-jarrah/6626 (accessed 1 May 2016).

Jeilani, Ismail, entrepreneur and educational instructor, founder of Satifs: www.satifs.com.

Joseph, Sarah, editor, *Emel* magazine: www.emel.com.

Khaku, Zohra, founder, HalalGems.com: Stacey Overton Johnson, 'Dubai to Get Best Halal Restaurant Finder', *National*, 10 November 2014, Available at www.thenational.ae/arts-lifestyle/food/dubai-to-get-best-halal-restaurant-finder (accessed 1 May 2016).

Khaled, Amr, Islamic television evangelist: 'One on one: Amr Khaled', Al Jazeera, posted 30 April 2011. Available at https://youtu.be/ PXBZGv8zjXE (accessed 1 May 2016).

Khan, Alia, founder, Islamic Fashion and Design Council: Rebecca McLaughlin-Duane, 'A Closer Look at the Islamic Fashion Industry with Dubai's Alia Khan', *National*, 3 March 2015. Available at www. thenational.ae/arts-lifestyle/fashion/a-closer-look-at-the-islamic-fashion-industry-with-dubais-alia-khan (accessed 1 May 2016).

Khan, Amir, boxing champion: Sophie McIntyre, 'Amir Khan Says He Is "More British than UKIP" and Describes Young Jihadis as "Brainwashed"', *Independent*, 12 April 2015. www.independent. co.uk/news/people/amir-khan-says-he-is-more-british-than-ukip-and-describes-young-jihadis-as-brainwashed-10171032.html (accessed 1 May 2016).

Khan, Nazma, creator of World Hijab Day: Emanuel Grinberg, 'World Hijab Day Encourages Women to Try Covering Up', CNN, 2 February 2015. Available at edition.cnn.com/2015/02/02/living/feat-world-hijab-day (accessed 1 May 2016).

Khan, Noorain, writer: 'Complete Guide to Bad Burqa Puns', Jezebel, 19 July 2010. Available at jezebel.com/5590215/your-complete-guide-to-bad-burqa-puns (accessed 1 May 2016).

Khan, Qaisra, curator, Hajj exhibition: Shelina Janmohamed, 'British Museum: Financier who Found Her Passion In Art Curates British Haj Exhibit', *National*, 18 February 2012. Available at www. thenational.ae/arts-culture/art/financier-who-found-her-passion-in-art-curates-british-haj-exhibit (accessed 1 May 2016).

Knight, Michael Muhammad, author: *The Taqwacores* (London, 2007).

Kossaibati, Jana, blogger, Hijab Style website and medical student: 'Hijab and Body Image', Hijabtrendz, n.d. Available at www.hijab trendz.com/2012/05/11/hijab-body-image/ (accessed 1 May 2016).

Lari, Zahra, figure-skater: Emmanuel Barranguet, 'Zahra Lari, the "Ice Princess" in the Hijab', Al Arabiya News, 17 April 2012. Available at english.alarabiya.net/articles/2012/04/17/208359.html (accessed 1 May 2016).

Lootah, Wedad, author and marriage counsellor: Jessica Hume, 'Marriage Advice by the Book', *National,* 11 July 2009. Available at www.thenational.ae/news/uae-news/marriage-advice-by-the-book (accessed 1 May 2016).

Mahee, Sumaiyah, high-school student: Sumaiya Mahee, 'I Am Muslim and From Bangladesh. That Does Not Mean that I Am a Terrorist', PRI, 27 May 2015. Available at www.pri.org/stories/2015-05-27/i-am-muslim-and-bangladesh-does-not-mean-i-am-terrorist (accessed 1 May 2016).

Mahfouz, Asma, Egyptian activist: 'The Woman Behind Egypt's Revolution', IslamiCity, 16 February 2011. Available at www.islamicity.org/4144/the-woman-behind-egypts-revolution (accessed 1 May 2016).

Makki, Hind, activist, blogger, creator of Side Entrance: sideentrance.tumblr.com.

Malik, Tausif, founder of Muslim Spelling Bee: Joe Jervis, 'Best Bits: Islam and Social Enterprise', *Guardian,* 13 March 2013. Available at www.theguardian.com/social-enterprise-network/2013/mar/13/best-bits-islamic-finance-ethical-capitalism (accessed 1 May 2016).

Mamdani, Mohammed Sadiq, founder of Muslim Youth Helpline and Al-Mizan Charitable Trust: 'A Listening Ear', *Guardian,* 25 May 2006. Available at www.theguardian.com/society/2006/may/25/10 (accessed 1 May 2016).

Al Mansour, Haifaa, director of *Wadjda*: Xan Brooks and Henry Barnes, 'Wadjda: Haifaa al Mansour on Becoming Saudi Arabia's First Female Feature Film Director – Video Interview', guardian.com, 16 July 2013. Available at www.theguardian.com/film/video/2013/jul/16/wadjda-saudi-arabia-female-director-video (accessed 1 May 2016).

Maruhom, Maguid, executive director of Ummah Fi Salam: 'A Discussion with Maguid Maruhom', Berkley Center for Religion, Peace and World Affairs, 3 December 2009. Available at berkleycenter.georgetown.edu/interviews/a-discussion-with-maguid-maruhom-executive-director-ummah-fi-salam (accessed 1 May 2016).

Memon, Hajera, founder, Shade 7 Publishing: shade7publishing.com.

Mirza, Abrar, founder, London Beard Company: www.londonbeardcompany.com.

Mohammad, Nadia S., editor: AltMuslimah.com.

Muhammad, Ibtihaj, Olympic fencer: athlete profile, USA Fencing. Available at www.usfencing.org/page/show/700219-ibtihaj-muhammad (accessed 1 May 2016).

Musaji, Sheila, founding editor, *The American Muslim* (*TAM*): www. theamericanmuslim.org (accessed 1 May 2016).

Nasim, Iqbal, director of National Zakat Foundation: Shelina Janmohamed, 'Foundation Wants "Zakat" in the English Language', *National*, 24 July 2013. Available at www.thenational.ae/news/uae-news/foundation-wants-zakat-in-the-english-language (accessed 1 May 2016).

Nawaz, Zarqa, creator of TV series *Little Mosque on the Prairie*: 'Zarqa Nawaz: My Hijab Rebellion', National Post, 25 June 2014. Available at news.nationalpost.com/full-comment/zarqa-nawaz-my-hijab-rebellion (accessed 1 May 2016).

Niazi, Sofia, designer, artist, co-founder *One Of My Kind* (*OOMK*): Hana Nazuddin, 'Interview: *OOMK* Zine: One of a Kind!', Body Narratives, n.d. Available at www.thebodynarratives.com/interview-oomk-zine-one-of-a-kind (accessed 1 May 2016).

Nikolova, Elena, blogger, Muslim Travel Girl: www.muslimtravelgirl. com.

Radwan, Lutfi and Ruby Radwan, owners, Willowbrook Farm: Carla Power, 'Ethical, Organic, Safe: The Other Side of Halal Food', *Guardian*, 18 May 2014. Available at www.theguardian.com/lifeandstyle/2014/may/18/halal-food-uk-ethical-organic-safe (accessed 1 May 2016).

Rahman, Farzana, founder, Desi Doll Company: desidollcompany.com.

Rashad, Kameela, Muslim chaplain at the University of Pennsylvania: Antonia Blumberg, '#BlackMuslimRamadan Aims to Celebrate a Vibrant, Often-Neglected Community', *Huffington Post*, 10 July 2015. Available at www.huffingtonpost.com/entry/blackmuslim ramadan-aims-to-celebrate-a-vibrant-often-neglected-community_ us_55a02697e4b0ecec71bc2a7c (accessed 1 May 2016).

Rashid, Aaron Haroon, musician: Matt Shedd, 'Interview with Haroon, Creator of *Burka Avenger*', Peabody Awards, n.d. Available at www. peabodyawards.com/stories/story/interview-with-aaron-haroon-rashid-creator-of-burka-avenger (accessed 1 May 2016).

Rehab, Ahmed, creator of MyJihad campaign: myjihad.org.

Ridha Payne, Muhammad, founder, Abraham Organics: 'Briton Muslim Farmer: "You Are What You Eat"', *Brunei Times*, 13 April 2007. Available at www.bruneitimes.com.bn/classification/life/features/2007/04/13/briton_muslim_farmer_you_are_what_you_ eat (accessed 1 May 2016).

Rizvi, Nasim, founder of Nasim's Halal Baby Food: Hannah Abdulla, 'The Bitesize Interview: Nasim's Halal Baby Food Founder Nasim Rizvi', Just-Food, n.d. Available at www.just-food.com/interview/nasims-halal-baby-food-founder-nasim-rizvi_id129894.aspx (accessed 1 May 2016).

Rizvi, Syed, physicist: 'Is There Such a Thing as Halal Foie Gras?', PETA blog, August 2010. Available at prime.peta.org/2010/08/is-there-such-a-thing-as-halal-foie-gras (accessed 1 May 2016).

Robert, Naima B., author: naimabrobert.co.uk.

Saleem, Shazia, founder of ieat foods: Will Smale, 'The Young Muslim Entrepreneur who is Hungry for Success', BBC News, 23 February 2014. Available at www.bbc.co.uk/news/business-26187624 (accessed 1 May 2016).

Al Salman, Yassin, 'The Narcicyst', journalist and hip hop MC: 'Arab Hip-Hop and Revolution: The Narcicyst on Music, Politics and the Art of Resistance', Democracy Now, 2 March 2011. Available at www.democracynow.org/blog/2011/3/2/arab_hip_hop_and_revolution_the_narcicyst_on_music_politics_and_the_art_of_resistance (accessed 1 May 2016).

Shahin, Abrar, student: Stephanie McNeal, 'A Muslim Girl who Wears a Hijab Was Voted "Best Dressed" by Her Senior Class', BuzzFeed, 15 July 2015. Available at www.buzzfeed.com/stephaniemcneal/hijab-wearing-fashionista#.favWOgAvX (accessed 1 May 2016).

Shaikley, Layla, creator of the Mipsterz video: 'The Surprising Lessons of the "Muslim Hipsters" Backlash', *Atlantic*, 13 March 2014. Available at www.theatlantic.com/entertainment/archive/2014/03/the-surprising-lessons-of-the-muslim-hipsters-backlash/284298 (accessed 1 May 2016).

Sheikh, Shihab, founder and chief strategist of Hiba Brandcom: sheikhism.blogspot.co.uk.

Sobh, Mariam, founder of Hijabtrendz: 'Eco-Hijabs on the Rise Among Muslim Fashionistas, Interview with Mariam Sobh', Green Prophet, 24 January 2011. Available at www.greenprophet.com/2011/01/eco-hijabs-on-rise (accessed 1 May 2016).

Stone, Heba Amin and Caram Kapp, artists: Associated Press, 'Graffiti Artists Hired by "Homeland" Mock "Racist" TV Show in Aired Scenes', Al Jazeera America, 15 October 2015. Available at http://america.aljazeera.com/articles/2015/10/15/homeland-is-racist-on-graffitied-show.html (accessed 1 May 2016).

Tabassum, Azra, blogger: 'I'm a Young Muslim Woman. I Am Not Oppressed by My Hijab', blog, n.d. Available at 5000letters.tumblr.com/post/47486288572/im-a-young-muslim-woman-i-am-not-oppressed-by-my (accessed 1 May 2016).

Taj, Saba, artist: www.artbysaba.com.

Taki, Amir, director and executive producer of Ahlulbayt TV: 'When Journalism Becomes a Tool for Social Enhancement and Education', Shafaqna, 5 March 2015. Available at en.shafaqna.com/news/8621 (accessed 1 May 2016).

Wilson, G. Willow, Ms Marvel author: Anthony McGlynn, 'Why Kamala Khan Is the Most Important Superhero in the World', Mary Sue, 10

December 2014. Available at www.themarysue.com/kamala-khan-important (accessed 1 May 2016).

Yasmin, Farzana, Bangladesh: 'Bangladesh Bride Disowns Her "Dowry Demanding" Husband', BBC News Asia, 15 November 2011. Available at www.bbc.co.uk/news/world-asia-15739640 (accessed 1 May 2016).

Younus, Zainab bint, the Salafi Feminist: thesalafifeminist.blogspot. co.uk.

Zaman, Dina, writer: 'Portrait of the Middle Class Muslim in Malaysia', Malay Mail Online, 21 March 2014. Available at www. themalaymailonline.com/opinion/dina-zaman/article/portrait-of-the-middle-class-muslim-in-malaysia (accessed 1 May 2016).

Zameer, Roshan, Pakistan: 'I Am a Sunni and I Married a Shia', *Express Tribune* blog, 27 March 2014. Available at blogs.tribune.com.pk/ story/19600/i-am-a-sunni-and-i-married-a-shia/ (accessed 1 May 2016).

Zanetti, Aheda, founder of Ahiida: Madeleine Coorey, 'Australia's Burkini Set to Put Muslim Women in the Swim', Middle East Online, 16 January 2007. Available at www.middle-east-online.com/ english/?id=19189 (accessed 1 May 2016).

Some of the Other People Mentioned

Bands: Deen Squad, Junoon, Outlandish, Poetic Pilgrimage, Raihan, Seven8Six.

Singers: Salman Ahmad, Shila Amzah, Zain Bhikha, Ahmed Bukhatir, Yusuf Islam (formerly Cat Stevens), Humood Al Khudher, Yuna, Rafli, Mo Sabri, Kareem Salama, Fatin Shidqia, Dawud Wharnsby, Sami Yusuf, Maher Zain.

Poets and spoken word artists: Dasham K. Brookins, Alia Gabres, Hissa Hilal, Khalil Ismail, Kamal Saleh.

YouTube and Blogger Celebrities: Amenakin, Humza Arshad, Yousef Saleh Erakat, Adam Saleh and Sheikh Akber, Dina Toki-O.

Stand-up comics: Allah Made Me Funny, Sadia Azmat, Nazeem Hussain, Aasif Mandvi, Sakdiya Ma'ruf, Mo Amer, Riad Moosa, Preacher Moss, Nemr Abou Nassar, Dean Obeidallah, Imran Yusuf.

Shows: *Halal in the Family, Here Come the Muhammads, Legally Brown.*

Fashion Designers: Iman Aldebe, Sarah Elenany, Alia Khan, Nailah Lymus, Dian Pelangi.

FURTHER READING

Books

Aslan, Reza, *No God but God: The Origins, Evolution and Future of Islam*, revised edition (London, 2011).

Bunt, Gary, *i-Muslims: Rewiring the House of Islam* (London, 2009).

Esposito, John L. and Dalia Mogahed, *Who Speaks for Islam?: What a Billion Muslims Really Think* (London, 2008).

Grant, John, *Made With: The Emerging Alternative to Western Brands from Istanbul to Indonesia* (London, 2014).

Jafari, Aliakbar and Özlem Sandikci (eds), *Islam, Marketing and Consumption: Critical Perspectives on the Intersections* (London, 2016).

Janmohamed, Shelina Zahra, *Love in a Headscarf: Muslim Woman Seeks the One* (London, 2009).

LeVine, Mark, *Heavy Metal Islam: Rock, Resistance, and the Struggle for the Soul of Islam* (New York, 2008).

Lewis, Reina, *Modest Fashion: Styling Bodies, Mediating Faith* (London, 2013).

Matin, Ibrahim Abdul, *Green Deen: What Islam Teaches about Protecting the Planet* (San Francisco, 2010).

Nasr, Vali, *Meccanomics: The March of the New Muslim Middle Class* (London, 2010).

Seneviratne, Kalinga, *Countering MTV Influence in Indonesia and Malaysia* (Singpore, 2012).

Weintraub, Andrew (ed.), *Islam and Popular Culture in Indonesia and Malaysia* (London, 2011).

Reports, Studies and Articles

Ahmad, Hafsa, 'I Am Not a Lollipop or a Pearl', altmuslimah, 14 March 2014. Available at www.altmuslimah.com/2014/03/i_am_not_a_lollipop_or_a_pearl (accessed 1 May 2016).

Arab Social Media Report, 'The Role of Social Media in Arab Women's Empowerment', 2011. Available at www.arabsocialmediareport.com/User Management/PDF/ASMR%20Report%203.pdf (accessed 1 May 2016).

Arab Youth Survey, 'Inside the Hearts and Minds of Arab Youth: Asda'a Burson-Marsteller 8th Annual Arab Youth Survey', 2016. Available at www.arabyouthsurvey.com/en/home (accessed 1 May 2016).

DinarStandard, 'State of the Global Islamic Economy Report 2015', 2015. Available at www.dinarstandard.com/state-of-the-global-islamic-economy-report-2015 (accessed 1 May 2016).

E27, 'Eat, Pray, Shop: Indonesian e-Commerce During Ramadan', 1 August 2014. Available at https://e27.co/eat-pray-shop-indonesian-e-commerce-during-ramadan-20140801 (accessed 1 May 2016).

Economist Intelligence Unit, 'E-Readiness Rankings 2009: The Usage Imperative', 2009. Available at graphics.eiu.com/pdf/E-readiness%20 rankings.pdf (accessed 1 May 2016).

Gallup Organization, 'Muslim–West Facts Initiative', 2007. Available at media. gallup.com/MuslimWestFacts/PDF/MWFFLYERv3ENGLISH. pdf (accessed 1 May 2016).

—— 'Gallup Coexist Index 2009: A Global Study of Interfaith Relations', 2009. Available at www.olir.it/areetematiche/pagine/documents/News_2150_ Gallup2009.pdf (accessed 1 May 2016).

Gani, Aisha, 'Younger Generation of British Muslims Showing Shift in Attitude to Gender Roles', *Guardian*, 23 July 2013. Available at www.theguardian. com/world/2015/jul/13/british-muslims-gender-roles-attitude-shift (accessed 1 May 2016).

Huffington Post, 'Muslims "Give Most to Charity", Ahead of Christians, Jews and Atheists, Poll Finds', 21 July 2013. Available at www.huffingtonpost. co.uk/2013/07/21/muslims-give-most_n_3630830.html (accessed 1 May 2016).

Janmohamed, Shelina, 'Designing a Game-Changing Islamic Brand', Spirit21, 2010. Available at www.spirit21.co.uk/2010/05/designing-a-game-changing-islamic-brand (accessed 1 May 2016).

Lewis, Reina, 'Faith-Based Fashion and Internet Retail', project report, University of the Arts, London, 2011. Available at ualresearchonline.arts. ac.uk/4911/1/LCF_modest_fashion_online.pdf (accessed 1 May 2016).

Muslim Global Fund for Women, 'Infographic: How Does the Media Portray Muslim Women?', n.d. Available at muslima.globalfundforwomen.org/ content/muslimwomeninthemedia (accessed 1 May 2016).

Online Project, The, 'Social Media in Ramadan: Exploring Arab User Habits on Facebook & Twitter', July 2013. Available at theonlineproject.me/files/ newsletters/Social-Media-in-Ramadan-Report-English.pdf (accessed 1 May 2016).

Pew Research Center, 'How People in Muslim Countries Prefer Women to Dress in Public', 8 January 2014. Available at www.pewresearch.org/ fact-tank/2014/01/08/what-is-appropriate-attire-for-women-in-muslim-countries (accessed 1 May 2016).

—— 'Why Muslims Are the World's Fastest-Growing Religious Group', 23 April 2015. Available at www.pewresearch.org/fact-tank/2015/04/23/ why-muslims-are-the-worlds-fastest-growing-religious-group (accessed 1 May 2016).

—— 'Muslims and Islam: Key Findings in the U.S. and Around the World', 7 December 2015. Available at www.pewresearch.org/fact-tank/2015/12/07/ muslims-and-islam-key-findings-in-the-u-s-and-around-the-world (accessed 1 May 2016).

Rohde, David, 'The Swelling Middle', Reuters, 2012. Available at www.reuters. com/middle-class-infographic (accessed 1 May 2016).

TradeArabia News Service, 'Women's Purchase Drivers "Key to Marketing"', 12 June 2012. Available at www.tradearabia.com/news/MEDIA_218873.html (accessed 1 May 2016).

Twenge, Jean M., Julie J. Exline, Joshua B. Grubbs, Ramya Sastry and W. Keith Campbell, 'Generational and Time Period Differences in American Adolescents' Religious Orientation, 1966–2014', PLoS ONE, x/5 (2015). Available at journals.plos.org/plosone/article?id=10.1371/journal.pone.01 21454 (accessed 1 May 2016).

Journals, Magazines and Websites

Âlâ: https://aladergi.com.
American Muslim Consumer Consortium: americanmuslimconsumer.com.
Aquila Style: www.aquila-style.com.
Arab Social Media Report: www.arabsocialmediareport.com.
Critical Muslim: criticalmuslim.com.
Digital Islam: www.digitalislam.eu.
Dubai Islamic Economy Development Centre: www.iedcdubai.ae.
Gallup Centre for Muslim Studies: www.gallup.com/topic/muslim_studies. aspx.
Global Islamic Economy Summit: www.giesummit.com/en/gie-summit.
Green Prophet: www.greenprophet.com.
Halal Gems: halalgems.com.
Hijabers community: hijaberscommunity.blogspot.co.uk.
International Museum of Women, Muslima: Muslim Women's Art and Voices: muslima.globalfundforwomen.org.
Islamic Monthly: theislamicmonthly.com.
Journal of Islamic Marketing: www.emeraldinsight.com/journal/jima.
Malaysia International Halal Show: www.mihas.com.my.
Mvslim: mvslim.net
Muslim Girl: Muslimgirl.net
Muslim News: muslimnews.co.uk.
Muslimah Media Watch: www.muslimahmediawatch.org.
Pew Forum on Religion and Public Life: www.pewforum.org.
Salaam - Global Islamic Community Gateway: www.salaamgateway.com
TwoCircles: TwoCircles.net
World Islamic Economic Forum: wief.org.
Zilzar: www.zilzar.com.

Ogilvy Noor Publications and Internet Sources

Brands, Islam and the New Muslim Consumer (2010).
A Little Empathy Goes a Long Way: How Brands Can Engage the American Muslim Consumer, 2010. Available at www.ogilvynoor.com/pdf/Ogilvy%20Noor_A% 20Little%20Empathy%20Goes%20A%20Long%20Way.pdf (accessed 1 May 2016).
Young, Miles, 'Muslim Futurism and Islamic Branding', speech given by Miles Young, CEO Ogilvy & Mather, at the Inaugural Oxford Global Islamic Branding and Marketing Forum, 26 July, 2010. Available at www.wpp. com/wpp/marketing/marketing/muslim-futurism-and-islamic-branding (accessed 1 May 2016).
Ogilvy Noor: www.ogilvynoor.com.
Ogilvy Worldwide: www.ogilvy.com.

Twitter: @OgilvyNoor

INDEX